Murder on the Mountain

Murder on the Mountain

• •

Crime, Passion, and Punishment in Gilded Age New Jersey

PETER J. WOSH AND PATRICIA L. SCHALL

Rutgers University Press

New Brunswick, Camden, and Newark, New Jersey, and London

Library of Congress Cataloging-in-Publication Data

Names: Wosh, Peter J., author. | Schall, Patricia L., author.
Title: Murder on the mountain : crime, passion, and punishment in Gilded Age New Jersey /
    Peter J. Wosh and Patricia L. Schall.
Description: New Brunswick : Rutgers University Press, [2022] | Includes bibliographical
    references and index.
Identifiers: LCCN 2021031065 | ISBN 9781978829145 (cloth) | ISBN 9781978829152 (epub) |
    ISBN 9781978829169 (pdf)
Subjects: LCSH: Capital punishment—New Jersey—History—19th century. | Murder—New
    Jersey—History—19th century. | Crime—New Jersey—History—19th century.
Classification: LCC HV8699.U6 N596 2022 | DDC 364.6609749—dc23
LC record available at https://lccn.loc.gov/2021031065

A British Cataloging-in-Publication record for this book is available from the British Library.

∞ The paper used in this publication meets the requirements of the American National Standard for Information Sciences—Permanence of Paper for Printed Library Materials, ANSI
Z39.48-1992.

www.rutgersuniversitypress.org

Manufactured in the United States of America

For our friends, colleagues, students, and family who have provided sustenance, humor, love, and learning over the years. You know who you are.

Contents

Preface

This project began with a holiday gift. Several years ago, one of my academic colleagues at New York University presented me with a reproduction of an 1881 property map that detailed the section of West Orange where I live now. The map itself had been prepared by a company called Historic Map Works. This enterprise, physically based in South Portland, Maine, boldly describes itself as "an Internet company formed to create a historic digital map database of North America and the world." Its website contains an impressive array of over 1,500,000 U.S. maps that have been culled and scanned from tens of thousands of atlases. Historic Map Works constitutes a useful geospatial database available via ProQuest, and it will also custom print and mount atlas sections for interested individual customers. The sepia-toned backgrounds convey a sense of age and historical authenticity. The company invites consumers to "track your ancestors to their homes; see the roads they traveled on and the names of neighbors they talked with." For historians and genealogists, both the site and the related products offer seductive insights into the built environments of the past and allow for some intriguing comparisons over time. Given my own interest in such matters, I appreciated the gift and resolved to do a bit of digging to learn more about the past history of my neighborhood.

I quickly discovered that my own street, Rock Spring Avenue near the intersection of Northfield Avenue in West Orange, did not exist in 1881. Rather, as I later learned, it had been laid out in the early twentieth century when the neighborhood began to grow and develop into a solid suburban

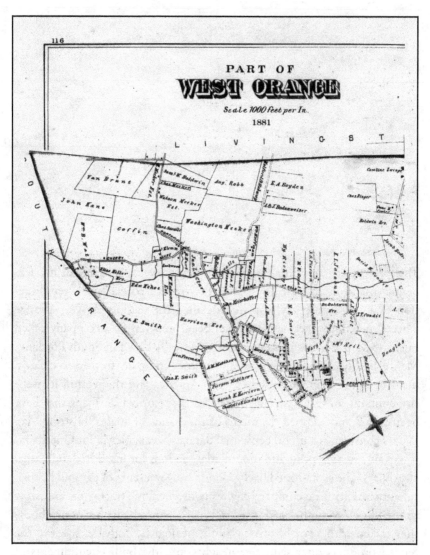

FIG. P.1 "Part of West Orange, 1881." The John Meierhofer farm is roughly in the middle of this map, along Northfield Road and extending to Swamp Road. It lies directly across the street from the Harrison Estate and immediately to the left of the tract owned by Mary Buchan. The cluster of homes in the lower right-hand corner of the map composes the Saint Cloud neighborhood. Courtesy of the author.

enclave. A small cluster of houses had been built a bit north of my current address, but the area mainly consisted of large, undeveloped acres with a sprinkling of farmhouses, residences, and outbuildings. As best as I could determine from the map, my current home appeared to be at the intersection of two tracts owned by individuals named Mary A. Buchan and John Meierhofer. This stimulated me to conduct some searches on Ancestry.com and Google in order to determine whether any information existed concerning these nineteenth-century landowners. Mary Buchan turned out to be a thirty-seven-year-old single White female who in 1880 lived with her younger sister, Martha, up the road in a fashionable new development known as Saint Cloud. She owned a large tract of land in the community and apparently came from a wealthy background, having been born in New York City, where many West Orange summer residents maintained their primary dwellings. My Google search for "John Meierhofer," however, generated a completely unexpected set of facts. The search engine produced one result, a link to a New Jersey genealogy listserv that contained the entry, "John Meierhofer, d. 1879, shot in head." Needless to say, I found this intriguing. I next decided to scan the readily available older issues of the *New York Times* to determine whether that newspaper might have covered the shooting. Sure enough, a front-page article dated 11 October 1879 carried the sensational headline "A Tramp Kills a Farmer," with two alluring subheads: "The Victim's Wife a Party to His Murder" and "A Tale of Crime in Orange Valley—John Meierhofer Shot Dead and Kicked into a Cellar."

This new revelation naturally piqued my curiosity. At first, I pursued the project as something of an antiquarian hobby, primarily conducting some occasional online research in digitized newspapers and other sources that had become readily available on various internet sites. I also involved my wife, Patricia L. Schall, in the project. Pat had been a professor in the Education Department in the College of Saint Elizabeth and a former English teacher at Watchung Hills Regional High School. She knew a good story when she saw one. Pat found the entire incident compelling as new details began to emerge, and she quickly became a valuable research and writing partner. We learned that John Meierhofer had been a Civil War veteran who had earned a reputation for erratic behavior in the community. The Meierhofer family operated a farm on the main road now known as Northfield Avenue, surprisingly typical for the mountainous terrain that extended westward into Livingston Township and Morris County. After piecing together the trial, we discovered that his wife, Margaret, along with a hired hand named Frank Lammens, both were found guilty of murder in the first degree and hanged at the Essex County Jail in January 1881. Further, Margaret Meierhofer became the last woman ever executed by the state of New Jersey. Gradually, as we read more about the story, primarily through available online sources, the episode began to take on greater historical significance.

It also became something of an obsession. We began taking research trips throughout the state to such locales as Newark, Orange, New Brunswick, and Trenton to consult primary sources. Local newspapers covered the trial and execution in extraordinary detail, though none of those press outlets had been digitized. We thus reacquainted ourselves with microfilm collections at Rutgers University and the State Archives in Trenton. We found the manuscript records of the Essex County Court of Oyer and Terminer, which conducted the trial, as well as John Meierhofer's Civil War records. Nineteenth-century county histories, city directories, manuscript census reports, and property atlases proved to be invaluable in reconstructing the history of the community and biographies of the individuals who played a major role in the story. We visited cemeteries and churches, tracked down addresses where our principal subjects had lived, and spent a day exploring the extant ruins of the Essex County Jail, where the hangings took place. Digitized sources considerably helped. It likely would not have been possible to complete the book without the voluminous data available through such sites as Ancestry.com and Find-A-Grave.com. Of course, we hit many dead ends. The project once again served as a reminder of the difficulties involved in researching and writing nineteenth-century social history. Excepting the trial transcripts, the principal actors in this story left behind few documents that chronicled their lives. Incomplete sources, inexplicable gaps in the historical record, frustrating attempts to track down prison and insane asylum records, tantalizingly seductive informational nuggets, inaccurate newspaper stories, and conflicting first-person accounts all proved problematic. Generally, however, we marveled at the breadth of information that we were able to unearth in order to transform this largely forgotten historical episode into a reasonably coherent narrative.

Most historical projects begin by posing "big" questions. This one started as an antiquarian curiosity that seemed like an opportunity to learn something about local history and make some discoveries about our own physical environment. As the project developed and deepened, however, a larger picture emerged. I typically started out by asking all the wrong questions. Why, I wondered, was Margaret Meierhofer the last woman executed by the state of New Jersey? How could two people have been put to death for the same crime when no witnesses came forward and the case depended purely on circumstantial evidence? Did the trial "prove" that Margaret Meierhofer and Frank Lammens conspired to murder the unfortunate farmer? Had the jurors made a correct decision in finding both guilty? When we discussed the project with friends and neighbors, they all wanted to know our opinion about whether Margaret really committed the murder or not. Did she do it? At the distance of 140 years, most of these issues appear impossible to resolve without excessive speculation. Other more significant questions, however, soon took precedence. Why did the trial receive such widespread local and national attention? What does that fact say about the structure of information, entertainment, and the legal profession in late nineteenth-century America? How did issues concerning family, gender, class, justice, community, immigration, and democracy play out in this Victorian drama? The overriding question became not why Margaret Meierhofer became the last woman executed by the state of New Jersey but rather why social and cultural factors in the late 1870s led to her conviction and hanging at that particular historical moment. Although it has become something of a historical cliché to argue that any era under examination seems to be a time of "crisis" and "transition," those terms aptly apply to post–Civil War America. The Meierhofer trial appeared to open a revealing window on the nature of ordinary life and death at a time that seems both inexplicably foreign and disturbingly familiar. Hopefully readers will learn how we grappled with that tension in the pages that follow.

The research and writing for this book proved to be rewarding on many levels. Family, friends, dental assistants, hairstylists, and gravediggers expressed considerable interest in—or at least remained tolerant of—our relating the latest research finds and obstacles. Neighbors exhibited shock and surprise that this infamous nineteenth-century murder occurred in their quiet little corner of the universe. We spent many pleasant hours sitting on our backyard deck during the summer and autumn months enjoying dinner while staring out at the wooded area next door where the Meierhofers worked their farm on the top of First Mountain. The landscape, an often underrated element in historical scholarship, helped place the entire episode in context. Physical proximity to the crime scene made everything appear much more vital and current. Our speculations and theories owed as much to these leisurely conversational evenings as to the days that we spent immersed in archival research. Archivists and librarians proved extremely helpful along the way, as they inevitably do with historical scholarship, and we would like to thank the following people: Bette Epstein and Don Cornelius at the New Jersey State Archives in Trenton; Fernanda Perrone, Al King, and Christie Lutz at the Rutgers University Department of Special Collections and University Archives in New Brunswick; Father Augustine Curley at the Benedictine Archives in Newark; Alan Delozier at the Seton Hall University Archives in South Orange; Greg Guderian at the Newark Public Library; Natalie Borisovets at Rutgers University in Newark; Brian Keough at the State University of New York in Albany; Kathy Thau at Holy Sepulchre Cemetery in Newark; Andrew Lee at New York University; Rita DiMatteo at Llewellyn Park in West Orange; the staffs at the Orange Public Library and the Essex County Hall of Records; the Dennis Historical Society on Cape Cod; Joseph Fagan, the West Orange Township historian; Russell Gasero at the Reformed Church in America Archives; Gary Saretzky; Myles Zhang; and the following Meierhofer family descendants: Patricia Brunker, Jean Geater, George F. Meierhofer, and Thomas Meierhofer III. Special thanks are due to Nicole DeRise, Margaret McGuinness, Fernanda Perrone, and Caryn Radick for reading through the text and offering comments. Peter Mickulas at Rutgers University Press did a wonderful job of shepherding the manuscript through the publication process and transforming it into a book, as did Scribe Inc.

As mentioned, this project began with a holiday gift. It unfortunately ended with a personal tragedy. Approximately one and one-half years ago, my beloved partner and coauthor, Pat Schall, received a bad cancer diagnosis. She passed away in April 2020 during the height of the pandemic in New Jersey and tested positive for COVID-19 during her final hospital stay. It greatly frustrated her when it became clear that she could no longer work on the project or see it forward to completion. She made me promise to finish the book, and I did so over the summer. Hopefully, I have done justice to the Meierhofer saga. Even more important, I hope the completion of the book honors the memory of Patricia Schall, a truly wonderful, ethical, substantive, kind, and caring person with a wide-ranging intellect. Here's to you, Pat.

Peter J. Wosh
October 2020

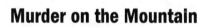

Murder on the Mountain

The Gallows

● ● ● ● ● ● ● ● ● ● ● ●

Margaret Meierhofer, sentenced to death for murdering her husband, John Meierhofer, walked steadily to the gallows in the Essex County Jail on Thursday, 6 January 1881, just as she had promised.[1] Two men escorted Margaret on her final journey. John Wood, a twenty-eight-year-old Newark policeman, bore the unenviable task of walking her from her cell to meet her final fate. Father Gerard Pilz, a Benedictine monk from the Newark Abbey who had spent considerable time with the condemned woman over the previous several months, also remained by her side. Margaret dressed all in black for the grim occasion. The sheriff placed a black cap on her head. One reporter observed that her "usually sallow face was bleached to an ashy white" as her hands were tied behind her back. Father Gerard and Father William Walter, who served as prior of the Benedictine Abbey in Newark, prayed over her in a scene that was illustrated and sensationalized by the *National Police Gazette*, a trashy tabloid newsweekly. Margaret responded to the monks' ministrations occasionally but showed no sign of fear or weakness as "her keen black eyes burned brighter than ever." One local reporter, who had anticipated witnessing "a woman of Amazonian proportions and strength" based on previous newspaper accounts and the melodramatic coverage of the trial, was surprised to see "a thin, skeleton-like, cadaverous looking creature, looking already more like a corpse than a strong woman." He concluded that "though she lacked flesh, she had plenty of nerve and never quivered." As she stood on the gallows, gazing at a crucifix that she held in her hand, Margaret spoke her final words: "I am as innocent as Jesus there."[2]

Now it came time for the Essex County deputy sheriff, Colonel Ebenezer W. Davis, to play his part in the macabre proceedings. Davis dutifully performed his responsibilities. He turned Margaret around on the gallows, slipped the noose over her head, and tightened it as other officers secured a strap around her legs. The Benedictines prayed constantly throughout the entire process. Essex County sheriff Stephen Van Courtlandt Van Rensselaer next stepped behind a screen and waited for Davis to signal him that the machinery of death was ready. Van Rensselaer sprang the mechanism. With a sharp click and a thud of the weights, Mrs. Meierhofer's

FIG. 1.1 "Execution of Mrs. Meierhoffer at Newark, N.J." The Meierhofer murder, trial, and execution made national news. This montage from the 22 January 1881, edition of the *National Police Gazette*, which depicted her hanging and the ministrations of Benedictines from Saint Mary's Abbey in Newark, appears to be the only extant visual depiction. Courtesy of the General Research Division, New York Public Library.

body popped up into the air and dropped to the end of the rope, turning around three times and stopping with her back to the twenty-four official witnesses at the hanging, including three physicians and William Fiedler, mayor of Newark. The *Newark Daily Advertiser* gruesomely observed that "there were a few convulsive twitchings of the arms and feet, a slight heaving of the chest, but beyond this, no struggle. She continued to breathe heavily for a few minutes."[3]

Two medical men also presided over the execution. Peter Van Pelt Hewlett, who recently had been elected to the post of Essex County physician, and David S. Smith, a forty-eight-year-old doctor from neighboring Clinton Township, checked Mrs. Meierhofer's pulse and heartbeat at several intervals after the hanging. From the time that her body dropped at 10:30 a.m., they reported with a clinical commitment to scientific accuracy as follows: "3 minutes the pulse was 140 and irregular. She gasped and there was a slight heaving of the chest; in five minutes there was another gasp and at 8 minutes the heart was still. At 9 minutes the pulse was 160; at 12 minutes 80; at 14 minutes 64; at 15 minutes 56; and at 16 minutes the pulse had ceased, and she was pronounced dead." The physicians' report indicated that it took her sixteen minutes to die. Doctors Hewlett and Smith noted that the body was "black around the lips and her tongue protruded from the mouth." They both "thought her neck was not broken but that she died of strangulation."[4] No one could realize it at the time, but Margaret Meierhofer would earn the dubious distinction of being the last woman ever executed by the state of New Jersey. Her body was left hanging until 11:00 a.m., when it was removed to a nearby room so that Frank Lammens, the man convicted of the same murder, could be hanged next.

At 11:13 a.m., Sheriff Van Rensselaer and his deputy proceeded to Frank Lammens's room in the jail. Davis read him the death sentence and asked him if there was anything more that he wanted to say. Lammens declared his innocence, protesting, "Oh, God! How can they hang an innocent man?" and asked if the jury that convicted him was present so that he might talk to them one last time.[5] The lawmen patiently explained to Lammens that his trial had ended and that the jury was not available. They secured his arms behind his back and placed the black cap on his head. Dressed in a clean shirt and pants, his "head completely shaded by the bulky roll of the black cap, and only the lower part of his face" visible "above his long and shaggy, grizzled beard,"[6] Lammens walked steadily to the gallows. Davis again led the grim procession, but the supporting staff differed somewhat from the men who accompanied Margaret to her execution. Two other Benedictine monks from the Newark Abbey, Frederick Hoesel and James Zilliox, took responsibility for preparing the nervous loner to meet his fate. Elias W. Osborn, a thirty-five-year-old veteran of the Newark police force who lived in the rough-and-tumble Ironbound section of town, had watched over Lammens the night before and now walked with him as well. While the monks prayed continuously, Lammens exhibited little sign of distress other than a slight trembling. The lawmen adjusted the noose around his neck, tied his ankles, and offered him a crucifix to kiss. Press accounts reported that at precisely 11:37 a.m. "the drop fell. Lammens rose with a bounce, fell back, struggled a little and swayed slightly to and fro. The arms dropped to the side and the fingers of the right hand twitched nervously a few times and that was all." The doctors dutifully recorded Lammens's pulse rate as "one minute 103; three minutes, 160; four minutes, 165, five minutes, 168; eight minutes, feeble and irregular." Soon the heart "stopped and life [was] pronounced extinct." Death came for Frank Lammens in fourteen minutes.[7]

Newark jail employees cut down the bodies and removed them to the prison laundry room for postmortem examinations. At this point, things began to get a bit unruly. John Klem, accompanied by one of his brothers, arrived around noon to claim their sister Margaret's body. Despite their insistent demands and their vocal objections to an autopsy, the local medical and scientific establishment overruled familial concerns. The physicians' interest in popular scientific theories of the day prevailed. During the late nineteenth century, a variety of sociologists, psychologists, alienists, and medical professionals sought to make the study of deviance and crime a more exact science. In 1877, Richard S. Dugdale published his landmark study "The Jukes," which had been commissioned by the Prison Association of New York. Dugdale studied a family of habitual criminals over the course of several generations, attempting to determine scientifically the extent to which heredity determined social deviance. In 1881, the same year as the Meierhofer execution, Moriz Benedikt's influential *Anatomical Studies upon Brains of Criminals* had been translated into English, positing the notion that "the brains of criminals exhibit a deviation from the normal type, and criminals are to be viewed as an anthropological variety of their species, at least among the cultured races." By 1885, Cesare Lombroso, an influential Italian positivist, would coin a new term, *criminology*, to describe the emerging discipline. These pseudoscientific investigations and theories all revolved around the notion that "born criminals" who had a hereditary predilection for evil could be identified by physical traits and characteristics. The criminology craze, somewhat related to such earlier pursuits as phrenology and craniology, focused on the scientific examination of miscreants and the precise measurements of their brains and bodies as methods for predicting individual behavior. Just as police departments throughout the world enthusiastically adopted Alphonse Bertillon's "mug shots" and anthropometric measurements as standard identification and predictive practices in the 1880s, medical professionals believed that autopsies and postmortems could provide scientific insights into deviant behavior. John Klem's emotional protestations counted for little when juxtaposed against the perceived social benefits that might accrue from examining the brains and bodies of the deceased. The Klem brothers were rebuffed and asked to leave until the medical professionals concluded their planned work.[8]

Four doctors conducted the postmortem, including the aforementioned Hewlett and Smith. They were joined by Henry A. Korneman, a German immigrant who served as the physician for the Essex County Jail and whose surgical skills might prove particularly useful in the autopsy. Dr. Alexander N. Dougherty, the fourth doctor present at the autopsy, maintained a lucrative allopathic practice in an elite Newark neighborhood near Military Park and had been a past president of the New Jersey State Medical Society while also having earned a prestigious medical degree from the College of Physicians and Surgeons. All four physicians proved particularly interested in the condition of the brains. Several of the medical men wondered what the brains might reveal about the mental health of the deceased, especially Frank Lammens, who seemingly exhibited some signs of potential mental disorders. The examination of Margaret Meierhofer's brain led the doctors to conclude that it was "in a healthy state and weighed 44½ ounces, which is above the average weight of the brain of a woman." They noted that her skull was thicker than normal and that the "brain substance was of fine texture and the convolutions deep," indicating that "she was an intelligent woman." This seemed to confirm the wisdom of the jury, who viewed her as the mastermind behind the murder. Lammens's brain, on the other hand, was "much lighter than average, weighing only 41 ¼ ounces," and was "very narrow in the forepart and very broad behind," with the "gray matter" appearing "scanty and the convolutions shallow." The doctors also discovered "a bony tumor" in the "bone on which the medulla oblongata rests," though they concluded that his brain was otherwise healthy. Again, this fit well into the trial narrative, which tended to present him as a naïve dupe. Another newspaper account of the postmortem differs somewhat, stating that "the brains of both Mrs. Meierhofer and Lammens had at some time been 'out of order,'" but the doctors remained uncertain if "the derangement was sufficient to cause insanity." The physicians also dissected Lammens's body, though the newspapers made no mention of a dissection of Mrs. Meierhofer's body. Both newspapers stated that the necks of the two were broken. The death certificates list the cause of death as "suspensio" and "asphysixio," leaving open the possibility that they died of asphyxiation or some combination of broken necks and strangulation. One thing remains clear: neither Meierhofer nor Lammens died immediately after they dropped on the gallows.[9]

Following the postmortem, the physicians turned Lammens's body over to Enoch F. Woodruff, a local undertaker who served as one of Essex County's three coroners in 1880. Woodruff's undertaking establishment at 844 Broad Street, conveniently located next door to the Newark and New York Railroad Depot, also served as a county morgue. Woodruff had a particular talent for public relations and propriety, boasting that his business offered mourners "personal attention," remained "open day and night," and featured "an experienced female always in attendance." The Lammens corpse proved to be a good publicity boon for Woodruff, since newspapers noted that many people arrived to view it on the day of the execution. In a peculiar comment raising issues that hinted at racial, generational, and gender proprieties, the *Newark Daily Journal* disdainfully noted that while Lammens's body "was viewed by scores of men," several "boys and two young colored girls also saw it." Lammens had no family to mourn his passing, and his body would have been unclaimed if it had not been for the efforts of the Benedictines. On January 7, Father Zilliox blessed the body and said some prayers over it. The monks donated a grave for Lammens's eternal repose at Saint Mary's Cemetery in East Orange, a small suburban burial ground that had been established in 1857 for the German national parish in Newark. Lammens would spend eternity surrounded by pioneer Benedictine fathers and sisters, as well as many prominent parishioners. As one reporter observed, since he had "confessed and received the sacrament before his death, Christian burial, it is said, could not be denied him," and he was interred in consecrated ground.[10]

Lammens would have been pleased to know that he had not been buried in a potter's field as he originally expected, though he would not have been happy with the dissection. According to newspaper accounts, he spent some time the night before the execution worrying about the fate of his body. When his attendants insisted that he would have a proper burial, the convicted murderer sneeringly replied, "Yes, they will give it to the doctors for scientific purposes." At least, however, he had been spared the fate of many executed criminals who ended up as cadavers in medical schools, suitable for student dissection and study. Still, Lammens's fears were justified. The practice of dissecting criminals' bodies can be traced back to sixteenth-century England and to the earliest American colonies. In fact, the donation of criminal corpses to medical schools appeared in the English penal code in 1752. After the colonies gained independence from England, American judges were permitted to add dissection to a criminal's sentence, though it was not required by law. New Jersey's "Act for the Punishment of Crime," enacted in 1796, stipulated that for all murderers and for those who aided and abetted their deeds, "the court may at their discretion add to the judgment, that the body of such an offender shall be delivered to a surgeon for dissection." The state further stipulated that anyone attempting to "rescue the body of such offender out of the custody of the sheriff or his officers, or the surgeon or his agents" would be subject to a one-hundred-dollar fine and imprisonment with hard labor for a maximum of twelve months. At the time of Lammens's execution, twelve states still had such statutes on the books: Alabama, Arkansas, Colorado, Connecticut, Georgia, Illinois, Indiana, Kansas, Massachusetts, Missouri, Nebraska, and New Jersey. Further, reports on people who survived hangings compounded a convicted criminal's terror of dissection. At least one person was documented as living for a long time after a hanging in a brain-damaged state due to the lack of oxygen. For criminals with religious beliefs that included the resurrection of the body, the idea of dissection was exceptionally disturbing as it could prevent a soul's journey into the afterlife, leading to a double death in this life and the next. Despite these fears, some desperate criminals sold their own bodies to medical schools prior to their executions so they could obtain money for their families.[11]

Between three and four o'clock on January 6, John Klem returned to claim his sister's body and carry it to his brother's home for a viewing in East Newark, just across the Passaic River. John's Livingston homestead, located in the somewhat inaccessible and mountainous area west of New-ark, would have made visiting difficult for mourners. The family decided to hold the viewing in the more developed urban community of East New-ark, which proved a more convenient venue for her supporters but also attracted ghoulish gatecrashers. When word of the arrival of Mrs. Mei-erhofer's body spread throughout the neighborhood, the *Newark Daily Advertiser* noted that a steady procession "of curiosity seekers began to apply for admission to view the remains, and so many were the visitors that shortly after ten o'clock Mr. Klem was obliged to tack on the fence gate leading to the stoop the notice 'No admittance.'" Even the next day, around 2:30 p.m., as Margaret's body was in the coffin and ready for transporta-tion to the parish where her funeral would take place, about two hundred people showed up at the Klem household in hopes of catching a glimpse of her lifeless corpse.[12]

Augustus L. Erb, a forty-nine-year-old Newark undertaker who had been born in Darmstadt, donated his services to prepare Mrs. Meierhofer's body for viewing and burial. Erb operated his mortuary business, as well as two livery stables, near the heavily German "Hill" section of Newark. He relied heavily on the German immigrant community for his business and no doubt viewed this contribution as an altruistic endeavor that would contribute to a proper burial for a poor woman who had suffered a sad fate. Erb went beyond the bare necessities, providing a "handsome mahogany coffin with a silver plate" that bore Mrs. Meierhofer's name and date of death, as well as a hearse and two carriages to carry her to her final resting place. The funeral procession attracted much attention as it made its way through the streets from the Klem household, passing by about sixty spec-tators who waited on the bridge over the Passaic River that linked Har-rison with Newark. In a moment of dark irony, Enoch Woodruff, who was driving the coffin carrying Lammens's body to Saint Mary's Cemetery in East Orange, crossed paths with the Meierhofer funeral procession, which was on its way to Saint Mary's Church in Newark.[13]

Saint Mary's, a German national parish located on High Street in a heavily immigrant Newark neighborhood, had been established in 1842 and was placed under the jurisdiction of the Benedictines in 1856. The par-ish had seen its share of controversy in the past. Nativists damaged and desecrated an earlier church structure on the site in 1854 when the anti-immigrant American Protestant Association orchestrated a riotous march

FIG. 1.2 Saint Mary's Church in Newark (right), where Margaret Meierhofer's funeral took place, constituted part of an impressive complex of buildings that had been constructed by the Benedictines on High Street in Newark. They included (from left to right) Saint Benedict's College and the Benedictine monastery, as well as the church. This etching first appeared in the *Annual Catalogue of the Officers and Students of St. Benedict's College, Newark, N.J. for the Collegiate Year 1887–'88* (Newark, N.J.: Wm. A. Baker, 1888). Courtesy of the archives of the Benedictine Abbey in Newark.

through Newark to support the Know Nothing Party. By 1880, a beautiful Italianate church building stood on the site, nicely illustrating the growing power and prestige of the city's German community. Annual reports estimated that between three hundred and four hundred families belonged to the parish, and one Benedictine informed the bishop of Newark that "as far as I know all" parishioners made their Easter duty. A thriving parochial school provided German language instruction to 420 children each year, and the church boasted a wide array of confraternities and religious societies. Saint Mary's operated on a healthy budget that exceeded ten thousand dollars, and it received substantial support from both wealthy Germans "on the hill" and less affluent parishioners throughout the city who rented pews and contributed to Sunday collections. The thriving urban parish appeared a world removed from the isolated and sad circumstances that had dominated Margaret Meierhofer's life, but the Benedictines of Newark guaranteed that she would receive a proper funeral and burial.[14]

A "vast crowd" waited outside Saint Mary's as Erb and his hearse arrived on the scene. Mourners and onlookers filled every pew in the church, meaning that between four hundred and five hundred people turned out for the occasion. Father Gerard Pilz, who like Margaret Meierhofer hailed originally from Bavaria, received the coffin on the steps of the church, after which it was carried slowly down the aisle and placed on a bier at the altar railing. One poignant scene transpired when Theodore Meierhofer, Margaret's fifteen-year-old son, asked whether the coffin might be opened so that he could see his mother for one final moment. Theodore had spent time with her throughout her incarceration and had visited on the Friday before the execution but had not seen her since then. Father Gerard refused the request, however, concerned about the large number of people attending the funeral and worried that exposing the woman's body might create undue excitement. All told, the service at Saint Mary's lasted about ten minutes. The priests included in the service one of the penitential Psalms that constituted a traditional prayer for the departed known as *De profundis*—out of the depths—that seemed especially appropriate for this particular mournful occasion:

> Out of the depths I have cried to thee, O Lord: Lord hear my voice. Let thy
> ears be attentive to the voice of my supplication.
> If thou, O Lord, wilt mark iniquities, Lord, who shall stand it.
> For with thee there is merciful forgiveness: and by reason of thy law, I have
> waited for thee, O Lord. My soul hath relied on his word:
> My soul hath hoped in the Lord.
> From the morning watch even until night, let Israel hope in the Lord.
> Because with the Lord there is mercy: and with him plentiful redemption.
> And he shall redeem Israel from all his iniquities.[15]

Now it became time to transport Margaret's body to her final resting place. Holy Sepulchre Cemetery in East Orange and Newark, also known as "The Bishop's Cemetery," had been opened by the diocese in 1859 as an alternative to small parish burial grounds. It had been enlarged several times since then, eventually growing to one hundred acres in a wooded grove far removed from the hustle and bustle of downtown Newark. Its stately gated entrance, broad avenues, gentle slopes, and winding pathways owed some inspiration to the rural cemetery movement and stood in stark contrast to the simple rectangular designs and orderly plots that characterized Lammens's final resting place at Saint Mary's Cemetery in East Orange. The diocese also hoped that Holy Sepulchre would make Catholic funerals more orderly, so they established careful regulations concerning headstones, monuments, processions, decorations, and plantings. Perhaps the most striking regulation, and the one that might have been applied most directly to Margaret's case, involved the stipulation that "no person belonging to a secret society, no public sinner, no unbaptized person, or otherwise forbidden by the rubrics of the Roman Ritual, 'de exeauiis' is to be interred in any grave or lot." The Benedictines, however, bore this no mind. They purchased the plot, arranged for an orderly-if-small procession of carriages, covered the ancillary funeral expenses, and made sure that Margaret received a proper Christian burial. Father Gerard also acceded to young Theodore's wishes at this point. The lid of the coffin was removed, and Margaret's son tearfully gazed at his mother for the last time. A small bouquet was placed on the gravesite. Five months later, its withered remnants on a plain mound of light-colored earth constituted the only sign that Margaret Meierhofer lay beneath, eternally confined to what cemetery employees referred to as the "poor grave" section of Holy Sepulchre.[16]

The two pitiful funerals also buried the daily barrage of sensational newspaper headlines and journalistic speculation about the nature and delivery of justice. The genuine gallows humor and prurient gossip about the crime that had been reported on daily in the local, state, and national press subsided as the journalists returned to their routine beats. A review of newspaper stories that circulated on the evening before, the day of, and the day after the hangings reveals several themes. Newspapers expressed a general belief in the rectitude of the death sentences, the guilt of the unfortunate pair, and the approval of the grim processes leading up to and including the actual executions. Some dissenting voices also made their opinions known. The headlines tell the story. On 6 January 1881, the *Newark Daily Journal*, in a series of boldfaced banners that promised a complete accounting of the proceedings, screamed, "EXPIATION! TODAY'S DOUBLE EXECUTION. Last Act in the West Orange Tragedy. Mrs. Meierhofer Leads in the Death March. And Lammens Follows Her Soon After. Both Die Easily and Protesting Their Innocence. No 'Scene,' No Bungling, but Everything Orderly. The Woman Dies at 10:40 and Lammens an Hour Later. Scenes and Incidents Last Night and This Morning. Post-mortem Examinations—Last Scenes of All." The

Newark Daily Advertiser, generally a more staid paper, captured the scene with more economy of language. It especially highlighted the notion that justice had been properly discharged: "THE GALLOWS. *Two Murderers Pay the Penalty.*" A Newark German-language newspaper, *Die Zeitung*, published a special English-language edition on the day of the execution with these enticing headlines: "THE DOUBLE EXECUTION. John Meierhofer Avenged. Separately Hanged and No Public Confession. Terrible Scenes at the Gallows. the Night at the Jail and the Last Hours of the Executed. Strange Conduct of Lammens, and a Murderess' Stolidity. Many Minor Details of the Greatest Tragedy of Essex County." The *New York Times* headlined the story with less color: "*EXECUTIONS TODAY IN NEWARK.* PREPARATIONS FOR HANGING LAMMENS AND MRS. MEIERHOFFER." Several weeks after the execution, on 22 January 1881, the *National Police Gazette*, which devoted considerable space to crime stories and sporting events, blared, "DEAD, DEAD, DEAD. The Law's Awful Decree Carried Out with Mrs. Meierhofer and Her Paramour, Lammens." This particular article, riddled with factual errors, further sullied Margaret's already shady reputation by describing Lammens as her lover, accomplice, and confidante.

Public interest in the murder case and its denouement had remained intense throughout the trial and execution, so both local newspapers and out-of-state press outlets covered the story. These included, but were not limited to, the *New York Herald*, the *New York Tribune*, the *New York Times*, the *Brooklyn Eagle*, the *New York Sun*, the *Buffalo Sunday Morning News*, the *Highland Weekly News* (Ohio), the *Eaton Democrat* (Ohio), the *Somerset Press* (Ohio), the *Chicago Daily Tribune* (Illinois), and *Skaffaren* (a Swedish-language newspaper from Redwing, Minnesota). Essex County officials understood the value of maintaining positive relationships with the press corps and carefully cultivated journalistic good feelings. A reporter from the *Newark Daily Journal* praised the prison officials and police staff for the "courteous treatment" that journalists received, adding that "every facility possible was afforded to the pressmen to fulfill their duties." Officials high and low vied with one another in kind treatment of the reporters. In a self-congratulatory moment, one reporter added, "It is proper also to remark that the 'pressgang' in attendance at the jail during and preceding the executions proved themselves personally deserving of the treatment they received." He humorously concluded that one "New York scribe" who spent the night at the jail griped that "the reporters might be provided with cells, so that they could sleep a little." Four reporters stayed in the jail all night, keeping watch with the warden, Adolphus Johnson, and his staff: one from the *Brooklyn Eagle*, one from the Philadelphia press, and two from Newark. As the hour of the executions approached, all the reporters were asked to leave the warden's office. Before the reporters left, however, they were permitted a glimpse of Frank Lammens as he was being led down the stairs to be hanged.[17]

The detailed and steady press coverage provided a public forum for experiencing private executions. Newspapers even carried brief accounts of dark humor from conversations about the executions that had been picked up on the streets. One news story reported an exchange between a customer and clerk at Centre Market in Newark. When the customer inquired about the price of lemons, the clerk joked, "Lemons are reasonable today, but tomorrow Lammens will be high." Another report described the dialogue between two men who met on Wilsey Street, near the jail, just after the executions. The men speculated about which person had been hanged first. When the second man learned Mrs. Meierhofer was the first to die, he quipped, "That's right, ladies first." News stories were crammed with every grim detail of the Meierhofer and Lammens executions, from the menu of the condemned prisoners' last meals to the timing of their final gasps of air and the cessation of their heartbeats. These detailed accounts substituted for the eyewitness viewing of public executions that had been typical in the seventeenth and eighteenth centuries, constituting a relatively recent shift in the way in which Americans, some of whom believed that public executions were a deterrent to crime, viewed state-sponsored death.[18]

During the eighteenth and into the nineteenth century, the American criminal code was based largely on English law, considered the harshest in Europe. Capital offenses punishable by death included such crimes as murder, rape, highway robbery, theft, witchcraft, piracy, counterfeiting, blasphemy, idolatry, adultery, incest, bestiality, robbery, some kinds of perjury, and a variety of property crimes like arson. By the early nineteenth century, states began to revise their criminal codes, and local officials increasingly were required to move hangings indoors and out of the prying eyes of the general public. Connecticut was the first state to formally abolish public hangings in 1830. By 1836, New Jersey and five other northern states followed their lead: Rhode Island, Pennsylvania, New York, Massachusetts, and New Hampshire. By 1860, public hangings had been abolished throughout the north, as well as in Delaware and Georgia.

Mississippi and Alabama became the first southern states to move hangings into the jail yard, but public hangings persisted in many communities throughout the South. Southern states continued to disproportionately execute African Americans publicly, often before largely Black audiences so that the prisoners' fates might serve as grim racial warnings. The use of the electric chair, which began coming into vogue in the late 1880s, largely ended public hangings in the South, though in 1936, Kentucky hanged a Black man accused of rape before a rowdy crowd who tore off pieces of the hood covering the condemned man's head. Public executions formally ended once and for all in 1938, when the Kentucky legislature finally banned them. Private race-based lynchings, however, remained common throughout the South from the late nineteenth through the mid-twentieth century. They frequently received semiofficial sanctions from public authorities and law enforcement officials. These grotesque spectacles often attracted large throngs of picnickers, revelers, and celebrants. They served as convenient vehicles for asserting White supremacy and intimidating African Americans, even generating their own collectibles and souvenir postcards for spectators. Most average Americans, however, could no longer personally witness an execution by the 1880s. Still, many citizens retained a voyeuristic interest in the ugly details of these events. To satisfy the public's morbid curiosity, newspaper reporters wrote detailed and often sensational accounts of executions, a trend very much exemplified by the Meierhofer/ Lammens press coverage.[19]

The exceptional efforts of the Newark Police Department to protect the privacy of Margaret Meierhofer and Frank Lammens reflected their knowledge of crowd behavior at public executions in the seventeenth and eighteenth centuries, events that often attracted raucous masses of people who came to see their version of justice done. Citizens were drawn to executions as a form of violent entertainment and eagerly anticipated various common components of the spectacles. They longed to hear noted ministers, who valued the opportunity to deliver messages to large audiences, preaching mesmerizing sermons on sin and redemption. They sought to collect copies of gallows poetry published for the occasion. They eagerly listened to the condemned criminal's final words delivered frequently in the form of speeches from the gallows. Some parents eagerly brought their children, since they considered executions an appropriate and instructive event for them to experience as a moral message about the wages of sin. In watching the grim delivery of justice, witnesses could gain reassurance that the criminal's death would restore the broken bonds of community trust.[20]

The Essex County officials responsible for the Meierhofer and Lammens hangings were especially cognizant of a more recent execution in New Jersey. They were determined not to repeat the riotous, macabre scene that created a circus atmosphere at an 1867 hanging, still fresh in the public's mind in 1881. It appears worthwhile to recount this murder and execution in some detail here, since the 1867 events reverberated clearly in the minds of Newark authorities, especially given the fact that this constituted the most recent time that a woman had been sent to the gallows. A jury in New Brunswick had convicted a twenty-two-year-old Irish immigrant servant, Bridget Durgan of murdering her mistress, Mary Ellen Coriell, on the evening of 25 February 1867.[21] Mrs. Coriell, a thirty-one-year-old mother of a two-year-old baby, Mamey, was the wife of a prominent physician in Plainfield. Her husband was away delivering a baby on the night that his wife was killed. The case drew national attention much like the Meierhofer affair and raised similar issues concerning class, ethnicity, and familial dysfunction. Bridget, who believed Dr. Coriell had shown a romantic interest in her, decided to kill Mrs. Coriell supposedly so that she could develop a relationship with her husband.

Bridget tried to blame the murder on burglars and, leaving the house in disarray, she ran with little Mamey to a neighbor's home to report a break-in. When the neighbors arrived at the house to check on Mrs. Coriell, they made their way through dense smoke to a bedroom where they found her blood-spattered body pierced with at least fifty stab wounds. A strong scent of kerosene permeated the room, and the bloody kitchen knife was found in an outhouse. Bridget incurred cuts on her hands during the struggle with Mrs. Coriell, and the blood on her clothes pointed to her involvement in the killing. She was arrested shortly after the murder and was tried and convicted. She eventually confessed to the crime and to the failed attempt to conceal her misdeeds by burning the victim's body. Several published confessions circulated as lurid tracts complete with illustrations. Various enterprising individuals, including some municipal officials and jail employees, hawked their own versions of Bridget's confession to the public. They made a special offer to sell the confessions to *New York Times* reporters covering the execution for extraordinary prices ranging from fifty to one thousand dollars.[22]

FIG. 1.3 The 1867 execution of Bridget Durgan, an Irish domestic servant who had been convicted of murdering her mistress in Plainfield, turned into a botched fiasco at the Middlesex County Jail in New Brunswick that prompted calls for reform. It also generated a lively trade in true crime pamphlets such as this one, complete with illustrations and sensational revelations. Courtesy of Special Collections and University Archives, Rutgers University Libraries.

As the day of the execution approached, Sheriff Clarkson, the official responsible for the hanging, tried to secure a professional hangman. His first choice declined the offer, chivalrously stating that he "hung men, not women." The second request went to a reputable local detective, Isaac Edsall, who ignored it because he did not consider hanging within his line of work. Therefore, the sheriff had no choice but to assume responsibility for the execution himself, and according to newspaper accounts, he bungled everything from Bridget's confinement in prison to her death on the gallows. Bridget found little privacy, comfort, or peace during her time in jail and especially throughout her last night on earth. The *New York Times* noted that "it was variously declared that ghosts, whiskey and excitement, religion, turnkeys, and reporters kept her awake until 1 o'clock." Bridget was hanged at 10:15 a.m. in the jail yard of the New Brunswick prison on 30 August 1867, before what *New York Times* reporters described as approximately one thousand of "the roughest, rudest and most ungentlemanly crowd of men we ever saw," bloodthirsty eyewitnesses who paid admission to gawk at the unfortunate woman as she met her fate by a mechanism of death morosely labeled an upright "jerker." She twisted and turned at the end of the rope, and her partially pinioned arms flew up and had to be secured by jail staff on the gallows. The hanging failed to break her neck, and her breath and pulse persisted for thirty minutes. After her body was cut down, Sheriff Clarkson disregarded the objections of the priests who served as Bridget's spiritual counselors as well as her own stated request not to allow people in attendance to see her face. The lawman theatrically removed Bridget's hood so that the crowd could revel in one final glimpse of her ashen countenance. Her body was placed in the waiting coffin, and friends accompanied it for burial in consecrated ground.[23]

While the site of Bridget's execution met the letter of the law banning public executions, it was by no means private, nor did the New Brunswick legal officials make any attempt to maintain even a shred of dignity as they snuffed out the condemned woman's wretched young life. The reporters described the grisly tableau that they observed as Bridget marched to the gallows, stating that it was "a scene we hoped never again to witness." They disdainfully mocked the melee of men jockeying for a better view, pushing and shoving: "The crowd surged to and fro. Every man pushed for position. Oaths and profane ejaculations of the most outrageous nature mingled with cries and calls as one may hear at a circus. For five minutes we stood in the midst of these brutes, and wondered of what stuff and refuse they were made." The same reporters wryly observed that Sheriff Clarkson handled the details of the execution "to the best of his ability, but they could not have been worse," and they criticized the "bustle and confusion" caused by the crowd of men, women, and children surrounding the prison, dressed in their best clothes for the auspicious occasion. They derided the amateur "militia" employed to guard the prison entrance: "Boys and men in red or white shirts and black trousers, walking up and down with muskets on their shoulders, shouting, hurrahing and having a gay old picnic (without provisions) all to themselves, and greatly to the edification of the country people who gazed at them with awe." People peered from the jail windows and others scrambled up on the roof of the jail and a nearby barn for an unobstructed look at the proceedings. A boisterous assemblage of gawkers swarmed up on a platform outside the jail yard to secure a better view of the gallows only to crash land when the structure collapsed under their weight. All in all, the execution of Bridget Durgan epitomized a clumsy and incompetent unprofessionalism that discredited the law enforcement field and, in the minds of sophisticated urban journalists, satisfied the bloodthirsty desires of the hicks and rubes that populated the hinterlands.[24]

The officials in Newark charged with hanging Margaret Meierhofer and Frank Lammens remained determined not to repeat the ghastly spectacle of Bridget Durgan's execution. Consequently, they guarded the entrance to the jail; limited access to the prisoners to legal officials, attorneys, family, and spiritual counselors; endeavored to correctly install and test the gallows; and arranged for crowd control to keep the prying eyes of the public from witnessing any aspect of the executions. Deputy Sheriff Davis sought assistance in assembling the gallows from James Van Hise, an experienced master carpenter who also served as the courthouse janitor.[25] As the deputy and his assistants erected and tested the gallows, prisoners other than Meierhofer and Lammens watched from their cell doors. Reporters witnessing the construction of the gallows sat at a table in the shadowy light of two lamps and commented that "the hall was dimly lighted and the one or two lanterns that shed their flickering light down upon the sanded floor or against the newly whitewashed walls only served to make the scene more weird and solemn." The reporters watched as Davis and Van Hise tested the pullies, rope, spring, iron, and treadle with a 120-pound sandbag used to mimic an average person's body and another bag with a 450-pound weight designed to fall into a large hole dug in the cellar floor, jerk

FIG. 1.4 The Meierhofer and Lammens hangings took place in this courtyard at the Essex County Jail, where a gallows was built specifically for the event. The only windows that would have existed at the time of the 1881 executions were the slit windows in the jail wall at the right of the photograph. The large glass windows were added in the early twentieth century during a subsequent renovation. Courtesy of the Historic American Buildings Survey Photographs, Library of Congress Prints and Photographs Division, Washington D.C.

the prisoners up, and drop them. While the gallows were being built and tested, Coroner Woodruff arrived at the jail, having driven through the snow and ice in a sleigh carrying two coffins, which were quietly carried to an empty cell and stored until they were needed the next day.[26]

At 7:00 a.m. on the day of the executions, the prisoners whose cells faced the gallows were released from their quarters, led to water troughs to wash, served a half a loaf of bread and a dipper of coffee for breakfast, and marched past the gallows to the other side of the jail. They were housed temporarily in cells with other inmates "where it was impossible to see anything of the execution." At 8:30 a.m., forty policemen arrived to cordon off the surrounding streets, stretching "ropes across New Street, at the corner of New and Wilsey streets, and stationed themselves along the line to do guard duty." The warden, Adolphus Johnson, ordered the windows of the jail that faced Wilsey Street to be covered with "stout muslin, to prevent anyone from witnessing the execution from the outside." Sheriff Van Rensselaer guarded the Essex County Jail entrance and allowed none to enter who were "without proper passes." Only those individuals acting in some official capacity remained. Jurors who had been empaneled to witness the execution, consisting of twelve men appointed by the trial judge, David A. Depue, were sworn in. A second twelve-person jury of witnesses appointed by the sheriff arrived shortly thereafter. Two members of the condemned prisoners' families were permitted to attend the execution, but Margaret's relatives declined the invitation and Lammens had no family to attend. Colonel Gustav N. Abeel, the prosecutor who had won the convictions of Meierhofer and Lammens, appeared with what newspapers reported were two conditional pardons from New Jersey governor George McClellan. If either Frank or Margaret confessed their guilt prior to the executions, Abeel would produce a gubernatorial pardon to save the life of the other convicted murderer. Also in attendance were Essex County Jail physician Henry Korneman, law enforcement officials, and newly appointed Newark chief of police William H. Meldrum. Only one individual other than these official observers stayed in the warden's office: "The operator on a telegraph instrument, which was put up there" to broadcast news of the executions to press outlets throughout the nation.[27]

Outside the jail, a crowd began gathering around 8:00 a.m. and peaked at 11:00 a.m. Reporters estimated the size of the throng at less than three hundred men and boys. As the curious onlookers spotted the reporters leaving the execution site, they strained at the police ropes and called out for news. Several reporters suggested that the "dreadfully inclement weather with rain above and the slush below, rendered the presence of the police outside the jail almost unnecessary," and the curiosity seekers "quietly dispersed" after the executions. All newspaper reports indicated that the police officials successfully provided the crowd control and privacy absent in the execution of Bridget Durgan. Newspaper editorials offered conflicting assessments of the nature of the justice that the two executions delivered. An editorial in the *Newark Daily Journal*, revealing its conclusions in its title, "*Justice!*," asserted that Meierhofer and Lammens had received fair trials, including an appeal for Lammens, with a competent judge and impartial juries. It praised the Newark officials for carrying out dignified executions, noting that "it is gratifying to observe that both executions were conducted without any unseemliness, and that there was no 'scene,' no disturbance and no confusion. The wages of sin is death." The Newark newspaper contrasted the "comparatively humane course" of the current executions with the "barbarism of the past," especially the public executions, while still acknowledging that greater efforts needed to be made to provide a "painless and instantaneous death." The *Daily Journal* concluded with a question and expressed doubt about whether any threat of execution, public or private, would "prevent men and women from giving way to passion and temper and murdering each other."[28]

In contrast to the editorial in the *Newark Daily Journal*, a New York newspaper, the *Sun*, published an opinion piece with a title revealing its perspective: "*Trial by Rope*." It pointed to the remaining doubt about who actually had committed the murder and decried the mistaken assumption that either Meierhofer or Lammens might confess as death became imminent. Either one could have been innocent but, according to public opinion, there was a greater chance that Margaret would confess, so they sent her to the gallows first. She died professing her innocence, as did Lammens. The *Sun* asserted that "we have nothing to do with the doubts and expectations of the public in this respect, save as they were reflected in the course of the officers charged with the execution of justice." It criticized the notion that the life of one person should depend on another who might confess based on "terror of imminent death." The *Sun* denounced the fact that "two wretches" went to the gallows "with the question of their guilt and innocence of murder still undetermined." The editorial disparaged Governor McClellan's "experiment" in providing two potential pardons, which utterly failed to resolve the "awful doubt" that remained as both of the condemned criminals died.[29]

The *Newark Daily Journal*, clearly perturbed by the *Sun*'s editorial, fired back with a second editorial accusing the *Sun* of failing "to remember certain facts in connection with this whole matter which satisfy intelligent people that, no matter how much doubt may exist in the public mind here or elsewhere as to the guilt or innocence of the deceased persons, justice has not miscarried in either case." It pointed to John Meierhofer's brutal murder and the assumed motivation of Margaret and Lammens to "live together without anyone to look ugly" at them for their relationship so that they might "enjoy the farm" where John had once toiled. The *Journal* went on to argue that the jury heard firsthand the actual testimony of the accused and the witnesses rather than secondhand accounts from newspapers. It extolled Judge Depue as "a man learned in law, a just, conscientious and exceedingly careful Judge, who would not willingly permit the state to take the slightest advantage of the prisoners, and on all occasions

leaned, if at all, to their side." Observing that one jury found both Meierhofer and Lammens guilty and a second jury rejected Lammens's appeal,
the newspaper editorialists argued that the proceedings failed to produce
"a scintilla of evidence to show that the murder was committed by other
parties." The *Sun*, according to this account, misconstrued the presence of
Prosecutor Abeel with the possible pardons on the day of the executions
as a sign that the determination of guilt or innocence was left to be "solved
by the rope." Rather, the *Journal* claimed, these appeals conveyed the fact
that "human judgment is fallible and that Governor McClellan, yield-
ing to the dictates of his own judgment and the promptings of his tender
and humane nature, resolved to go to the foot of the gallows, as it were, and
exercise his right to respite should anything occur to give proper excuse
therefor." The editorial went on to question whether the decisions of juries
and the court should be accepted as "being in accord with truth and justice
or are the stubborn protestation of innocence on the part of the murderers to be accepted as truth," citing an old saying that "a lie well stuck to is
as good as the truth." The newspaper concluded with firm support for the
decisions made about the executions and with a bit of wounded Garden
State provincial pride: "We believe, and we believe the court which passed
the death sentence firmly believe that Jersey Justice has made no mistake."
New Jersey journalists thus unanimously concluded that the system had
worked flawlessly, justice had been delivered, and citizens could continue
to maintain great confidence in the courts. This proved a fitting claim for
a public culture that increasingly viewed its institutions and processes as
rational, efficient, progressive, scientific, and orderly. No more needed to
be said.[30]

The stories of Margaret Meierhofer and Frank Lammens disappeared
from the public forum shortly after their funerals. A search of newspapers
for a month after the executions and funerals yielded no further stories, nor
did a search of newspapers on key dates, such as the anniversaries of the
murder and the executions. The account of the Meierhofer murder and its
resulting trial and executions faded as quickly into history as the flowers on
the two graves that remain unmarked to this day. John Meierhofer perished
with a bullet through his head at the foot of the cellar stairs in an old farmhouse on the Northfield Road. Two people died on the gallows for one
murder without any concrete evidence pointing to the person who actually pulled the trigger. Two sons lost both their father and mother. Still,
these tragic events did not occur in isolation. Rather the Meierhofer story

remains embedded in the historical, social, and political context of the nation as well as in the small, but growing and diverse, community of West Orange. Before examining the details of the murder itself, a close attention to the immediate surroundings that enveloped the family's day-to-day existence offers revealing insights into their cultural milieu and to the events that subsequently transpired.

2

Communities

• • • • • • • • • • • • •

West Orange, boasted a typical late nineteenth-century guidebook, "contains within its boundaries some of the most beautiful and picturesque drives and avenues in Essex County, and some of the most elegant and costly villas in Northern New Jersey." Town boosters encouraged visitors to explore its "many and attractive drives, with fine paved road beds, broad streets, romantic scenery, ever changing vistas of hill and mountain, woodlands and fields, wild and rocky mountain ledges." As they marveled over the beauties of untamed nature, however, awestruck tourists might further pause to consider the "stately mansions and charming villa sites, with well-kept lawns and spacious grounds" that also characterized this bucolic suburban township. And in fact, such idealized descriptions contained an important element of truth. West Orange residents, who largely lived in dispersed homesteads on a sparsely settled and mountainous terrain, had sought independence from the more urban and densely populated city of Orange in the early 1860s. They especially complained about supporting schools and services that appeared largely designed to benefit valley dwellers in the downtown area. Mountain residents identified more closely with the less populated and more rural towns of Livingston and Caldwell in western Essex County. After some legislative wrangling and boundary adjustments, West Orange formally became a separate township in 1863. But if the municipal independence movement primarily reflected the economic concerns of small freeholders, hardworking artisans, and frugal businessmen, the new community quickly became identified in the public mind with wealth, social prominence, style, and natural beauty. Three settlements within the growing village especially reinforced these general perceptions.[1]

Llewellyn Park, a gated residential development located within the township's boundaries, received the most extensive attention and commentary. Llewellyn Haskell (1815–1872), a wealthy pharmaceutical merchant in Philadelphia and New York City, conceived this planned suburban community in the 1850s. At that time, the dispersed settlements along the mountainous ridge that he targeted for purchase remained administratively part of Orange. Haskell began buying up tracts of land from the lower valley up through the First Watchung Mountain, where he was entranced by the spectacular views, scenic beauty, dense forests, and wild mountainous splendor that provided the area with a distinctive character. He partnered with his personal friend Alexander Jackson Davis (1803–1892), one of the nation's premiere landscape architects, to try to create a unique type of private residential park that would attract a wealthy and tasteful clientele. The enclave included a rustic gate lodge at the main entrance, winding roads, a large park that contained miles of drives and walks, rocky outcroppings that offered stunning views of the surrounding countryside, and the sixty-acre "Ramble," a sprawling ravine with rustic paths and bridges that traversed the middle of the park. Expert landscaping created ponds, waterfalls, flower beds, rockworks, and sylvan glens throughout the property. Haskell and his associates imported exotic trees and shrubs to enhance the terrain, with evergreens, weeping willows, rhododendrons, azaleas, magnolias, holly, doggerel, and laurel proliferating in the park. The bridges, benches, and shelters scattered throughout the property were constructed of native stone and rough-barked wood, thereby adding to the picturesque quality of the setting.[2]

Haskell and Davis initially envisioned this rustic retreat as a land of country homes where the modest villas constructed in quasi-vernacular styles would blend into the surrounding landscape. Early in the process, they claimed the most spectacular vistas near the top of the Eagle Rock for themselves, building romantic Gothic Revival dwellings that they named "The Eyrie" and "Wildmont," respectively. Davis created several prototype designs for country homes in Llewellyn Park, relying especially on the Gothic Revival, Swiss, and Italianate styles popular for rural estates

FIG. 2.1 The Llewellyn Park Gatehouse, which was designed by Alexander Jackson Davis and built in 1857, still serves as the entrance to the neighborhood. The rustic look illustrates the scenic beauty and the naturalistic landscape that is evident throughout the park. This sketch, attributed to James David Smillie, appears courtesy of the Llewellyn Park Archives, West Orange, New Jersey.

throughout the 1850s and 1860s. He emphasized such architectural features as irregular shapes with broken silhouettes, verticality, deep contrasts of light and shadow, and rough textures when constructing individual homes. One typical example, still standing in the park, is the Nichols-McKim Cottage, which was built in 1858–1859 as a home and studio for the Hudson River landscape painter and Haskell associate, Edward W. Nichols. This one-and-one-half-story, three-bay frame dwelling with its tall interior brick chimneys, low-pitched hipped roof, and open-timbered ceiling on the second floor to house the studio exemplified Davis's Gothic Revival style. The board-and-batten siding highlighted the home's rusticity, and its commanding eminence on a hilltop with a sweeping lawn and stately trees lining the property boundaries conveyed a sense of refined rural living. Approximately thirty similar structures, supplemented by a few French-style Second Empire homes featuring mansard roofs that achieved popularity in the post–Civil War period, had been erected in the 750-acre park by 1870.[3]

From the outset, Haskell marketed his development with a particular type of buyer in mind. He early on adopted the slogan "country homes for city people." This catchphrase aimed at attracting urbane and sophisticated

FIG. 2.2 The Nichols-McKim Cottage in Llewellyn Park, completed in 1859 and still standing today, reflects the Gothic Revival style of romantic country homes favored by Alexander Jackson Davis and Llewellyn Haskell. It typified many of the early cottages occupied by the more middle-class residents of the development. Courtesy of the Llewellyn Park Archives, West Orange, New Jersey.

residents who wished for a comfortable and genteel style of living in the West Orange suburb, far removed from the daily stresses and strains endemic to city life. Several advantages received particular emphasis. Haskell suggested that Llewellyn Park could function as a commuter suburb "only one hour from [the] Barclay and Christopher Street ferries" in New York City. The park entrance also remained in close proximity to a local train station on the Morris and Essex Railroad and was well situated to take advantage of connecting horsecars that traveled regularly between Orange and Market Street Station in Newark. Further, the bustling and growing adjacent city of Orange itself offered Llewellyn Park residents "good schools and churches of the various denominations" as well as the urban convenience of having "butchers, bakers, and icemen coming to their very doors." Haskell succinctly summarized the development as "planned with special reference to the wants of citizens doing business in the city of New York, and yet wishing accessible, retired, and healthful homes in the country."[4]

As the foregoing quote suggests, however, the park's primary appeal for potential residents owed first and foremost to the fact that it was located "fairly in the country." The newly incorporated community of West Orange retained its rural character, "comprising many old farms, with their orchards, green fields, and native woods" as well as a "ready supply of pure spring water." Mid-nineteenth-century Americans often associated health and vitality with country living, and Haskell took full advantage of these popular perceptions. He claimed that the development's location on the southeastern slope of the First Mountain left it "sheltered from the prevailing winds of winter" while fortuitously catching the summer sea breezes. Llewellyn Park offered more than simply a healthful home in the country. Haskell made sure to emphasize that property owners also purchased elegance, style, and exclusivity. The picturesque gatehouse provided a stylish point of entry, and the winding circular avenues emanating from that point offered a fine approach to the homes and villas that dotted the mountainside. Further, Haskell enthused, *"Llewellyn Park is a Private Park."* He contrasted this with the newly opened Central Park in New York, observing that his creation "is strictly *private*, to be used only by the owners and their friends." Gatekeepers made sure that all visitors and strangers presented proper identification and signed a guest book prior to gaining admittance. A board of managers elected annually by the proprietors carefully tended to the grounds and maintained the properties, placing governance somewhat outside municipal boundaries.[5]

Affordability, convenience, and community constituted core principles that shaped the development. Haskell articulated his primary goal as "to enable a family occupying a small place in the country, costing only a few thousands of dollars, to enjoy all the advantages of an extensive country-seat, without the expense or trouble attending the latter." Each plot consisted of between one and twenty acres, with the average estate consisting of six acres by 1870. Individual villas initially proved mostly modest and cozy, architecturally interesting but avoiding garish ornamentation and excess. A relatively modest fee of ten dollars per acre each year supported park maintenance and staff. Large communal spaces, such as "The Ramble," proved to be natural gathering places and became centralized venues that hosted events and parties. Residents eschewed fences, separating their properties only with hedges and natural barriers. Deed restrictions proved minimal, though the park clearly attempted to minimize commercial activity within the grounds. Haskell inserted clauses against "the erection of grog shops, factories, hotels, etc., etc., etc.," thus defining the park as a separate sphere for raising families and enjoying domestic life, clearly distanced from the urban economies and businesses that financed and made possible the property owners' lifestyles.[6]

Scholars have long recognized the development's significance, frequently observing, in the words of the historian Jane B. Davies, that it has been "considered to be the first major romantically landscaped residential park in America." Though Llewellyn Park clearly drew upon such precedents as English resorts and metropolitan suburbs, as well as rural cemeteries and urban parks in the United States, it received widespread attention from planners and landscape architects throughout the nineteenth century. Initially, Haskell attracted an eclectic group of artists, intellectuals, freethinkers, communitarians, spiritualists, fellow Swedenborgians, and transcendentalists to occupy most villas. The aforementioned Nichols-McKim Cottage illustrates the early settlement pattern. Edward W. Nichols (1812–1891) frequented the intellectual spheres that gravitated toward Llewellyn Haskell during the mid-nineteenth century. Haskell operated within a smart circle of literary figures, artists, and architects that included Washington Irving, William Cullen Bryant, Andrew Jackson Downing, Calvert Vaux, and Alexander Jackson Davis. Nichols, who began creating art in the late 1840s after pursuing earlier careers as both music teacher and lawyer, had studied under the prominent Hudson River School artist Jasper Cropsey and spent the mid-1850s in Europe refining his craft. At the same time that he commissioned Davis to design his Llewellyn Park villa, Nichols set up operations in the Tenth Street Studio Building in New York City, which quickly became an important center for the growing artistic community that settled around the Greenwich Village area. At Tenth Street, Nichols interacted with such prominent artists as Winslow Homer, Albert Bierstadt, and Frederic Church. He made his own name by executing Hudson River-style landscapes of such areas as the White Mountains in New Hampshire, Lake Champlain, Lake George, and the Connecticut River Valley. He exhibited regularly at the Boston Athenaeum and the National Academy of Design, which elected him a member. Haskell himself commissioned Nichols to design some promotional materials for Llewellyn Park, and his iconic sketch of the gatehouse provided the development with its most enduring symbol. He personified the union of economic and artistic impulses that contributed to the vitality of the early park, solidifying the popular image of West Orange as a unique and desirable nineteenth-century destination.[7]

When Nichols decided to sell his villa and move to Peekskill in 1866, the new purchaser also reflected the progressive intellectual currents that flowed throughout the park. James Miller McKim (1810–1874) had been ordained as a Presbyterian minister with degrees from Dickinson College and Princeton Seminary, but his widespread fame owed mainly to his activities as a committed abolitionist. A founding member of the American Anti-Slavery Society in 1833, McKim lectured widely for the organization, eventually serving as its corresponding secretary. He also gained national notoriety in 1849 when he became a recipient of the package containing Henry "Box" Brown, who smuggled himself from slavery to freedom by sealing himself inside a crate that abolitionist supporters then shipped from Richmond to Philadelphia via the Adams Express Company. McKim pushed abolitionist boundaries and supported "fugitive slaves" throughout the antebellum period, even accompanying John Brown's wife to Harper's Ferry in 1859 to witness her husband's execution. He continued his political and social activism after moving to the park, serving on the American Freedman's Union Commission until its dissolution in 1869 and becoming a founder of the *Nation* newspaper. His daughter Lucy married Wendell Phillips Garrison, son of the famous abolitionist William Lloyd Garrison, who also moved to the park. James's son, Charles, became a partner in the renowned Gilded Age architectural firm of McKim, Mead, and White. The McKim family itself remained in residence at the cottage into the twentieth century.[8]

By 1880, however, Llewellyn Park already had taken on a somewhat different character from the freewheeling experimentation and utopian overtones that informed its early years. Both the Civil War and economic depression during the 1870s had slowed land sales. The 1880 census revealed that only thirty-seven families resided in the development, indicating sluggish growth. Haskell himself suffered some health setbacks owing to a railroad accident and a series of financial reverses. He died in 1872, though his son continued selling properties in the park until he moved to California in 1877. More significantly, the park's population itself underwent significant changes. An elite cadre of bankers, merchants, manufacturers, and attorneys owned most of the acreage in the development. Indeed, nearly 32 percent of the residents worked in the financial, mercantile, and professional sectors, far greater than in any other township neighborhood and vastly exceeding the 14.9 percent who pursued these occupations in West Orange as a whole. Further, the householders hailed overwhelmingly from New York, New Jersey, and Connecticut, again atypical for a town where the foreign-born population over fifteen years of age comprised 42 percent of the community. In one respect, though, the population proved typical, as sixty-eight foreign-born residents (40 percent of the adults over the age of fifteen) resided in the development. These overwhelmingly Irish (forty-six), Scottish (eight), and English (five) Llewellyn Park inhabitants largely worked as domestic servants, laborers, coachmen, and gardeners in the villas, residing with their employers and ensuring that all labor in the development was spared the homeowners and their families. Indeed, virtually every household head lived with between one and three servants to handle domestic chores. Further, Llewellyn Park's housing styles themselves began to change in the late nineteenth century. Many of the older and more modest cottages endemic to the mid-nineteenth-century growth spurt were enlarged or demolished, with larger and more expensive Gilded Age mansions becoming increasingly commonplace. Formal gardens often replaced the more rugged and idiosyncratic plantings that respected the contours of the natural environment. The park appeared to lose its philosophical purpose, beginning its transformation into a less romantic and more typical residential suburban enclave.[9]

Another small settlement, less extensive than Llewellyn Park, exerted an even greater influence on local culture and institutions owing to the social prestige of its inhabitants. Erastus Edgerton Marcy (1815–1900), one of the most prominent homeopathic physicians in the United States, planted the seeds of this wealthy enclave when he purchased two hundred acres of wild and virtually inaccessible forest land at the summit of First Mountain in 1860. At the time, Marcy maintained both a home and a lucrative private practice on Fifth Avenue in New York City, where he also wrote extensively on Samuel Hahnemann's alternative medical theories and edited the *North American Journal of Homeopathy.* He quickly threw himself into the Orange Mountain project, however, likely envisioning the location as a healthy alternative and country retreat from urban life. Marcy's property spanned the divide between two major east-west arteries, the Northfield Road and Mount Pleasant Avenue, which originated in the Orange Valley and provided travelers with a navigable route up through the mountains and westward toward Livingston and Morris County. Marcy cleared the forest, opened a road from the mountain to Mount Pleasant Avenue, constructed a substantial Victorian Gothic home, engaged a prominent landscaper to cultivate the grounds, and even arranged for gas pipes to be laid from Orange Valley up through the mountain to his property.[10]

More significant for the development of the town, however, Marcy's vision to create a secluded country retreat soon attracted a small group of wealthy and influential neighbors who contributed to West Orange's reputation as a highly desirable place of residence. Erastus first interested his brother to build an estate nearby in the early 1860s. Randolph Barnes Marcy (1812–1887) was a successful career army officer, eventually attaining the rank of brigadier general. A rugged sportsman who enjoyed hunting in the Rocky Mountains, he fought in the Mexican War, conducted a variety of exploratory expeditions in the southwest, served in military campaigns against the Seminoles and Mormons during the 1850s, and attained national notoriety for his work with the Army of the Potomac in the early days of the Civil War. He also struck up a close friendship with General George B. McClellan (1826–1885) beginning in 1852, when "Little Mac" had been assigned to serve as engineer, commissary, quartermaster, and second-in-command under Marcy to map and discover the sources of the Red River in Texas. The two West Point graduates became regular correspondents and, partly owing to the urging and intervention of his older friend, McClellan aggressively courted Randolph's daughter Nelly (1835–1915), eventually marrying her in 1860. When he received his appointment to command the Union forces in 1861, McClellan requested that Randolph Marcy be appointed as his chief of staff. They served together in the Civil War until Abraham Lincoln relieved McClellan from his command after the Battle of Antietam in 1862. Both shared a deep antipathy to the president as well as an affinity with the conservative Democratic politicians known as "Copperheads," who sought to restore the Union but also allow the continuation of slavery in the South.[11]

Nelly began spending more time at the estates of her father and uncle on "Mountain Ridge," as the elite West Orange settlement became known, in the early 1860s. General McClellan's wealthy friends and Democratic operatives, including the prominent merchants John Jacob Astor and William H. Aspinwall, presented him with a fully furnished four-story brick house on West 31st Street in New York City in 1862, however, and the couple relocated there. McClellan soon discovered that it might prove expedient to cultivate some distance from the public pressures and highly charged ideological environment that characterized New York politics, so he began renting out the 31st Street property in 1863 and retreated with his family to West Orange. The mountain became his base of operations throughout 1864, as his political supporters and managers worked to secure his presidential nomination at the Democratic Convention in Chicago. After news of his nomination reached the Oranges, a torchlight parade up the mountain ensued. Supporters gathered near the Marcy front porch to hear McClellan's triumphal remarks. The 1864 campaign, however, proved to be a disaster as Republicans convincingly portrayed their opponents as disunionists, borderline traitors, and the party of treason. McClellan carried only three states (New Jersey, Delaware, and Kentucky), received a mere 45 percent of the popular vote, and suffered a decisive defeat in the Electoral College, 212 to 21.

For the next several years, the general and his family traveled throughout England and the Continent, living comfortably on rental income and stock investments brokered by wealthy New Yorkers. After returning to the United States in the late 1860s, McClellan decided to build his own estate on Mountain Ridge, next to that of Randolph Marcy. In 1870, he completed the rambling three-story Second Empire-style mansion, featuring a mansard roof, broad verandas, a stone fence around the property, and formidable iron gates controlling entry. Both natural and imported ornamental trees filled out the landscape and lined the pathway to the entrance, where a "star" flower bed greeted visitors and a small grove sheltered the grave of McClellan's trusty steed, "Daniel Webster." He named the estate "Maywood" after his only daughter, and McClellan's literary executor observed that he "brought around him treasures of literature and art, memorials of faithful friends, of far travel, of scenes in his life which were pleasant to remember." Maywood remained McClellan's primary residence throughout the 1870s, though he also escaped the August heat by taking lengthy excursions to the White Mountains of New Hampshire and Mount Desert Island in Maine and often spent winters at another home in New York City's Gramercy Park. After New Jerseyans elected McClellan to a four-year gubernatorial term in 1877, he spent most of his time on Orange Mountain, typically traveling to Trenton on Tuesday mornings to conduct state business and returning to his secluded retreat in the evening. The office took a physical and mental toll, however, and

McClellan wrote his mother in February of 1881 that although "I got through with my governorship all right, I am very glad to be done with it, as it was becoming a nuisance to be obliged to go to Trenton in all weathers."[12]

McClellan and the Marcys exerted an outsized influence on the broader West Orange community and its developing institutional structure during the 1870s in several ways. First, they supported a variety of religious and fraternal organizations as the town's center of social gravity began shifting up the mountain. An earlier generation of town dwellers—personified by such families as the Williamses, Condits, Harrisons, and Dodds—often traced their lineage to colonial times and owned the large tracts of farmland and pastures that became carved up into such settlements as Llewellyn Park and Mountain Ridge. These more established townsfolk tended to identify as Episcopalians and worshipped at the handsome Saint Mark's Church in the valley area, which they built in 1828 and enlarged significantly throughout the 1850s and 1860s. By the time that McClellan completed work on Maywood in 1870, the beautifully constructed Gothic Revival brownstone church in the valley featured a steeply pitched slate roof with decorative trusses and brackets designed by Richard Upjohn Jr., pointed arch windows, and valuable stained glass. Its towering steeple, located on a commanding downtown eminence, dominated the cityscape of the valley and constituted a worthy monument to the town's traditional elites. McClellan and Marcy, however, represented a newer generation of town dwellers with different values and interests. As devout Presbyterians and mountain dwellers who rarely ventured into the valley, they worked with their neighbors to establish a new institution that would rival Saint Mark's in wealth and style. They engaged a prominent New York City architect with an international reputation, William Appleton Potter, to design a handsome brownstone Gothic Revival church up the hill that blended beautifully into the mountainous landscape. Architectural historians have praised its "pyramidal bell tower, shaped window openings, steeply pitched roof and bold entrances" as reminiscent of the work of Henry Hobson Richardson. Further, after the new Saint Cloud Presbyterian Church opened in 1877, it became an important social center in the mountain neighborhood, hosting musical recitals, dramatic presentations, and lectures as well as religious services. A new institutional venue now existed to serve the cultural and religious sentiments of a more sophisticated and urbane audience than the older landowners who populated more modest estates in the valley.[13]

McClellan also brought a new social style to the mountain. Llewellyn Park residents typically employed between one and three servants to manage their more modest households. McClellan's household staff included three domestics, two of whom were born in Ireland, an Irish coachman to handle his driving needs, and a Louisiana-born African American waiter. Many neighbors engaged even more elaborate staffs. William Adams (1807–1880), a prominent minister on Mountain Ridge who served as president of Union Theological Seminary during his residency there, employed eight women domestics (seven from Ireland and one from Scotland), a coachman, and a German-born gardener to maintain his substantial estate. Other outbuildings and smaller cottages on Mountain Ridge sheltered complex households containing maids, coachmen, grooms, laborers, waiters, governesses, and gardeners from such diverse locales as England, Ireland, Scotland, France, Canada, Baden, Wurttemberg, Saxony, and the West Indies. Nelly McClellan especially became noted for her popular soirees, and the eclectic combination of businessmen, professionals, and arts enthusiasts on the mountain created a lively intellectual scene, albeit one a bit less radical than the freethinkers, former abolitionists, and mystics who gravitated to the somewhat more freewheeling atmosphere that characterized the early Llewellyn Park.[14]

A few examples illustrate the larger point. William Adams, the aforementioned clergyman with ten servants, possessed impeccable Presbyterian credentials with degrees from Yale College and Andover Theological Seminary. During his tenure at Madison Square Presbyterian Church, according to his successor Charles Parkhurst, "no church in New York City at that time exercised a wider or more commanding influence, not only in the city but throughout the country; the congregation largely was composed of the cultivated people of the town, prominent in every department of secular and religious activity." Brown moved easily within the circles of the wealthy and the powerful. Indeed, one of his daughters married James Brown, the founder of Brown Brothers, one of the most prominent global financial firms in the United States. A second daughter married Eugene Delano (1844–1920), who lived with his father-in-law on Mountain Ridge in 1880. Delano also became a partner in Brown Brothers; his sister became the mother of Franklin Delano Roosevelt, and his son William Adams emerged as one of the most acclaimed architects in the early twentieth century, whose commissions included the Rockefeller home in Pocantico Hills. Francis Beatty Thurber (1842–1907) also gravitated to Mountain

Ridge. During his residency in West Orange, his firm had the "reputation of being the largest wholesale grocery house in the world," according to his obituary. He also authored the delightfully eccentric book *Coffee: From Plantation to Cup* while living on the mountain and subsequently achieved some national notoriety as the oldest law student in the United States after his firm went into bankruptcy. Thurber's wife, Jeannette (1850–1946), became one of the first substantial patrons of classical music in the United States, played an instrumental role in establishing the National Conservatory of Music in New York City in 1885, and was responsible for bringing Anton Dvorak to America in 1892 to head her company. Although many of these Mountain Ridge residents moved back and forth between New York City and West Orange and some resided for only a few years in the community, they provided the town with a reputation as a premiere setting that attracted some of the nation's most prominent political, economic, and cultural elites. Marcy and McClellan clearly provided the glue that cemented this small and closely bound settlement of approximately fifteen families.[15]

Another cluster of homes near Mountain Ridge also received some notoriety as a desirable residential community in the 1860s and 1870s. This neighborhood owed more to classic real estate speculation and standard nineteenth-century urban development patterns than either Llewellyn Park or Mountain Ridge, but it also contributed to West Orange's upscale reputation. Benjamin Franklin Small (1832–1882) bore the principal responsibility for developing this area, which he named Saint Cloud. Small had grown up in the small town of Harwich on Cape Cod, where his father, Zebina, had amassed considerable real and personal property by becoming a pioneer in cranberry cultivation on the peninsula. Benjamin gravitated more toward white-collar work and urban living than cranberry bogs and marshes, however, and by 1850, he had moved to nearby New Bedford, where he boarded with a successful merchant and worked as a clerk in his landlord's firm. Shortly thereafter, he became inducted into the Masons, indicating his growing social status as a young man on the rise in the mercantile world. For some unknown reason, Small found his way to northern New Jersey in 1860, where he discovered the rugged and enchanting landscape on the summit of First Mountain. He decided to turn his attention from the countinghouse to real estate, using his family money and his earned income to purchase a huge tract of vacant and largely unimproved farmland in the region. Small then began dividing up plots, laying out streets, and marketing the properties to potential buyers.[16]

Saint Cloud contained neither the innovative and utopian planning that informed Llewellyn Park nor the exclusivity and substantial wealth that characterized Mountain Ridge. Rather, Small laid out main streets named Edgewood, Fairview, Ridgeway, and Benvenue according to a fairly standard grid plan. He also attempted to make the development more accessible by macadamizing Northfield Road, obtaining six thousand dollars from the New Jersey state legislature in 1869 to pave the rocky and irregular terrain from the valley and up into the mountain. Small's efforts initially proved quite successful. He created, according to the *Newark Daily Advertiser* in 1882, a "pretty little settlement which has since become so popular a place of Summer residence." Indeed, early settlers occupied small lots on the main streets, constructing a combination of relatively modest cottages, shingle-style dwellings, and Second Empire homes in the neighborhood. Though Saint Cloud existed in close proximity to Mountain Ridge, both a formidable stone wall and significant social class distinctions separated the two settlements. Saint Cloud contained approximately twice as many households (twenty-nine) as its more prosperous neighbor in 1880 but fell short in other categories indicating wealth and prestige. Only eleven of the twenty-nine households employed servants, for example, as opposed to virtually every homeowner in both Mountain Ridge and Llewellyn Park. Further, ten of the eleven homes with hired help housed only one or two domestics. Household heads in Small's settlement tended to work in banking, commerce, real estate, law, medicine, and education, but their sphere appeared smaller and more local than in the more prestigious developments. Dry goods salesmen, clothing merchants, life insurance clerks, accountants, real estate agents, and physicians with practices in Newark predominated. Most householders appeared at a relatively early stage in their careers, ranging in age from their early thirties through their middle forties. Many Saint Cloud dwellers still possessed sufficient resources to maintain substantial primary residences in New York City, and virtually all lived comfortable upper-middle-class existences. Few, however, exhibited the cultural sophistication and the national connections that characterized West Orange's more elite residents.[17]

William James Appleton Fuller constituted the one idiosyncratic exception proving the rule. Born in 1822, he was a generation older than most of his neighbors. A native Bostonian with a distinguished ministerial lineage, Fuller early exhibited considerable intellectual prowess through his attendance at the Boston Latin School and admission to Harvard University. Academic pursuits held little attraction for the young man, however, and he soon abandoned Harvard Yard for more thrilling and adventurous endeavors that made his life somewhat nefarious and definitely "eventful—more so than falls to the lot of ordinary men," in the words of one biographer. Another chronicler of his life noted that he spent the 1840s and early 1850s sailing around the world as a seaman, hunting whales in arctic climes, spending time in exotic locales ranging from Cuba to California, winning and losing occasionally outlandish wagers, earning his living as a teacher and newspaper editor, and becoming a chess master who popularized the introduction of that game into the United States and helped found the American Chess Congress. After he returned to the east coast in the mid-1850s, Fuller became a popular orator and stump speaker for John C. Fremont's presidential campaign as well as a committed abolitionist who commanded a regiment of Massachusetts's volunteers during the Civil War. He also turned his attention to the law and, after moving to New York City in the early 1860s, struck up a partnership with a rising New Jersey Democratic politician named Leon Abbett, who eventually became governor of the Garden State. As an attorney, Fuller became known as the "Patent Rubber Man" for his tenacious work in prosecuting anyone who tried to infringe on the Goodyear fortunes. One chronicler of New York society—after praising his quick wit, energy, tenacity, and fairness—opined that his success owed "to his keen and thorough knowledge of men (for which his checkered and eventful life eminently fits him), great readiness, the power of thinking rapidly on his feet, never losing his self-control; and unlike most New York lawyers, he attends to his business—never neglects it."[18]

Fuller had also befriended Brigadier General Randolph Marcy, perhaps during the war, and McClellan's father-in-law no doubt drew his attention to the pleasures and benefits of life on First Mountain. The 1870 census found Fuller living in West Orange, though he also maintained a home on Thirty-Fifth Street in New York City, participating fully in the social scene and club life of the great metropolis. By 1880, he was living with his wife and six of his eight children in the most substantial and elegant home in Saint Cloud. His household also included five servants: two African American maids from South Carolina, the birthplace of his wife,

Charlotte; two Irish domestics; and one male German-born laborer who maintained the property. Fuller's guile and good luck enabled him to live on a scale and in a style that far exceeded most of his neighbors in Saint Cloud. He remained a prosperous and well-connected attorney throughout his old age, frequented the Union Club and founded the Whist Club in New York City, traveled regularly to the Continent with his wife and children, and doubtless enlivened social gatherings and public events on the mountain. Some of his neighbors, as well as the Saint Cloud development itself, proved less fortunate.[19]

The 1870s featured the longest depression in American history. The Panic of 1873, precipitated by both global events and bank failures owing to overextended credit and shady financial speculation in the United States, ushered in a period of economic instability that lasted over five years. Bankruptcies numbered in the thousands annually, businesses collapsed, and the New York Stock Exchange closed for the first time in its history. Unemployment and layoffs among the growing class of wage-earners skyrocketed. Small-scale entrepreneurs failed and previously independent producers often sought jobs as laborers to make ends meet. Farm profits plunged and banks repossessed land at an alarming rate. Scholars have estimated that the unemployment rate exceeded 15 percent by 1878, with over 30 percent of the workforce experiencing at least one hundred days of unemployment during that year. Structural unemployment led to a host of serious social problems throughout the nation, including homelessness, poverty, and a rising crime rate.[20]

Benjamin Small turned out to be an early victim of the downturn. His obituary noted that "the Panic of 1873 put a quietus upon the real estate market," and he soon "found the load heavier than he could carry, and he lost a large part of his property." Small eventually managed to recoup some of his fortune by the early 1880s. He turned his attention to raising and breeding pure blood Alderney cattle and operated a successful dairy farm. Small's memorialist claimed that "his stock was some of the finest to be found in the country," and he maintained a thriving business in New York at the time of his premature death in June 1882. Saint Cloud itself, however, stagnated and never realized its early promise. The prosperous homes that had been built in the late 1860s and the early 1870s remained, but Small's plans to expand the development throughout the mountain collapsed. Much land remained vacant and fallow. Although the three elite West Orange neighborhoods—Llewellyn Park, Mountain Ridge, and

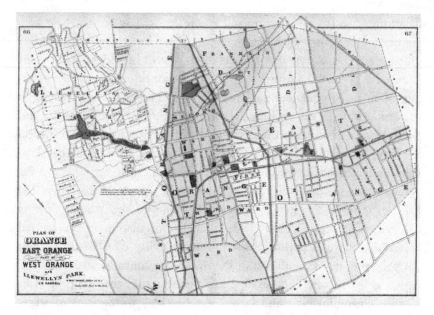

FIG. 2.3 "Plan of Orange, East Orange, Part of West Orange, and Llewellyn Park" from
F. W. Beers, *State Atlas of New Jersey* (New York: Beers, Comstock & Clines, 1872). Hatters
in West Orange dominated the streets to the immediate left of the Third Ward of Orange,
near the bottom center of the map. The Mountain Ridge neighborhood, settled by the
Marcys and McClellans, can be found to the west and north of the hatting district. Llewellyn
Park is located north and east of Mountain Ridge. Saint Cloud and the Meierhofer residence
on Northfield Road are not contained on this map but can be viewed in fig. P.1.

Saint Cloud—still attracted summer vacationers and year-round residents
in 1880, none of them grew substantially during the depression decade.[21]

West Orange itself, however, enjoyed a modest population increase from
2,106 to 3,385 between 1870 and 1880. Though impressive by statistical
standards, since the 1,279 new residents amounted to a 62 percent growth
rate over the course of the decade, the town remained a small and dispersed
community largely consisting of the three planned residential enclaves, a
densely settled neighborhood in the valley, and some scattered farmsteads.
Its 1880 population paled in comparison to neighboring Orange, which
had developed into a thriving small city that exceeded 13,000 inhabitants,
as well as the regional hub of nearby Newark, which counted approximately 136,500 residents. Further, West Orange's population growth illustrated some surprising trends between 1870 and 1880. The percentage of
residents employed in service-related occupations—including maids,
coachmen, gardeners, waiters, washerwomen, and laundresses—declined

slightly from 34 percent to 31 percent, perhaps reflecting the general economic stagnation and lack of growth in the middle-class neighborhoods. West Orangers employed in manufacturing enterprises, however, increased from 18 percent to over 21 percent, with the hatting industry exhibiting an exceptionally marked expansion. Indeed, the number of men and women employed in this trade more than doubled during the decade. Further, unskilled laborers, who made up less than 9 percent of the 1870 labor force, constituted 14 percent of community residents who reported an occupation in 1880. Despite the town's reputation as a wealthy and comfortable suburban community and healthful summer retreat, West Orange also housed a less visible, more diverse, and poorer group of citizens whose lives had little in common with the Llewellyn Park intellectuals and successful businessmen on the mountain.[22]

Hatting largely dominated the town's industrial economy. A visitor to neighboring Orange, in the words of one late nineteenth-century industrial directory, "cannot fail to notice the number of hat-manufacturing establishments located there and the multitude of workpeople engaged in them." Hatting, according to this 1882 guide, "is the great industry of the place," as craftsmen produced "fur hats of all sizes and qualities" for export throughout the United States. Although small hat shops had existed in the Orange Valley during the early 1800s, by midcentury, the industry had matured, grown, and consolidated. Orange boasted a knowledgeable labor force, enjoyed close proximity to the fashion capitals of New York and Philadelphia, and carefully cultivated connections to furriers who provided the skins from rabbits, muskrats, and other small animals needed by local manufacturers. Enterprising factory owners in the community successfully competed with their rivals in such midsized towns as Danbury, Connecticut, and even held their own with manufacturers in the larger cities of Newark, Philadelphia, and Boston. By 1854, Orange boasted twenty-nine hat factories that employed nearly one thousand people. Hat manufacturers included relatively substantial companies with national reputations and attractive retail showrooms, such as Frederick Berg and the Stetson Brothers, who employed hundreds of formers, finishers, and trimmers. Other small commission shops consisted of just a few hired hands, rented tools and space in dilapidated factories, and operated on the margins. Orange companies particularly specialized in manufacturing the soft hats made from fur felt that had become fashionable in the 1850s and proved especially popular with soldiers during the Civil War. Although production and sales declined somewhat during the depression years of the 1870s, which also witnessed the derby hat craze that shifted the center of the industry elsewhere, hatting remained an important element of Orange's local economy well into the twentieth century.[23]

Hat factories concentrated in a tightly packed area of the central city, located primarily on streets and alleys a few blocks removed from the town's more fashionable commercial sector. Manufacturers typically built their facilities near the east branch of the Rahway River, which provided a useful water supply for washing hats and also formed part of the boundary between Orange and West Orange. They further benefited from close proximity to the Morris and Essex Railroad Station, which linked them directly with the great metropolises and commercial emporiums of Newark and Jersey City. Hatting connected the valley areas of Orange and West Orange, both of which featured densely packed concentrations of cheap one- and two-story wooden homes that sheltered workers and their families. If large estates and well-manicured properties characterized mountain life, valley people operated in an environment dominated by railroad tracks, coal yards, boardinghouses, billiard parlors, and saloons. Labor historians have observed that hat finishers, who successfully resisted the deskilling and mechanization of their craft for much of the nineteenth century, cultivated work traditions characterized by extensive apprenticeships, trade loyalty, manly independence, periodic unemployment, tramping, and heavy drinking. One admittedly temperate and pious West Orangeman recalled, when reminiscing about his late nineteenth-century childhood, that "the hat makers were well paid when they worked, but their work was irregular, and whatever they made beyond a bare living they spent at the corner saloons."[24]

Such stereotypical renderings contained an important element of truth, but real life in the valley differed somewhat from these broadly conceived caricatures. West Orange hatters did live in close quarters and within easy walking distance of the factories. Sixty-seven percent of the individuals involved with the trade in 1880 resided on one of seven streets in the valley: Main, White, Mitchell, Stockman, Tompkins, Freeman, and South Valley. These congested little arteries housed approximately 23 percent of the community's adult working population. As a contrast, the much more spacious and sprawling Llewellyn Park settlement sheltered only 8 percent of West Orangers over fifteen years of age. Hatters definitely dominated the aforementioned seven streets: 45 percent of all jobholders who lived there worked in some aspect of the industry. And the area's economic profile differed dramatically in other ways from the rest of the town. Only 12 percent of these valley residents were connected with service-oriented occupations as opposed to 31 percent for West Orange in general. Further, domestic servants in the valley tended to live with their families or as boarders, commuting daily to their jobs rather than living with wealthier householders, which characterized domestic servitude up the mountain. Hatting also contributed to the area's particular ethnic character. Immigrants and first-generation Americans proved especially prominent in the trade, consistent with national employment patterns. South Valley Street, which contained the largest concentration of hatters, illustrates this trend. Irish immigrants and their children who lived on this street accounted for 64 percent of the industry's employees. Another 19 percent hailed from the German States of Prussia, Hesse-Darmstadt, Wurttemberg, Holstein, and Baden. Only 13 percent of South Valley residents who worked in hatting had been in the United States for at least two generations.[25]

Despite these neighborhood characteristics, it would be misleading to view the valley purely as an insular immigrant, working-class enclave. The percentages of foreign-born residents on the seven hatter-dominated streets (25 percent Irish and 12 percent German) roughly reflected West Orange's overall ethnic composition (23 percent Irish and 10 percent German). Further, the area contained a fair amount of economic diversity. Tompkins and Freeman Streets, in the heart of the hatting district, housed a number of craftsmen, including bakers, carpenters, shoemakers, butchers, and even an organ-builder who had been born in the German state of Hanover. John C. Morgan, a young native-born physician, maintained a home and a practice on the corner of Tompkins and Mitchell. Claude Sellier, an enterprising French immigrant born in the 1820s, worked as a teamster, operated a livery stable, and eventually opened a saloon in the valley though he described himself as a "veterinary surgeon" in the 1880 census. Somewhat surprisingly, several wealthy hat manufacturers also made their homes on Tompkins and Freeman. Nineteenth-century hatting featured a fair amount of internal mobility as finishers and factory owners often started their careers as apprentices or journeymen, gradually working their way up and accumulating capital while also remaining loyal to craft traditions. Napoleon Stetson (1821–1901), who maintained his Tompkins Street home until his death, best exemplifies the ties that sometimes bound bosses and workers. Napoleon's father, Stephen, had migrated to Orange from

Connecticut early in the nineteenth century and had established a small hatting business in the valley. By the 1850s, Stephen's firm grew into one of the largest in the area, earning a reputation for superior quality and providing a good living for his four sons. Napoleon partnered with his brother Henry to manage the concern until 1853, when the latter was killed in a tragic train accident on the Hackensack River. Napoleon then took over sole management of the business and also became active in public affairs, joining the New Jersey National Guard, serving on the Orange Town Council, and earning election to the Essex County Board of Freeholders. His other brother, John, moved to Philadelphia and earned national notoriety both for developing the western-style, ten-gallon "Stetson Hat" and for pioneering various employee welfare programs and philanthropic endeavors. Napoleon, however, remained rooted in Orange Valley, living in close proximity to his workers until ill health forced him to winter at the family compound in DeLand, Florida. He also became an active communicant at Saint Mark's Episcopal Church in West Orange, and his seven children continued to engage in various civic activities throughout the region. Napoleon never cultivated the national connections or influence that would have placed him in the orbit of, for example, the Marcys and McClellans who lived on Mountain Ridge, but he exerted a significant influence on economic, social, political, and religious life in the somewhat more limited and self-contained world of the valley.[26]

The Stagg family, who lived at 384 South Valley Street in West Orange, also provides some insight into the complex changes that were shaping local life by 1880. Amos L. Stagg, the patriarch, boasted a distinguished New Jersey ancestry, though he grew up in modest circumstances. Born in 1819, his mother's early death and the family's meager prospects led him to be bound out as a shoemaker's apprentice at the age of seven. By 1835, he had run away from home, established an independent household, and decided to earn his living as a cobbler. Orange had boasted a reasonably lively shoe trade in the 1830s and 1840s, but the local market dried up shortly thereafter. Small producers and craftsmen in towns like Orange quickly became eclipsed by national industrial magnates who opened extensive and highly mechanized factories in New England. The shoe industry consolidated, labor became more routine and less reliant on craft skills, and large-scale producers marketed their wares throughout the United States, marginalizing more modest shops in small towns and cities. Stagg managed to eke out a living in West Orange, but he could not hope to remain competitive with the national brand names, and financial pressures increased. By 1880, Amos still needed to support his fifty-five-year-old wife, Eunice, and seven children ranging in age from twenty-nine to twelve. For years he had supplemented his income by hiring himself and his two sons, George and Amos Alonzo, out to harvest grain and cut hay on the salt meadows of Newark Bay. This grueling job involved cutting and cradling grain by hand, battling the mosquitoes that bred wildly in the swampland, and carrying the heavy and wet hay by using black walnut poles to bring them to piling. Such exhausting seasonal labor proved endemic to working-class life.[27]

The Stagg family's employment patterns indicated the blurring of lines between white-collar work, the trades, and unskilled labor that existed throughout the valley. Amos's oldest son, George, for example, began his working life in the late 1860s as an apprentice for a blind and sash man-ufacturer in West Orange. By 1880, however, the twenty-nine-year-old was working as a bookkeeper in a local firm though still living at home and continuing to earn extra income as a laborer to help out his father. George eventually moved away from South Valley Street but remained in the area, working as a foreman in a local factory and serving as president of the West Orange Board of Education. Ultimately, George purchased a home in the attractive Essex County suburb of Irvington after achieving a coveted corporate managerial position as superintendent for the Lehigh Valley Coal Company. Sarah and Hattie, the two oldest daughters in the family, pursued different paths. Both began their working careers follow-ing eighth-grade graduation. The 1870 census listed their occupations as hat trimmers when they were seventeen and fourteen years old respec-tively. Trimmers essentially consisted of female operatives in hat factories who sewed in linings and often affixed ribbons to the finished prod-ucts right before they went to market. Irish women tended to dominate this job in the valley, but the Stagg girls found good opportunities in Orange's fur hat factories. By 1880, Sarah continued to work in a local hat shop, but Hattie had shifted gears and moved into the white-collar workforce as a "saleslady" for a dressmaking establishment. Sarah never married, found steady employment as a hat trimmer into the 1920s, and continued to live at the family home on South Valley Street after her par-ents died. Hattie worked herself up to the position of sales agent in her firm and married a man named Ridgeway, but she was widowed by 1920 and moved back to the family homestead with her son to live with Sarah and her two unmarried youngest sisters, one of whom taught at a local private school. Amos Alonzo Stagg, seventeen years old in 1880, became the most famous member of the family by carving out a career in the world of collegiate sports. Christianity and higher education became his ticket out of Essex County. Both fellow communicants at First Presbyterian Church in Orange and high school classmates recognized his potential. They secured a position for the young man at Phillips-Exeter Academy in New Hampshire, where the son of Orange's mayor paved the way. This provided Amos Alonzo with the educational training necessary to secure admission to Yale University, where he became a baseball star and divinity student. Stagg went on to work at the prestigious Young Men's Christian Association Training School in Springfield, Massachusetts, where he tutored under such physical education pioneers as James Naismith and Luther Halsey Gulick. He became perhaps the most famous and influential football coach in the nation at the University of Chicago during the first three decades of the twentieth century.[28]

The Stagg family story indicates the ways in which ordinary West Orange families found diverse ways to grapple with the town's changing economic and social world at a transitional moment in the nineteenth-century economy. Sarah found stability in such traditional economic trades as hatting, taking care of her aging parents and managing the family homestead. Her household became the focal point for her sisters, each of whom moved back to South Valley Street at some point. She remained tied to home and family, but her decision not to marry meant that she needed to support herself with an independent income. George moved easily between blue- and white-collar jobs throughout his life. His craft apprenticeship never led to long-term employment in the blind and sash industry, but his youthful industrial experiences no doubt facilitated his rise to the position of factory foreman. Ultimately, he took advantage of the new managerial opportunities available in large capitalist enterprises to create a comfortable suburban lifestyle. Hattie took advantage of the new opportunities available to women in a Gilded Age retail world increasingly characterized by glitzy department stores, conspicuous consumption, and the rise of a national fashion industry. Amos Alonzo managed to create a completely new career for himself in the sports industry by navigating national educational bureaucracies and mastering the art of public relations. The Orange Valley provided both economic opportunities and constraints for its late nineteenth-century denizens. The Staggs largely succeeded in achieving their financial goals, but other West Orange residents who had fewer options and could not adapt to changing circumstances proved less fortunate.

Farmers appeared in a particularly precarious position by 1880. Agriculture once constituted the primary occupation for West Orange's mountain dwellers. Good natural drainage produced fertile fields despite the hilly and rocky terrain. Streams, brooks, and rivers flowed throughout the town, naturally irrigating soil on the mountainsides and in the valleys. Ordinary farming proliferated and proved profitable, as settlers carried grains, vegetables, and fruit down the valley to grocers and retailers in Orange and Newark. The land also seemed especially adaptable to apples, and pioneers in the eighteenth and early nineteenth centuries planted hundreds of orchards throughout the area. Some farmers also owned substantial numbers of cattle, which led to a thriving dairy industry. Others trafficked in pork. Indeed, one of the principal east-west arteries linking Orange and West Orange originally bore the name "Swinefield Road," owing to the fact that local inhabitants drove their pigs by this route west to Livingston for summer pasture. Up until the mid-nineteenth century, virtually all the wealthiest families in West Orange—the Harrisons, Williamses, Condits, and Freemans—owed their fortune to farming and held substantial acreage. This pattern persisted somewhat through the 1860s. The 1870 census revealed that the four wealthiest farmers in West Orange—Simeon Harrison, Ira Harrison, Charles Williams, and Charles Harrison—accounted for nearly 43 percent of the total value of farmland, despite constituting only 6 percent of the agricultural households in town. Their property valuations ranged from $50,000 to $125,000. Even more strikingly, the wealthiest seventeen farmers, who comprised 27 percent of the total number, included four Harrisons, five Condits, and five Williamses. This interconnected group owned nearly 80 percent of the valued farmland in the community. By contrast, the bottom 49 percent of West Orange farmers accounted for only 9 percent of the assessed agricultural land, with their modest farmsteads typically worth between $1,500 and $3,000. A striking contrast existed between the first families whose lineage could be traced to colonial times and the more modest and recently arrived farmers who eked out a hardscrabble existence on much smaller landholdings.[29]

Beginning in the 1860s, however, the town's wealthiest citizens began moving away from agriculture. Such visionary developers as Llewellyn Haskell and Benjamin Small began buying up large plots of land to carve out their real estate ventures. The leading farm families sold off vast tracts for profit, often sent their male heirs to prestigious colleges to learn a profession, attempted to arrange favorable marriages for their daughters, diversified their economic interests, and appeared less interested in cultivating their substantial estates. Orlando Williams (1831–1911) offers one good example of the way in which agricultural pursuits became more complicated and marginal over time. The son of a prominent farmer known as Squire Jonathan Williams, Orlando grew up on a fifty-five-acre farm located near Pleasant Valley Way that had been in the family for three generations. Jonathan had five children to provide for, however, and his inheritance could not support everyone on the ancestral homestead. In the late 1840s, he encouraged Orlando to turn his attention to hatting, recognizing the long-term potential in this growing Orange industry. After a few years, the young man decided that other pursuits better suited his interests and skills, even though his brother, Samuel, continued working in the hat trade. Orlando instead turned his attention to shoemaking, which offered lucrative opportunities during the Civil War given the increased demand for footwear among northern troops. He opened a small shop on the John P. Condit estate in town, taking in work from local manufacturers. As the shoe business collapsed and his health declined, however, Orlando shifted gears once again. He returned to farming, not under any illusion that it provided a dynamic career choice, but rather "thinking that the open air would be a benefit to his health." Orlando lived out his life on the family estate with his wife, Hannah Condit, one unmarried daughter, Marie Antoinette, and an assortment of relatives and servants, never worrying about finances but not particularly committed to the occupation. He enjoyed the prestige of serving several terms on the town council, joined the Sons of the American Revolution as a way to pay homage to his distinguished heritage, and trafficked with the local elite. His family line, and the Williams estate itself, however, ended with his death.[30]

Farming generally declined in West Orange between 1870 and 1880. The absolute number of individuals employed in this sector decreased from 128 to 115. Even more strikingly, the percentage of the workforce involved in agricultural pursuits shrank from 16 percent to 9 percent. Furthermore, farmers now concentrated almost exclusively in particular areas of the town. Fully 73 percent of the farmers resided on six streets that accounted for only 31 percent of the adult population. These streets included the three major east-west thoroughfares that ran up the hill from Orange to Livingston: Eagle Rock Avenue, Northfield Road, and Mount

Pleasant Avenue. Eagle Rock Avenue, it should be noted, had changed its name from "Swinefield Road" as developers sought to brand the area with a more bucolic and romantic image and move away from the stigma associated with the pork trade. The other three byways dominated by farmers constituted the major north-south arteries of West Valley Road, Pleasant Valley Way, and Prospect Avenue. Highway locations made the farmsteads convenient stops for teamsters who carried produce to market and also allowed for some smaller farms to sell their wares directly to travelers and passersby. Ethnically, West Orange agriculturalists also differed significantly from their earlier nineteenth-century counterparts. Only 47 percent of the farmers in the 1880 census had been born in the United States with native-born parents. Thirty-six percent were immigrants, and 17 percent were first-generation Americans whose parents had both been born in Europe. Germans predominated among the foreign-born farmers, making up 63 percent of this population, with a sprinkling of French, Irish, Scottish, Swedish, and English émigrés accounting for the remainder. The immigrants tended to cultivate smaller plots along the main roads. Many struggled to make ends meet, sometimes taking in boarders and occasionally using transient hired hands during peak busy seasons. The local economic center had shifted elsewhere, more lucrative agricultural operations had migrated westward beyond the town borders, and local farms offered more of a romantic engagement with the past than realistic prospects for future prosperity.[31]

By 1880, West Orange appeared to be a diverse and fragmented township, difficult to categorize. Distinctive neighborhoods, ethnic diversity, changing economic conditions, seasonal residents who left some affluent areas virtually deserted in the winter, and the gradual dispersal of the traditional local landowning elites made for an unsettled situation. Perhaps most significantly, if not surprisingly, the institutional infrastructure remained weak and underdeveloped. West Orangers relied almost exclusively on neighboring Orange for municipal services. The town did not establish a police department until 1884, failed to organize a fire department until 1892 after a disastrous conflagration destroyed a downtown city block, and held its township committee meetings in a structure that was condemned for safety reasons in 1890. West Orange did maintain four elementary schools, one in the valley adjacent to Saint Mark's Episcopal Church and three on the mountain. Any local child wishing to matriculate beyond grammar school, however, had to travel to Orange and pay tuition to that community until 1890, when townspeople finally established their own high school. West Orange had no newspaper. The community relied on spotty coverage in the *Orange Journal*, as well as occasional tidbits in the Newark press, for print journalism. The Orange post office handled all local communications until West Orange finally received its own facility, named after George McClellan, in 1885. Residents even depended on Orange bankers to handle all financial services until 1909, when the First National Bank of West Orange was organized.[32]

Religious, social, and cultural life centered in Orange. Only two churches existed in West Orange in 1880: Saint Mark's Episcopal in the valley that still largely served traditional local elites and Saint Cloud Presbyterian that offered a more evangelical alternative to residents in the area of Mountain Ridge. Irish Catholics needed to travel to Orange, where Saint John's Church and Our Lady of the Valley sought to satisfy their spiritual needs. German-speaking immigrants had few religious options in the immediate area. Saint Mary's and Saint Peter's in Newark constituted the closest Catholic parishes that offered German language services. A German Presbyterian Church did, however, exist in Orange. In terms of secular clubs and associations, West Orange contained virtually no fraternal, social, or civic organizations. Orange, contrastingly, boasted a full complement of masonic lodges, odd fellows halls, temperance councils, total abstinence unions, improvement associations, a Grand Army of the Republic post, and even a Mendelssohn Union. A spectacular music hall opened near the corner of Main and Day Streets in Orange in the late 1870s, bringing high culture to the city and offering residents a veneer of social sophistication. On a somewhat less elevated tone, the 1883 Orange City Directory counted fifty-three saloons within the municipal limits, as opposed to only two in West Orange. Clearly, the newer town had established few of the institutional and social elements that would prove necessary for transforming a dispersed group of idiosyncratic neighborhoods and individual householders into a unified and coherent community.[33]

Few newsworthy events occurred in West Orange during the 1870s and 1880s. Llewellyn Park attracted some national interest, though the gated community discouraged outsiders from entering the grounds. Reporters occasionally covered lavish weddings and social events on the mountain, but these remained private affairs, off-limits for curiosity seekers. For most Essex County residents, West Orange seemed something of an afterthought. Local traffic on the major arteries proved steady during peak agricultural seasons, but few commercial vehicles spent much time in town except to pick up some produce from local farms. Hunters might take advantage of the plentiful woods on the mountain to track and bag small game, but the paucity of local saloons and absence of any restaurants or oyster houses made it unlikely that they would find much refreshment in the community. More distant travelers might spend some time at one of the town's two lodging houses: the Llewellyn Park Hotel on Main Street near the foot of Eagle Rock Avenue or the Saint Cloud Hotel near the Rock Spring on Northfield Road. Even these appeared to be modest operations. The 1880 census recorded only eleven boarders at the first hotel and three families staying at the second spot. West Orange occasionally intersected with the outside world in other ways. Several industrial quarries had opened on the mountain to take advantage of the rich supply of trap rock. Essex County residents became accustomed to the noise generated by steam rollers on the mountain, and stone wagons carried crushed rock from West Orange to construction projects throughout the region. Generally, though, the town prided itself on remaining quiet, peaceful, and largely nondescript. The split from Orange relieved townsfolk from the financial burden of supporting municipal services, but it also meant that few outsiders had much reason to think about the community. This relative insularity, isolation, and calm became shattered by a shocking event in 1879 that briefly turned the eyes of the region, and even the nation, on West Orange. The family tragedy that lay at the heart of this story generated widespread horror as well as prurient interest and sensational press coverage. In the process, it also exposed some of the tense social relations, insecure ethical foundations, and fragile community bonds that existed at the heart of Gilded Age culture.

3

Murder

● ● ● ● ● ● ● ● ● ● ● ●

Many northern New Jerseyans viewed the advent of autumn through a romantic lens. The *Newark Daily Advertiser* eloquently described it as the time when "the sunshine kisses the falling leaves as though loath to part with them; the peach introduces us to the pear, the pear to the apple, while other fruits and vegetables continue to ally the season to the prolific soil." The changing weather patterns offered a welcome break from the summer heat as it remained "warm enough and bright enough to woo men from active work" yet "clear and cool enough to be thoroughly enjoyable." The *Advertiser* advised its largely urban readership to head for the woodlands, specifically Schooley's Mountain, an attractive nearby ridge with sweeping views of the Musconetcong Valley and home to a few small iron mines. At Schooley's, city folk might "note the colors that nature is laying upon the landscape, listen to the chirp of the bird and the hum of the bee and breathe an inspiring draught of October air mixed with October sunshine." Contemplating the bucolic mountain scenery, the rivers that ran through the valley, the wildlife that roamed the rocky terrain, and the songbirds gearing up for their annual migratory journeys, the reporter who penned these words enthused that "there is nothing like it." And indeed, seasonal rhythms provided the overarching structures and organizing principles for a people who largely depended on natural sunlight, reliable rainy seasons, and productive agricultural cycles to shape the pace of their daily lives and local routines. Autumn always signaled significant disruption and change. In 1879, Essex County residents who contemplated the months ahead as the days grew shorter had reason to exhibit both hope and concern.[1]

Newark businessmen and manufacturers viewed the coming season with guarded optimism. The nation finally appeared to be recovering from the economic depression that had settled in six years earlier. A survey of Newark industries indicated that fall orders had picked up considerably for carriage and harness makers, trunk manufacturers, jewelers, cloak makers, and leather entrepreneurs, all critical concerns in the area. Indeed, prospects appeared brighter than they had been since 1873. Businessmen had confronted an extended period of turmoil, uncertainty, and instability throughout the 1870s. The misery for workers and wage earners proved far worse. Long-term unemployment and wage contractions seemed to be producing a permanent class of transients and wanderers who could not support themselves or their families. Widespread hunger and malnutrition, petty crime, infectious disease, and hopelessness all appeared on the rise. Some feared that capitalism itself might be on the verge of collapse. Strikes and work stoppages often ended in violence and death as both the state and private industrialists brutally repressed job actions and labor revolts. By 1879, however, serious worker uprisings had declined as suppression tactics proved effective. The more favorable business climate did not mean that things would be returning to post–Civil War boom times. Declines in per capita income for unskilled workers, a new recognition that unemployment and underemployment constituted a semipermanent state for many wage-earners, and increased concentrations of wealth in the hands of a few produced a sense that the northern economy appeared to be changing in some permanent and unforeseen manner. Still, businessmen welcomed the promise and possibility of better times ahead in the last few months of 1879.[2]

In other ways, familiar seasonal changes produced the illusion of continuity as autumn approached. Essex County public schools planned their annual opening for September 1, with the growing number of private schools throughout the area slated to begin their terms throughout the rest of the month. Anxiety and anticipation appeared among students and teachers as August drew to a close. John C. Pierson, a young West Orange schoolmaster, no doubt looked forward to the new school year with eager excitement. He had secured a position at School Number 42, located on Northfield Road near the West Branch of the Rahway River.

The small township boasted only four elementary public schools in 1880, with the other three being Saint Mark's, located downtown on Valley Road near the Episcopal Church, Number 40 up the hill on Eagle Rock Avenue near Pleasant Valley Way, and Number 41 in the Saint Cloud development on Mount Pleasant Place near Mount Pleasant Avenue. Excepting Saint Mark's, all of these elementary schools had been established in the mid- and late-1870s, as the population in the mountain areas grew with the rise of new developments. The township still proved too parsimonious to provide any secondary training for local students, in keeping with the antitaxation impulses that initially stimulated the residents to incorporate their own community. Parents who wished to send their children to public high school thus still needed to make an arrangement and pay tuition to neighboring Orange. For Pierson, however, teaching the sons and daughters of farmers, artisans, and laborers on the hill offered a useful entrée to a possible career and a leg up on the many educated young men who sought temporary positions in local districts. Pierson no doubt felt fortunate that he had secured a suitable living situation as well. He made arrangements to rent a room at the Meierhofer farm on Northfield Road, just a short walk from his new assignment, where he would be provided with meals and lodging for a modest fee.[3]

Perhaps most exciting of all for local residents, the Essex County Courts planned to reopen on September 2 following their long summer hiatus. Trials provided popular entertainment, endless grist for local gossip mills, and an exciting diversion from everyday life. High-profile cases attracted large audiences in the courtroom, newspapers titillated subscribers with detailed daily accounts of testimony, and everyone could become a trial expert, arguing over verdicts and applying their own standards of justice to real and imagined community transgressions. The *Newark Daily Advertiser* excitedly announced that the fall 1879 session looked especially packed with interest as forty-nine supreme court and fifty-two circuit court cases already appeared on the clerk's list with the promise that "more will probably come in," a large increase over the spring docket. Perhaps the most sensational case in the fall lineup involved the trial of Joseph A. Blair, a bank teller and well-to-do citizen of Montclair, who had shot and killed his thirty-two-year-old Irish coachman in a dispute that revolved around perceived insubordination, class conflict, familial discord, and intoxicating liquor. Another high-profile trial involved a local Newarker accused of assaulting one of the city's most prominent Presbyterian clergymen. Then there were the more routine cases of domestic abuse, assault and battery, and petty crime: "The Italian who stabbed his wife one Sunday on the Hill in a fit of jealousy; one Squires, who cut his wife's throat; Thompson, the man suspected of being implicated in the robbery of Mrs. Fuller of Montclair; Cornelius Beatty, accused of robbing his father's store and conspiring against him." Add to these a series of cases involving libel, forgery, illegal liquor sales on Sunday, and the leftover trial of Adam Wolf, "who was indicted at the last term of court for shooting his wife but who fled from the city and was only arrested the other day," and the session seemed alive with prurient promise and salacious possibilities.[4]

Generally, though, life seemed to move forward in a methodical and systematic manner in the communities of Orange and West Orange with little overt drama. Orange, which had some urban pretensions and attempted to cultivate a sense of style and sophistication, had begun construction on its new downtown music hall in September. When it finally opened the following year, this grand hall contained approximately one thousand seats and cost sixty-five thousand dollars, a substantial municipal investment. The outlying areas of West Orange had more parochial and mundane concerns. Horace Stetson, who reported on the area for the 1880 census, noted that the age of large-scale agriculture on the mountains appeared to be over, as most farmers had sold their land for development and moved west to Ohio and Illinois. As a result, subdivided and less productive tracts had been purchased "chiefly by small German and some French-Canadian farmers." The countryside produced only limited goods for Orange residents and consisted of "generally small" operations that yielded "a moderate supply of all the ordinary products except wheat, barley, and flax." Small farmers in the mountains marketed dairy products, potatoes, apples, and some vegetables, but they struggled every year to make ends meet. In Stetson's view, "a widely extended suburban region" constituted the most likely future possibility for the area, and the modest farmsteads appeared destined for extinction.[5]

West Orange farmers had a reason for particular pessimism in 1879. A relentlessly hot and dry summer gave way to an even more foreboding fall. The New Jersey Department of Agriculture held out little hope for the potato crop in Essex County: "Drought and bugs will make the crop light." In terms of hay and pasturage, the state forecast a "short crop: pasturage retarded by drought." Apple trees, which grew in abundance on the mountainside, offered little hope. The *Daily Advertiser* warned in early

September that "the apple crop is said to be almost a total failure this year and the cider makers will have little to do." In addition to drought, pests added to the problem. The newspaper noted that "many of the farmers in different sections of the state are complaining of a small black worm, averaging in size from a half to a full inch that has made its appearance and is playing sad havoc with the apple trees." September and October brought additional bad news. From September 15 through the end of October, the area witnessed "only four rainy or partially rainy days and the total rain fall during all this time has been only 37/100 of an inch." The extended dry spell "has not been noticed in all the years over which these records extend," and farmers grew increasingly desperate. Unseasonably hot weather exacerbated tensions. Throughout October, temperatures exceeded eighty degrees on four days and registered over seventy degrees or more on nineteen days. For small-scale agriculturalists who had experienced several lean years owing to the national depression and falling prices due to the overproduction of crops elsewhere, this recent run of bad weather offered little promise for relief.[6]

Other factors also contributed to tensions on the mountain during the late summer and early fall. New Yorkers with summer residences in the Saint Cloud and Mountain Ridge neighborhoods often shuttered their homes for the winter during this time, returning to the metropolis and leaving behind vacant structures until the late spring. This created opportunities for petty thieves and drifters to raid their premises during the winter, but the crime season seemed to start early in 1879. William J. A. Fuller, the eccentric attorney profiled in the preceding chapter, reported in August that his Ridgeway Avenue home had been burglarized as thieves broke a downstairs window while he tended to his sick wife in an upstairs bedroom. The intruders managed to escape with his gold watch, some silverware, jewelry, a check, and approximately seventy-five dollars in cash. A neighbor on the corner of Ridgeway and Benvenue, Robert P. Anderson, also reported a break-in, with the loss of some silverware. On September 1, burglars forced open a ground floor window at the picturesque "Eyrie" villa on Eagle Rock Avenue, which had been built and previously occupied by Llewellyn Haskell, escaping with a small quantity of clothing. Low-level crime occurred with some frequency throughout the Oranges in the late 1870s, based on newspaper accounts, yet the recent wave of burglaries on the mountain appeared exceptional. West Orange had no police force at all given the small number of transgressions and relied on neighboring

Orange to handle its law enforcement. The Orange force, which consisted of one marshal, one sergeant, one roundsman, and ten part-time patrolmen, typically attended to simple cases of drunkenness and breaches of the peace, which accounted for nearly four hundred of the six hundred arrests recorded in 1879. Indeed, the police department's annual report, issued in March 1880, chronicled only eight arrests for burglary during the previous year and noted that "few cases of robbery have been reported." Further, the marshal made certain to inform the citizenry that "in our complex city, with so many of its streets sparsely settled, it should not be expected that with our present limited force we can give that protection which the different sections of our city demand." Certainly, the minor "crime wave" that hit Saint Cloud at the end of the summer of 1879 provided enough concern to unnerve the locals, who no doubt had little confidence that the Orange force would apprehend the perpetrators.[7]

These small-scale crimes paled, however, before a shocking incident that took place in West Orange on October 1. Thomas Ogden Woodruff, a seventy-five-year-old lifetime county resident and former Essex County freeholder, was found shot in the head at his Prospect Avenue home. Woodruff, who had been born in nearby Caldwell, owned a substantial amount of property in the township that he devoted largely to farming, though he also had engaged in shoemaking. His daughter had married a Prussian immigrant, Anthony Kunick, and the couple had moved to Virginia, with Woodruff holding a mortgage on their farm there. After Woodruff's daughter died, Kunick became estranged from his father-in-law, proved unable to keep up with mortgage payments during the depression decade of the 1870s, and grew increasingly unhinged. Woodruff decided to foreclose on the Virginia property, which threw Kunick into a rage and caused him to travel to Newark to meet with his father-in-law. A bitter argument ensued, after which Kunick followed Woodruff to West Orange, bringing along his five-barreled Smith and Wesson revolver. Kunick burst into the house, fired on Woodruff (inflicting a superficial scalp wound), then turned the gun on himself and committed suicide by blowing his brains out. Woodruff survived and subsequently took in his two grandchildren, aged twenty and seventeen, but the entire incident shook the normally quiescent community. The familial discord, economic tensions, passionate violence, nativist fears, and disturbing implications of the Woodruff affair encapsulated many of the social issues that appeared to be tearing apart the fabric of American culture in the 1870s. Ironically, however, at the very moment that Anthony Kunick was being laid to rest in Rosedale Cemetery on October 9, an even more horrific event was playing out on Northfield Road. Before turning to the particulars of that tragedy, however, it appears essential to examine the previous life stories of the three individuals who collided on that fateful fall day.[8]

Margaret Klem (Meierhofer), John Meierhofer, and Frank Lammens all remain murky and mysterious historical characters. Basic facts concerning their lives either cannot be reconstructed from the historical evidence or remain in dispute. They aptly illustrate the difficulties inherent in documenting the lives and thoughts of ordinary people who lived in relative obscurity. As immigrants with marginal economic resources, they arrived in America quietly and without fanfare. They labored in a variety of tenuous trades, scrambling to earn their livelihoods and leaving little overt marks on their communities. At various moments, they passed through public and private institutions that regulated the tempo of daily existence for the poor in a harsh and unforgiving society. Occasionally, they resorted to illegal activities and shady practices in desperate attempts to better their fortunes. Each one experienced the stress of constant movement, the hardship of civil war, the empty promises of peacetime, and the debilitating effects of economic depression. Their personal lives played out against the pleasures, frustrations, and hardships that characterized life in the mid- and late-nineteenth-century United States. If not for their involvement in a grisly and controversial murder, they likely would have disappeared completely from the historical record without a trace. As it stands, their tragic personal lives earned them a fleeting moment of fame and notoriety in Gilded Age America.

Margaret Klem, owing largely to her extensive trial testimony and corroborating evidence, lived the best-documented life of the three individuals at the heart of this story. Margaret was born in Bavaria in 1841, the youngest in a family of at least five children. Indeed, her mother, Catharine, was forty-four years old at the time of Margaret's birth. Her childhood coincided with a period of severe economic crisis and deprivation in the southern German states. Bavaria, similar to nearby Baden and Wurttemberg as well as the southern Rhine River valley, bore the brunt of distress. A devastating potato rot especially worsened conditions in agricultural areas. Grain and potato prices rose dramatically during this period leading to widespread famine and hunger riots throughout the region. German farmers who previously supplemented their incomes by taking on seasonal

660   HARPER'S WEEKLY.   VOLUME XXVII., NO. 1400

BI-CENTENNIAL OF THE FIRST LANDING OF GERMANS IN AMERICA—THE CELEBRATION IN NEWARK, NEW JERSEY.—DRAWN BY TAYLOR AND MEEKER.—[SEE PAGE 663.]

FIG. 3.1 "Bicentennial of the First Landing of Germans in America—the Celebration in Newark, New Jersey," *Harper's Weekly*, 1 October 1876. This triumphal municipal gathering reflected the growing political power and maturation of a large and influential body of immigrants who had settled in Newark and throughout Essex County. German immigration had increased exponentially in the 1850s, and by the 1870s, the "Hill" section of Newark, near Saint Mary's Church, had developed into an important social, religious, and cultural center. Courtesy of Special Collections, Newark Public Library, Newark, N.J.

textile work found that the Industrial Revolution virtually eliminated these opportunities. Rural overpopulation exacerbated the problems, and farming families increasingly discovered that the land could not support their progeny or guarantee survival for subsequent generations. By the early 1850s, bankruptcies reached record levels and desperation appeared to be the prevailing mood. Increasingly, families turned to migration as a solution and, paradoxically, as the only way to preserve their traditional way of life.[9]

Margaret migrated to the United States in 1852 or 1853, coinciding with the peak years of the early nineteenth-century German exodus to America. Immigration from the German states had increased steadily since 1800, averaging roughly 60,000 per year until 1851. Suddenly, the numbers increased exponentially. Indeed, German immigrants outnumbered the Irish from 1852 to 1854, with over 400,000 arriving in America during the latter year. New York City constituted the major port of entry, processing over 140,000 arrivals in 1852 and 1853. Some Germans, including

Margaret initially, remained in Manhattan and even created their own tightly knit ethnic enclave known as Kleindeutschland on the Lower East Side. Many others dispersed throughout the nation, however, most often settling in the "German triangle" bounded by Cincinnati, Milwaukee, and St. Louis. A substantial number of these émigrés sought land in the Midwest in order to pursue farming in a fertile area. Although historians have long suggested that political and religious motives played a large role in stimulating the German diaspora, no evidence suggests that the Klem family fled Bavaria for ideological reasons. Rather, given the rapidity with which Margaret's brothers acquired land and established farming households in northern New Jersey, they probably migrated for economic opportunity owing to the German agricultural crisis.[10]

It appears likely that the Klems came to America as a unit. All five siblings and the family matriarch clearly arrived in the United States in the early 1850s. Some subsequent census evidence, however, suggests that Margaret's older brother, Michael, may have made the trans-Atlantic journey alone in 1850 and sent for the rest of the clan a few years after establishing himself in Essex County. Whether or not she arrived with her entire family or as a result of chain migration, Margaret settled first in New York City and boarded with a family while serving as a nursemaid. Before long, however, she moved to Orange, likely so that she could be closer to her brother John, who had purchased a small farm in Livingston where he resided with his wife and two children as well as with Margaret's sixty-year-old mother. In Orange, she found employment as a servant in the reasonably fashionable but socially mixed Tory Corner neighborhood, which boasted several merchants, a clergyman, and a retired hat manufacturer among its residents. Margaret worked first in the home of Cyrus Harrison, a young hatter of some means who previously had engaged an African American woman to handle his household chores and nurse his young daughter. She then moved to the home of Caleb Gould Harrison (1815–1893), a wealthy carriage manufacturer with a growing family and several boarders. This proved to be a reasonably stable engagement, and she lived with the Harrison family for two years as his four sons reached maturity. During her time with the Harrisons, Margaret became acquainted with John Meierhofer, a laborer who boarded with a neighboring family and who also hailed from her home state of Bavaria.[11]

Germans typically met and married mates from their native states, owing at least in part to the tight-knit ethnic networks that formed once they arrived in America. Interestingly, Margaret's three Bavarian-born brothers proved exceptions to this rule: two married Prussians and a third had a wife who had been born in Wurttemberg. All of Margaret's nieces and nephews were born in the United States, indicating that these marital matches occurred after the Klems had immigrated to America. Margaret's story also appeared unique for another reason. John Meierhofer was in his mid-to-late thirties in 1859, more than fifteen years older than his bride, a generational divide that would ultimately contribute to the stresses and strains in their relationship.[12] Still, despite the age difference, Margaret and John quickly decided to marry, with the ceremony taking place at her brother's Livingston farmhouse on 3 March 1859. Margaret's widowed mother could now rest assured that all of her children appeared settled in stable familial situations despite the movement and mobility that had disrupted their life in Bavaria. The newlyweds moved in with John and his family after the wedding, but the rural location likely made it difficult for them to find sufficient work other than farm labor. Further, John Klem's real property was valued at only nine hundred dollars in 1860, among the lowest assessments in this largely agricultural community and indicating the modest nature of his dwelling. John and Margaret had increased the household size to seven, and soon after their arrival, a newborn infant further strained the living quarters. In December 1859, Margaret gave birth to their first child, Joseph, who was baptized at Saint Mary's German Church in Newark. Her twenty-nine-year-old sister, Catherine, along with her husband, Joseph Greiner, who owned a lager beer saloon in Newark, served as the sponsors. John and Margaret then decided to move out of Livingston and board with an Orange shoemaker name John Van Buskirk in an outlying ward of the sprawling city. John Meierhofer continued to pick up day laboring jobs throughout the area while Margaret kept house for the Van Buskirk clan, which included three children aged fifteen, fourteen, and nine.

In 1860, however, Margaret helped broker a partnership that would permanently alter her family's fortunes. She connected her brother Michael with her husband, John, and they jointly purchased twenty-seven acres of farmland from a French-born hatter named Peter Savonney for $1,350. The Northfield Road property, which was located on rocky and mountainous terrain in an area of Orange far removed from the town center, appeared among the more marginal and undesirable tracts in the community. The deed description, which described its boundaries as "beginning in the

middle of the main road near Rock Hill" and ending at "a point oppo-
site the centre of the road called Swamp Road," aptly captures the nature
of the terrain and the character of the acquisition. Based on 1870 census
estimates, the $1,350 price would have placed it as the fifth-lowest value for
any of the sixty-three farms in the area that became West Orange, where
the largest landholders had been assessed at over $50,000 and even mod-
est properties were valued at $5,000. It reflected the manner in which
large landowners had begun subdividing and cashing out their holdings.
This land originally constituted part of a much larger tract that belonged
to a member of the prosperous Williams family, who then sold this piece to
a farmer and speculator named Elias Meeker, who subsequently divided
his holdings on the mountain and sold this acreage to Savonney. By 1860,
this section of Northfield Road was home to some abandoned dwellings, a
few scattered farms owned primarily by German and French immigrants,
and a smattering of local craftsmen who were finding more work as Benjamin Small began building the neighboring Saint Cloud development.
Michael Klem and John Meierhofer, however, considered the purchase
a significant investment that offered the promise of economic mobility.
For the Klems, who quite likely worked as small farmers or agricultural
laborers in Bavaria, land connoted stability and an opportunity to transfer their skills to America. For John Meierhofer, who had knocked around
the Orange area as a day laborer boarding in several households, the farm
offered rootedness and a place to raise his family.[13]

The Klems and the Meierhofers erected a modest farmhouse on the
property in 1860, moving in together and no doubt facing the future with
guarded optimism. The *Orange Journal* subsequently described the two-
story homestead as "a little, old weather stained structure" standing close to
Northfield Road. The first floor contained a broad hall running down the
center with a sitting room and bedroom on one side, and the kitchen and a
second bedroom on the other. Some rickety stairs led down to a basement
where the family stored milk, potatoes, and other goods ready for market.
The second floor included additional bedrooms. All in all, the property
initially appeared perfectly adequate for Margaret and her extended family.
The Civil War decade, however, ultimately proved disruptive on several
levels. First, for unexplained reasons, the partnership dissolved. Michael
Klem, twenty-four years old in 1860, had moved into the farmhouse with
his wife and two-year-old daughter, Anne. By 1864, though, perhaps
owing to the fact that the couple planned to grow their family and decided

FIG. 3.2 "A Lonely Road, Orange Mountain." The rough and rocky terrain that led to the Meierhofer farm provided scenic thrills for tourists but also illustrated the relative isolation and difficult agricultural challenges that faced German and French farmers on the mountain. Courtesy of the author.

that this living arrangement no longer appeared adequate, he sought to end the arrangement. In February of that year, John Meierhofer bought out Michael's share for eight hundred dollars and the Klems acquired another nearby farm valued at approximately twelve hundred dollars. Two additional children, born in 1866 and 1868 respectively, also resided in Michael Klem's household by 1870.[14]

John Meierhofer, for his part, enlisted in the Union army in 1864. This meant that Margaret had to take on greater responsibility for managing the family economy. Before John joined his regiment, he granted Margaret power of attorney to transact all business in his name and also gave her full control over the property. Margaret further maintained a five-hundred-dollar bank account at the Newark Savings Institution, part of which she withdrew to build a barn on her property where she initially kept cows and various livestock. In March 1865, she received a $207 disbursement from the army connected with John's military service, thereby adding to her available capital. Gradually, she assumed control over the entire farming operation. She planted crops, raised produce, sold goods in Orange and Newark, hawked butter and milk to individuals and grocers who traversed the Northfield Road, and tended to the farm animals. As the neighboring

Saint Cloud area began to develop during the 1860s, she found other ways to supplement her income. Most notably, tradesmen and laborers required lodging on the hill as they were engaged to build the attractive vacation homes and estates springing up throughout the area. Margaret converted several vacant bedrooms into makeshift lodging spaces for transient carpenters and painters who found this arrangement more convenient than commuting daily from Orange, thus providing her with another steady source of cash. If Victorian novelists sentimentalized the home in the 1860s and 1870s as a domestic space that women cultivated in support of their manly providers and protectors, Margaret's experience reveals the other side of that equation. She functioned as an independent, competent, and reasonably successful businesswoman who transcended idealized gender roles and appeared in control of her own environment.[15]

Some neighbors apparently viewed her with suspicion and distrust and her growing independence eventually strained her marriage. John returned home from the war in June 1865, and approximately nine months later, Margaret gave birth to her second son, Theodore. The *Orange Journal* in 1879 claimed that Theodore was "an illegitimate child," incorrectly asserting that he had been born during John's military service. It also informed readers that Margaret "bears anything but an enviable reputation," in keeping with other newspaper accounts that typically described the Meierhofers as "none the best for the locality" and stating that the house had "acquired a bad reputation for disorder." Scandalous and salacious rumors circulated throughout the neighborhood about the goings-on at the home and the behavior of the various men who boarded there. The Meierhofer marriage showed increasing signs of stress and strain. John appeared more erratic and out of control following his return from the war. Margaret described him as "a quick-tempered man" under the best of circumstances and someone with wild mood swings who "soon got over his temper, and then cried and begged forgiveness." Still, during the late 1860s and early 1870s, John's behavior became less predictable and more violent.[16]

Margaret twice called the police to arrest her husband. In the early 1870s, she made a complaint before Police Justice Edward G. Smith that he had committed assault and battery against both her and her son Joseph. That incident caused her to flee the house and spend the night with her neighbor Albert Kirsten and his family, German immigrants from Saxony who lived down Northfield Road. After listening to the testimony, Judge Smith determined that John "could not be in his right mind," but he merely suggested that Margaret engage a veteran local physician, Dr. Edwin Thompson of Orange, to examine her husband. When Thompson approached the house, however, John Meierhofer thought that he was a local constable and fled the scene. The examination never took place, and no additional charges were forthcoming. Business proceeded as usual. In 1878, another ugly incident occurred at dinner when John, in Margaret's words, "threatened to cut my throat from ear to ear" over the sale of a cow and a dispute over some meat. Margaret contacted Willett Rendell, the local constable, who tried to arrest John and ultimately arraigned him before another West Orange justice of the peace, Edmund Condit. Again, the judge took no action and Margaret was left to deal with the situation as best she could. She avoided him during his "spells," eventually reaching an accommodation whereby John slept in the barn with the cows during the summer months and shared a bedroom upstairs with Theodore during the winter. Margaret and John quarreled frequently in German and English, the family rarely shared a meal together, and an argumentative atmosphere prevailed. Both Meierhofer children reinforced their mother's account, with Joseph observing especially that Margaret "was particular about his going to school, to church and to Sunday School and tried to bring him up right," while John "was very peculiar at times. . . . There was no getting along with him sometimes. . . . He would scold and quarrel when there was no cause for it." Tension pervaded the domestic circle.[17]

Margaret's extended family also suffered losses and unanticipated changes during this period. Her seventy-five-year-old widowed mother, Catharine, died in a Newark hospital after contracting a skin infection in 1872. Margaret's sister, Catherine, apparently began showing signs of mental illness during the 1870s and became confined to the Essex County Hospital for the Insane in Newark. Her brother Michael's two female children—Anne and Mary—may have died during the 1870s; at the least, they are no longer listed as residing with the Klem family on West Valley Street in the 1880 census despite their young age. And Margaret's son Joseph struck out on his own in 1873 or 1874. He moved to nearby East Orange, where he found work initially as a butcher and eventually became a clerk in a produce operation. For all these reasons, Margaret found herself increasingly isolated. Indeed, Joseph recalled that John complained vociferously whenever anyone visited Margaret, and he would "even object to her own relations" when they called on their sister. One might imagine that neighbors would have sympathized with Margaret's situation. In

1879, Margaret was a thirty-eight-year-old woman attempting to raise a fourteen-year-old boy with no help from her husband. She had no marital relations, had suffered physical and psychological abuse at the hands of her spouse, found no recourse in the courts, and had been instructed to simply deal with her partner's mental health issues on her own within the confines of the family. Her familial support structure had begun to erode, she remained an immigrant outsider in a community that did not have extensive German social and fraternal institutions, and she had only a rudimentary understanding of English.[18]

West Orange, however, proved unforgiving. Many historians have documented the ways in which anxieties over family and home dominated the concerns of Gilded Age Americans. Richard White, for example, in his masterful synthesis entitled *The Republic for Which It Stands: The United States during Reconstruction and the Gilded Age, 1865–1896*, observes that household issues "sat at the juncture of politics, public policy, gender relations, racial relations, social reform, the economy, and child-rearing" in the postwar United States. White middle-class Protestants obsessed over the dangers that challenged their idealized notions of family life. Chinese immigration and the growth of Roman Catholicism introduced alternative familial conceptions and values that threatened to overwhelm the native-born. Mormon polygamy loomed as a particularly menacing influence in the Far West. A large number of single-parent households, where women typically assumed charge over children, constituted one result of the massive slaughter of young men during the Civil War. Orphans became a particular social obsession, evident in the novels of Horatio Alger and the movement to place urban children with reliable farm families on the frontier.[19]

Victorians especially worried about independent-minded women who dominated the domestic sphere and threatened the traditional prerogatives of masculinity. Some guardians of morality agonized over the increased accessibility to pornography made possible by the new technologies of photography and cheap printing. Others fretted over the calls for more sexual freedom emanating from a radical generation of feminists. On the one hand, men fought back during this period by codifying laws and creating social movements to protect the Victorian family. Campaigns to eradicate plural marriage, legislative attempts to restrict immigration, nativist crusades to suppress Catholicism, and Anthony Comstock's New York Society for the Suppression of Vice in 1873 all received broad backing. Even the promulgation of the Homestead Act, which enshrined the self-reliant family farm as a bastion of American independence, exemplified these goals. Independent-minded women, on the other hand, pursued their own agendas. Victoria Woodhull emerged as a national celebrity in the 1870s through her advocacy of free love and her belief that personal satisfaction and emotional connections transcended marital bonds. On the conservative side, the Women's Christian Temperance Union conducted campaigns to eradicate alcoholism as part of an effort to banish domestic violence and desertion from American life. All of these trends and movements signaled a fundamental disconnect between Victorian rhetoric and reality. The social ideal of the manly breadwinner and the submissive wife who tended home and hearth appeared to be breaking down. Women who cultivated their own financial independence, violated sexual and gender norms, and dominated the men in their households posed particular dangers to social stability. When these women came from immigrant backgrounds, the threats appeared particularly insidious, akin to a foreign invasion. Margaret Meierhofer necessarily engendered suspicion. Her immigrant status, limited command of English, firm control over household affairs, rumored sexual liaisons, and economic independence made her much more than merely a disreputable and eccentric figure in West Orange. On a fundamental level, she threatened the social order. The details of her life history crystallized for many community members the forces that appeared to be tearing apart American culture.

John Meierhofer, on the other hand, never even had an opportunity to tell his story or explain his actions. Under the best of circumstances, such men left behind few historical records. Excepting an 1879 burial entry at Rosedale Cemetery in Montclair that listed his cause of death as a "pistol shot wound" and provided a plot number for his unmarked grave, official documentation concerning his life and career appear virtually absent. The few sources that do exist often contradict each other. Census reports and military records routinely misspell his name. Sources sometimes claim that he emigrated from Baden, other times from Bavaria, and most frequently only list "Germany" as his place of origin. His exact age remains a matter of dispute. No immigration records document his arrival in the United States. He appeared to have no known or close relatives in America. At the least, none ever attended the trial of his murderers and no record indicates that anyone took responsibility for his body. The press ignored his funeral and burial. His children never bothered to provide him with a headstone. All indications point to the fact that he led a sad and solitary existence, largely ignored by his neighbors except as an object of curiosity and occasional derision. In an age that celebrated manly independence and enshrined free labor as a core value for White males, Meierhofer appeared as an especially tragic figure, unable to support himself or his family. Everything about his life suggested humiliation and failure.

First, consider his physical appearance. Civil War muster rolls indicated that John had blue eyes, brown hair, and a light complexion—nothing exceptional there. They also listed his height at 5 feet, 2½ inches, and his slight and sickly build offered a remarkable contrast to Margaret. The *National Police Gazette* described Margaret as "nearly six feet in height, straight, strong, and vigorous, with jet black hair and eyes." Newspaper reports typically characterized her as "Amazonian" with both reporters and attorneys regularly remarking on her formidable and intimidating presence. One pressman described her as "remarkably tall and muscular." Another observed that she possessed "bones and muscles of no common strength." Margaret herself noted that, owing to her work on the farm, she possessed "a great deal of strength" and had bulked up to 169 pounds at one point, though she did not believe that "I weighed as much as that within twenty pounds at the time of my husband's death." Their troubled marriage and frequent arguments often resulted in physical confrontations, according to the *Newark Daily Advertiser*, "but the woman being the larger, stronger, and strongest-willed always came off the victor." One attorney at the trial drew the appropriate lesson, depicting Margaret as "strong and vigorous" while noting that "John Meierhofer, having been weak, imbecile, and cumbrous to her," functioned in the marriage primarily as "an object of contempt." John Meierhofer, somewhere in his fifties at the time of his murder, had been cast as physically, emotionally, and intellectually inferior to his thirty-eight-year-old wife. He seemed incapable of performing his husbandly duties, literally dwarfed by his physically imposing spouse. Margaret dominated both the household and her husband, reducing him to a state of comic subservience that failed to meet proper Victorian standards. Based on this narrative, John functioned as a pathetic figure in the household, a short and sickly foil for his robust and physically imposing wife. When disaster struck, he proved incapable of even defending himself let alone providing for the needs of his household.[20]

John also remained economically and socially dependent on the Klem family throughout his life. When John first met Margaret in the late 1850s, he had dim prospects, approaching middle age and boarding in downtown Orange while eking out a meager living as a day laborer. By 1860, however, John became embedded in the extended Klem family. His marriage to Margaret took place at her brother's farmhouse. Her siblings and their spouses became the baptismal sponsors for both Meierhofer children. Michael Klem provided the capital that allowed the newlyweds to move from Orange to their farmhouse on the mountain. When John enlisted in the Union army, he transferred control over the property and other family finances to Margaret. Indeed, it remains questionable whether John played any economic role in the household at all. Some newspaper accounts referred to him as "a small farmer" or "the poor old demented German farmer," but the *Orange Journal* perhaps most accurately observed that he merely "continued to live on the farm" until his death. Margaret clearly played the major role in managing hired hands, transforming the household into a boardinghouse, building the barn, doing her own planting, tending to the cows and horses, and negotiating fair prices with the grocers and customers who traversed the Northfield Road. She described John's occupation as doing "day's work on the mountain" while she accomplished farming and household tasks. Once again, the Meierhofer domestic arrangements violated standard Victorian norms and proprieties: Margaret functioned as the breadwinner and financial manager, while also handling typical womanly chores. Her son Joseph confirmed these accounts. He viewed her as a loving and attentive mother who made every effort to instill solid moral values in her children and care for their needs. John took little role in family life, rarely even participating in family meals. According to fifteen-year-old Theodore, "Father was in the habit of eating when and where he pleased; if he wanted anything he went to the cupboard and got it." The Meierhofer children grew up in a household that appeared far removed from the middle-class ideals of manly independence and domestic tranquility that prevailed in such settlements as nearby Saint Cloud. No wonder that neighbors looked upon the goings-on at the little farmhouse with suspicion and disdain.[21]

John never functioned effectively as a household head or successful breadwinner, but his military service marked a clear dividing line and a key moment in his life history. Congress had passed a National Conscription Act in 1863, hoping to stem the tide of heavy desertion and widespread resistance that imperiled the Union war effort. Indeed, northern hopes appeared particularly precarious that year as Confederates scored a series of battlefield victories in Virginia and appeared on the cusp of invading the Union states. The legislation, however, proved wildly unpopular in many parts of the North. It authorized government officials to go house-to-house to enroll men between twenty and thirty-five, allowed provost marshals to summarily arrest evaders and resisters, and offered the wealthy and privileged the option to avoid conscription by paying for substitutes. In New York City, the draft set off what the historian Mike Wallace characterized as "the largest single incident of civil disorder in the history of the United States." A racial bloodbath occurred in the metropolis between July 13 and July 16 as predominantly Irish rioters ruthlessly beat and killed African Americans on the streets while also attacking policemen, destroying property, and targeting visible symbols of political Republicanism. The ultimate death toll numbered in the hundreds. New Jersey, perhaps surprisingly given widespread secessionist sympathies, proved more quiescent. The historian William Gillette characterized antidraft demonstrations in the Garden State as "mild affairs" that produced minimal property damage and no fatalities. Governor Joel Parker, who supported the war but routinely criticized the president, managed to convince Abraham Lincoln to delay the draft in New Jersey until the spring of 1864 to alleviate tensions. He also worked diligently to secure enough volunteers to roughly fulfill his state quota, further defusing the volatile situation.[22]

John Meierhofer registered for the draft in June 1863. The Conscription Act itself mandated registration for all men between the ages of twenty and thirty-five and unmarried men between thirty-five and forty-five. Meierhofer, married and in his forties in 1863, fell into neither of these categories. He registered as a matter of choice. Perhaps, given his marginal economic circumstances, John found the modest bounty, clothing allowance, future allotments, and even the widows' benefits attractive. Given the fact that he signed all his assets over to Margaret prior to enlistment, he clearly hoped to provide for his wife and son in some manner if he did not survive the war. When he was finally called to service in September 1864 along with the rest of the fellow recruits, John was assigned to the Thirty-Ninth Regiment, Company H, at Camp Frelinghuysen in Newark. The company headed south in early October, arriving at City Point, Virginia, a critical Union supply depot at the confluence of the James and Appomattox Rivers. For several months, the company saw no actual combat. City Point recently had been targeted by Confederate saboteurs, who had destroyed a wharf at the port, and Company H became involved in repairing the damage and fortifying the breastworks. The division also became involved in guarding the Southside Railroad, another key northern transportation facility that became even more critical during the siege of Petersburg. Things changed dramatically on the night of 1 April 1865, however, as General Ulysses Grant ordered a massive military operation designed to take Petersburg and thus threaten Richmond. The Thirty-Ninth Regiment's historian described the ensuing battle as "of the most stubborn and murderous character," with "very severe" losses to the regiment. Captain George W. Harrison, who commanded Company H, was killed, as was the lieutenant assigned to the same company. The rebels fought "with a tenacity which defied all attempts to dislodge" them, and deadly assaults continued throughout the next days. Ultimately the Union offensive successfully brought Petersburg under northern control, forcing Robert E. Lee to retreat and Jefferson Davis to flee from Richmond. The Petersburg campaign, however, which lasted 292 days from its inception in June 1864, left a trail of human casualties.[23]

Recent Civil War historiography emphasizes the difficulties that veterans faced in readjusting to civilian society. Many soldiers returned from the war both physically and psychologically damaged. Wartime injuries and battlefield trauma frequently resulted in amputated limbs, chronic intestinal maladies, cardiovascular ailments, and nervous disorders. Some returnees retreated into depression and uncontrolled drinking, others committed suicide, and many exhibited problems maintaining basic social relationships. Civil War pension files chronicled the violent outbursts, spousal abuse, paranoia, hallucinations, and delusions endemic to applicants. Civilian attitudes frequently exacerbated these problems. Many northerners, eager to forget the war and return to "normal" life, viewed ex-soldiers as malingerers, deadbeats, and cranks who appeared most interested in gaming the rudimentary welfare system. States and cities lacked any comprehensive social policies to address veterans' issues. Federal pensions only applied to soldiers who could prove that they had been physically injured or incapacitated on the battlefield. Governmental authorities did not take mental illness seriously with psychiatrists typically viewing it as an example of personal moral failing. This lack of social support caused veterans to create their own civilian subcultures, often centered on such fraternal and charitable institutions as the Grand Army of the Republic. John Meierhofer shared some common characteristics with fellow soldiers who experienced trauma. He served in a regiment that suffered heavy casualties, witnessed death and dismemberment on the battlefield, engaged in intimate violence, and likely suffered from such typical wartime conditions as malnutrition and fatigue. His service also differed from fellow recruits in some respects. He was older, thus perhaps making him less prone to nervous disorders, and served for a relatively short time. He returned from the war physically intact and never experienced the horrors of confinement in a prisoner-of-war camp. No evidence indicates that he suffered from substance abuse. Upon his return to the farm, however, John remained more isolated than many other veterans. No Grand Army of the Republic post existed in West Orange. His social circle and intimate connections appeared confined primarily to the Klem family. And farm labor constituted a largely solitary activity.[24]

For whatever reason, John Meierhofer's situation and behavior certainly changed after he returned from the war. John was mustered out of service on 17 June 1865. Precisely eight months and twenty-six days later, on 13 March 1866, Margaret gave birth to the couple's second child, Theodore. As mentioned, the infant's paternity generated rumors and ridicule throughout the mountain neighborhood. Suspicion centered especially on Henry Richey, a Prussian-born farmer who lived in the neighborhood and who subsequently claimed that he "was intimate with Mrs. Meierhofer" during the war and "frequently slept with her." Richey, a fairly wealthy farmer who claimed seven thousand dollars in realty and three hundred dollars in personal property in the 1870 census, would have been thirty-five years old during the period of his alleged liaison with the twenty-four-year-old Margaret. Richey also had a wife and six children at the time. He placed the blame for the affair squarely on Margaret's shoulders, insisting that "she solicited him" and that he typically "climbed in the back window and came at her request" during this period. At a certain point, however, Richey reconciled with his spouse, whereupon he decided that Margaret "was a bad woman" who "carried on too much with the men," and he had not been "on good terms with her" for many years prior to John's murder. Margaret, for her part, denied that she "had improper relations with Henry Richie." Neighbors clearly took Henry's side in the matter and gleefully referred to the Meierhofer child as "Theodore Richey" throughout the 1860s and 1870s. Theodore's baptismal record at Saint Mary's in Newark offers no evidence on the contested paternity, however, simply registering the baby as the son of John and Margaret, with two Klem siblings serving as the sponsors. No direct evidence supports the fact that John suspected this indiscretion, though the gossip that permeated the community no doubt contributed to the Meierhofer marital troubles.[25]

John's behavior clearly became more erratic, strange, and periodically violent following the war. Theodore recalled that "ever since he could remember," his father slept in the barn all summer and shared an upstairs bedroom with his son in the winter. Margaret attributed this behavior to "spells" and paranoia: "The barn had to be left open at night to give the cows air, and he therefore slept there to prevent thieves from coming in." She also emphatically denied that their marital relations had ended "because of my relations with other men" but rather claimed that John preferred to sleep upstairs in the winter "because he could look toward the barn" and spot potential intruders. Boarders and neighbors testified to the family patriarch's strange behavior, even though some blamed Margaret for confining him to the barn and refusing to perform such wifely chores as cooking. They observed that John often wandered aimlessly about the property, muttering to himself and exhibiting antisocial behavior. He frequently berated his spouse in German and English, and police confirmed that he once had been arrested and detained overnight for abusing and beating Margaret. Law enforcement officials agreed that one year prior to the murder he threatened to cut her throat over the sale of a cow. Perhaps the *Newark Daily Journal* best summarized John's situation when it described him as "one of the lowliest men that was to be found within [New Jersey's] borders—a poor, wornout, demented, and ignorant farmer." John may, like other veterans, have been permanently damaged by the brutal combat that he engaged in during his military service. He might have been embittered by the many years of dependence on Margaret and her family, frustrated by his inability to perform manly roles in the household. Or he could have been worn down by the constant rumors concerning his wife's behavior or infidelity. At this historical distance and given a lack of clear evidence, it is impossible to determine the precise sources of his mental illness. Clearly, however, his condition exceeded Margaret's ability to manage it within a household setting. Her occasional attempts to seek institutional help failed. She remained responsible for raising two children and coping with a husband who, in the words of one observer, "she always treated . . . like a child, and when she asked him to do anything she would say 'there's a good boy.'" And John himself became a bit player in the drama that occurred on Northfield Road, unable to articulate his own story or to take control of a rapidly escalating situation.[26]

Frank Lammens proved problematic in other ways. His attorney once remarked that it "is as though he dropped from the clouds." He appeared to leave no historical record in his wake. Census tallies, sacramental records, ship manifests, passenger arrivals, institutional reports, government documents, and personal testimonies all remain silent concerning the comings and goings of this mysterious character. No one seemed to know quite what to make of the drifter when he wandered onto the Meierhofer property in September of 1879. He spoke eloquently and loquaciously about himself, but his stories frequently changed. He altered his basic life facts, conveniently forgot about key moments in his past, and spun tall tales concerning his exploits and travels. He appeared to lack any close relations or known family, seemingly friendless and alone. Yet he charmed reporters and courtroom observers with his excessively formal speaking style, his apparent good humor, and his complete ignorance of legal procedures and norms. Lammens could always be counted on to produce an amusing story, a telling anecdote, or a witty aside. Despite his gregarious nature, however, he also possessed a more sinister and checkered background that began to emerge as people got to know him better. Further, when pressured, he became prone to incoherent outbursts and manic behavior. His emotions surged out of control; his actions grew increasingly bizarre. And his mental instability manifested itself in sudden illnesses and physical debility. He proved to be an enigma to everyone that he encountered, and there seemed little reason to challenge his attorney's conclusion that he constituted a "wreck of a man." Yet perhaps Frank Lammens himself spoke a more telling truth when he characterized himself simply as a "professional tramp."[27]

Lammens apparently had been born in a rural maritime province of Holland in 1835, making him approximately six years older than Margaret. Dutch immigration paled in comparison to the German diaspora in the nineteenth century. Historians have estimated that approximately two hundred thousand Netherlanders settled in the United States between 1820 and 1914, far fewer than the Germans who arrived during their one peak year of immigration in 1854. In many ways, however, the economic reasons to migrate remained similar. Holland experienced a severe potato crop failure in the mid-1840s, causing catastrophic food shortages. The general problems of overpopulation, land scarcity, and an inability to support families mirrored conditions in the German states. Governmental ineffectiveness also contributed to the difficulties. For Frank Lammens, who most likely hailed from a rural part of Holland though he claimed to set sail from the port city of Antwerp in 1852, economic motives no doubt played a role in his decision to migrate. His personal experience, however, differed considerably from many of his countrymen. Historians have characterized the Dutch as among the most family-oriented migrants to the United States, typically crossing the Atlantic with kin. They tended to cluster together more than many ethnic groups, often forming colonies and communities in rich farming regions throughout the Midwest. As a group, the Dutch experienced significant economic mobility after migrating. They proved successful at transmitting cultural traits, religious traditions, and language across generational lines. Lammens constituted an exception to that ethnic profile. He traveled alone to America as a seventeen-year-old youth without family or friends in the New World. Rather than attach himself to an established ethnic community, he proved rootless and consistently on the move. He remained on the East Coast and quickly adapted to his new environment by learning a highly formal and stilted form of English. Lammens never acquired property or significant personal holdings. He lived out of his knapsack. And religion seemed insignificant to him: though he had Catholic roots in Holland and even dubiously claimed that he spent several years studying in a monastery, he once observed that he "inclines toward the Baptists" in America while also acknowledging that ecclesiastical matters did not much concern him.[28]

Lammens led a peripatetic existence. Throughout the 1850s, he worked at a series of short-term farm laboring jobs throughout Connecticut, Pennsylvania, and New York. He finally settled down a bit in 1861, however, when he met an Irish woman named Bridget Fallon, who had been working for a farmer somewhere in the vicinity of Jamaica and Flushing on Long Island. They quickly had three children and moved to Brooklyn, whereupon Lammens decided to try his hand at a new trade. He recalled purchasing a horse and wagon and setting himself up as "a huckster" as he traversed the streets and peddled goods throughout the burgeoning metropolis. Frank quickly learned the tricks of the trade, developing a rapid-fire delivery and animated speaking style that translated well into running small-time scams. He apparently operated as a classic nineteenth-century confidence man, procuring enough cash to support his growing family for a brief period. By the end of the Civil War, however, his life unraveled. All three children had died, for reasons that Lammens could not recall. Frank remembered that he "was out of my mind a little." He abandoned his wife and traveled to the Cleveland area with two acquaintances. This led to a protracted period

FIG. 3.3 "The Tramp." Once viewed as somewhat benign misfortunates and traveling work-men, by the mid-1870s, tramps became identified with danger, crime, and menacing behavior, as this 1876 illustration from *Harper's Weekly* aptly demonstrates.

of petty crime, rootless wandering, and an eventual return to New York, at which point he declared that he "got better." Frank never attempted to hold down a steady job after that experience. Rather, he continued to travel around and support himself through small-scale larceny. His behavior finally resulted in an arrest and conviction, whereupon he was confined to Sing Sing for a period in the late 1860s. Prison authorities soon decided that he suffered from some mental disorder, however, and they elected to transfer him to the Auburn Asylum for Insane Convicts in western New York state for treatment and hopeful recovery. This period of institutional-ization marked another significant turning point in Frank's life.[29]

The Auburn Asylum for Insane Convicts received its first patients in 1859, near the end of a period that witnessed the large-scale construction of special-purpose state institutions to confine and treat mentally ill indi-viduals. If the Meierhofer household illustrated the difficulty of addressing insane behavior within family-based contexts, institutions such as Auburn exhibited the problems that faced special-purpose institutional endeav-ors. Antebellum optimism fueled the rise of asylums as reformers justified their creation on humanitarian, financial, and scientific grounds. Before long, however, problems became apparent. State appropriations proved inadequate, overcrowding strained the facilities, and recidivism proved frequent among the inmates. The Auburn asylum received referrals from local and state institutions in the hopes that a regimented and routinized existence would teach inmates the steady regularity necessary for them to be at least "useful in performing simple duties." Auburn claimed to provide inmates with healthy and clean facilities, nutritious food, and instruction that would ease their transition to independent living. An adjoining farm trained asylum-dwellers in agricultural labor and also provided a small source of income for the institution. Most residents in the late 1860s had been born in the United States or Ireland, were under forty years of age, worked as laborers prior to their incarceration, and had been living in New York City, Kings County, Queens County, or Westchester County. Roughly two-thirds had been imprisoned on either burglary or larceny charges, and almost all had been diagnosed with "chronic mania" or some form of dementia. Auburn faced the same problems that plagued similar institutions. Originally constructed to house sixty-four patients, the building had over ninety occupants by 1864. The facility began deteriorating almost immediately, and staff struggled to plead with state legislators to fund routine maintenance. Further, administrators became frustrated with the class of "hopeless, incurable cases" that had been transferred to their care when they viewed their purpose instead as rehabilitating less severely impaired individuals. All in all, the utopian reformist zeal that inspired the creation of Auburn never matched reality.[30]

Lammens only stayed briefly at Auburn, but it served primarily to cut him off from his previous life. He lost touch with Bridget, who believed that he had died at the institution. Although deemed well enough to survive on his own, he never again sought out a more permanent job, and he abandoned his attempts at hucksterism. Rather, Frank decided that his future lay on the road. Like many aimless Americans in the 1870s who found themselves socially and economically marginalized by the economic depression, he set about "tramping" as a way to get by from day-to-day. Tramps, declared *Harper's Weekly* in 1876, "have of late become a recognized class in our community." The term itself, which generally came to include primarily White males who traveled throughout the nation with no visible means of support, came into vogue in the early 1870s and soon took on sinister connotations. *Harper's* described them as "dangerous stragglers, who wandered through villages, alarming women and children by their wild appearance and imperious demands for food and shelter." The tramp "infestation," according to this middle-class magazine, proved especially alarming in rural locales where these "thieves and robbers" appropriated anything they could lay their hands on "and, if necessary, use[d] violence, sometimes amounting to murder, rather than forego their plunder." Social work professionals took an even harsher view. Francis Wayland (1826–1904), a Yale law professor who prepared a special report on tramps for the Conference of Charities convention in 1877, described this dangerous class of wandering nomads in these terms: "A lazy, shiftless, sauntering or swaggering, ill-conditioned, irreclaimable, incorrigible, cowardly, utterly depraved savage. He fears not God neither regards man. . . . He will outrage an unprotected female, or rob a defenseless child." By the late 1870s, social anxieties over these unemployed drifters had created panic, calls for stricter vagrancy legislation, and demands for more workhouses. Newspapers, dime novels, and reformist tracts flooded the marketplace with worrisome stories about homeless wanderers who operated outside the traditional boundaries of town and home. Some feared that basic American institutions, such as stable and orderly communities, the middle-class household, and free labor, appeared on the verge of collapse. Tramps seemed to reject all the manners, the morals, and the steady habits that middle-class Americans had imbibed and promoted. During an especially tumultuous decade, rootless tramps seemed both symptomatic of contemporary disorder and possible harbingers of a chaotic and unruly dystopian future.[31]

The New Jersey state legislature formally codified the growing social anxiety concerning this class of individuals when it passed "an act to define and suppress tramps" in April of 1876, the first such law in the nation. The act defined tramps as any individuals "who have no legal settlement in the places in which they may be found" and those "who live idly and without employment, and refuse to work for the usual and common wages given to other persons for like work in the place in which they then are." Lawmakers decried drifters who "shall be found going about door to door" as well as persons who roamed New Jersey's highways and byways "to beg or gather alms, and can give no reasonable account of themselves of their businesses in such places." The legislation authorized local magistrates to incarcerate these vagrants in county farms, houses of correction, poorhouses, workhouses, and municipal jails. It also sought to transform tramps into productive convict laborers by directing county authorities to put them to work on road repair projects or, in some instances, bind them out to private third parties for fixed periods. Further, it allowed law enforcement officials and overseers of the poor to return these individuals to their original places of residence, provided that the expense did not exceed twenty dollars and that the tramp labored to earn this sum prior to removal. Finally, the legislators encouraged county freeholders to "erect and maintain buildings and enclosures suitable for the detention of persons convicted under this act." Enforcement proved sporadic and impractical as arrests rapidly overwhelmed local resources. Other states followed New Jersey's example in the late 1870s, however, as legislative attempts to stamp out vagabondage and to define homelessness as a condition that reflected nothing more than individual moral failings and poor personal work ethics intensified.[32]

Frank Lammens personified the tramper traits that many middle-class Americans found dangerous. One boarder at the Meierhofer house recalled that Lammens characterized himself as a "professional tramp" who "would not work long for anybody." He affirmatively wanted to be "on the road" as much as possible ever since his release from prison, enjoying his anonymity and his ability to move from place to place. Though a bit older than the classic tramp, who most often was in his twenties or early thirties, Lammens nonetheless adopted the masculine swagger and aggressive style that typified his fellow wanderers. He also chronicled a series of bafflingly random movements throughout Pennsylvania, New York, and New Jersey that had little rhyme or reason. At one point, he asserted that he had worked in Honesdale, Pennsylvania, near Scranton, in the coal mines for several years, but this seems highly unlikely given his constant mobility. He temporarily boarded with a farmer at Hempstead on Long Island in 1875 before heading back to Pennsylvania. In late 1876, he found himself in Philadelphia, where he recalled visiting the Centennial Exposition. He also outfitted himself with a firearm at that point, claiming that "in Philadelphia women carry pistols and niggers carry razors, and I took a notion for a pistol," though he subsequently insisted that he had never fired it. Another series of short-term farming engagements throughout southern and western New Jersey followed: Trenton, Annandale, High Bridge, Flemington, and Flagtown. In July 1879, he headed to New Brunswick, where he bought a horse for ten dollars and figured that he might take another try at the huckstering business that he had pursued in Brooklyn during the Civil War. The horse, however, "soon fell dead," and Lammens then decided that he would head to Brooklyn and see whether he could locate his estranged wife, Bridget. His efforts proved fruitless, and he next wandered around northern New Jersey over the summer looking for work and shelter. Around the beginning of September 1879, Frank happened upon the Meierhofer farmstead while traversing the Northfield Road. His life history soon took an even darker turn.[33]

Frank apparently saw Margaret at the front door and approached her to ask for a light of his pipe and some tobacco. They engaged in conversation and Margaret subsequently noted that "he was ragged and forlorn; had no shoes on, and looked like any other tramp." Still, she needed help with the fall harvest and with routine maintenance. Though Frank initially denied that he wanted any work, they ultimately reached an agreement whereby "she would give him what he was worth," somewhere between six and twelve dollars per month, in exchange for routine labor. She further allowed Lammens to occupy an upstairs bedroom as part of the arrangement. Frank, for his part, entertained some hopes of staying through the approaching winter when seasonal labor proved difficult for tramps to obtain. He began digging potatoes, cutting wood, milking cows, raking leaves, washing windows, and performing other simple farming chores on the property. For the first few weeks, things went well. Frank claimed that he believed Margaret to be a "nice respectable woman." She appeared satisfied with the drifter, observing that "he did any work that was given him." He also reached a grudging accommodation with John Meierhofer, who continued to wander around the property mumbling to himself and occasionally scolding Lammens for being an incompetent workman, even as the tramp proved himself to be an effective farm laborer. By early October, however, the relationship appeared to have run its course. Their stories began to diverge. Margaret recalled that Lammens approached her on October 3 and said "he wanted to go away" and resume his nomadic existence. She also claimed that Frank made some unwanted sexual advances toward her. Lammens, for his part, insisted that Margaret attempted to seduce him and arrange a series of nighttime liaisons during the week after he announced his intention to leave. At the same time, he increasingly felt that she "got suspicious of him" and no longer wanted him around the farm. By October 9, things had reached a boiling point. Their accounts of what transpired next dramatically differed. Their contested claims and counterclaims concerning the events of that day received complete exposition during the ensuing trial. Some basic facts and incontrovertible developments can be reconstructed, however, offering a skeletal framework for examining the subsequent controversies and testimonies.[34]

The sun rose at 6:04 a.m. on October 9. The unseasonably warm and dry weather that had plagued Essex County throughout the Fall continued on that tragic Thursday with, in the words of one local newspaper, "an old-fashioned August heat, the mercury rising to eighty-five degrees in the shade." Shortly after dawn, Margaret knocked on the first-floor bedroom window of John Clinton Pierson, the young schoolteacher who had been boarding at the farm. Pierson recalled that Margaret seemed in a state of great excitement and told the teacher that "for God's sake I must do something with this man [Lammens], he has threatened to kill me and my husband and blow up the place if I won't be his." She asked Pierson to write a note for her that would summon authorities. The note, dictated by Margaret, read as follows: "Mr. Philip Chickway: SIR: Come up immediately; there is a man here who threatened to shoot me and my husband and blow up my whole place if I will not go with him. There is a young man boarding here who wants to buy a horse, and you can come up as an excuse to see him, so as not to excite suspicion. Come as soon as possible, and be prepared. MRS. M. MEIERHOFER." The "Mr. Philip Chickway" referred to in the note actually was John Philip Jacqui, a Bavarian-born plumber and prominent citizen of Orange who also served as a fire warden. Margaret, who had a rudimentary command of English and lacked much understanding of the American legal system, believed that Jacqui had the power to arrest and incarcerate criminals owing to his position with the fire department and the fact that he could often be seen around town wearing what looked to be an official uniform with a badge. She entrusted the letter with her son Theodore, asking him to carry it to Orange prior to the start of the school day and also begging Pierson to dismiss students early so that he might return to the farm and monitor the tense situation. Theodore dutifully headed to Orange with the letter but could not locate Jacqui, whereupon he carried Margaret's missive to the police department. The constables proved completely disinterested in the entire issue, and Marshal Patrick Conroy refused to even open the envelope. Theodore therefore headed back home, arriving at the farm around 9:30 a.m. He then walked to his nearby school near Swamp Road, noticing that his father was tending to a horse near the brook that ran through their property and that Lammens was raking some leaves in front of the house.[35]

Pierson had already left for the school, but he remained uneasy about the developing situation at the Meierhofer farm. Before heading out, he heard John and Frank engage in a verbal confrontation. Meierhofer "called Lammens a loafer and told him to get out." Frank threateningly "shook his fist at the old man" and menacingly glowered at John. Despite Pierson's attempts to defuse the tension, neither man calmed down. At some point shortly thereafter, Lammens claimed that he went to the nearby home of Claude and Susan Jaillette, two elderly French immigrants who ran a small boardinghouse and tavern on Northfield Road near the Rock Spring. He brought back some whiskey and continued working around the yard. Although some individuals who traversed the main road remembered seeing John puttering around the property early in the day, by 11:00 a.m. or so he seemingly had disappeared. As Thursday progressed, however, in many ways it appeared to be a typical if unseasonably hot autumnal afternoon on the farm. Grocers and milkmen stopped by to purchase and sell goods. A few hunters knocked at the Meierhofer door seeking refreshments. Several Saint Cloud residents arrived at Margaret's doorstep hoping to procure some fresh produce. Nothing seemed extraordinary or unusual. When Pierson arrived home from school around 3:30 p.m., however, he discovered that things had taken a shocking turn for the worse. The schoolteacher asked Margaret about John's whereabouts, since he seemed nowhere to be found. At that point, Margaret "placed her hand on her breast, threw her head back, rolled her eyes and said in a low tone that he was dead." As the afternoon progressed, it became obvious to Pierson that she feared Lammens might continue on his rampage, and she also did not want Theodore to know what had happened. Margaret therefore concocted a story that John had gone down to Newark in order to purchase a new suit of clothes and would not be back until late at night, since he enjoyed walking home. Somewhat incredibly, Margaret then sat down to dinner with Pierson, Theodore, and Lammens though she subsequently claimed that she only "pretended to eat and could swallow none." Soon Lammens "complained of not feeling well" and left the tea table.[36]

As night fell, Margaret again attempted to summon the authorities. She asked Pierson to call on another neighbor, Albert Kirsten, who might take him to the Orange Police Station. Kirsten, whose German immigrant father had assisted Margaret years before when John threatened to kill her, was a twenty-year-old carpenter who lived on the Northfield Road with his parents and several siblings. He initially refused to help, scoffing at the notion that Lammens had murdered Meierhofer and further stating that he "was tired and did not want to go to Orange," since he had just made a similar trip down the mountain. Indeed, all of Margaret's efforts to obtain assistance from community residents and police officials thus far had ended in failure and frustration. Nobody seemed interested in her story, and everyone greeted the entire episode with apathy and disbelief. Finally, Pierson himself agreed to go down the mountain to Orange. At the last minute, he convinced Kirsten to accompany him, and they both departed for the police station at 7:30 p.m. Once again, Marshal Conroy stated that "he did not put much faith in the story," but he at least agreed to call in Willett Rendell, the constable who handled most of the crime that occurred in West Orange. Rendell subsequently testified that he also "objected at first to going to the scene of the shooting, as he believed the story to be a canard, as there was constant trouble about the place." For whatever reason, these two Irish-born police officers appeared remarkably unenthusiastic about responding to the pleas of the German immigrant woman on the hill. After some delay, however, they commandeered a third Irish policeman, reluctantly agreed to investigate, and headed up the mountain. By the time they reached the Meierhofer farmhouse it was already 11:00 p.m., and they clearly were not prepared for the scene that they witnessed. Margaret answered the door wearing a nightgown and white petticoat. She hurriedly told the trio that her husband had been murdered in the basement and that Lammens had been about to escape by climbing out the back window. Two constables ran to the back of the house, but Conroy hurried to Margaret's first-floor bedroom, where he found Lammens lying in bed undressed. Conroy then handcuffed Frank and assembled his team, at which point they all headed down to the basement with Margaret to check on the rest of her story.[37]

Rendell "threw the rays of his lantern under the stairway" and discovered the lifeless body of John Meierhofer. The deceased had been propped up into a sitting position, "his back resting against the partition, his head bent forward upon his breast, and one of his arms extended." Rendell ascertained that he had no pulse. At that point, he decided to handcuff Margaret as well and transport everyone to the Orange Police Station to sort out the situation. The policemen also secured the crime scene, bagged up evidence and belongings from Frank Lammens, and waited for the results of the county physician's postmortem examination. Dr. Peter Van Pelt Hewlett, the county physician, performed this task less than forty-eight hours later along with his assistant, Dr. Fayette Smith. They determined that John had been murdered with a .22-caliber bullet fired from a pistol that appeared consistent with one that the detectives had recovered at the scene. Their examination also indicated that "the bullet had entered the back of the head and ascended through the base of the brain." It appeared most likely that the victim had been executed from behind as he descended the stairs, and "death was doubtless instantaneous." Initial newspaper accounts primarily pointed toward Lammens as the murderer with an implication that Margaret might have been involved. "A Tramp Kills a Farmer" blared the headline for the *New York Times* on October 11, though a subhead declared, "The Victim's Wife a Party to His Murder." The *Orange Journal* ran a less judgmental story, stating simply in its banner headline "John Meierhofer Shot in His Own House in Broad Day Light" and noting in the body of the article that the murder was "probably" committed by a tramp. In any event, the gruesome details, the sexual suggestiveness, and the central role of that threatening new social figure known as the tramp meant that the ensuing investigation and trial would receive widespread attention. The murder involved all the most complex and controversial issues that appeared to be threatening American culture in the Gilded Age: uncontrolled immigration, unstable gender relations, the rise of a new breed of dangerous classes, and the breakdown of community cohesion. Viewed from one perspective, the murder might be considered a purely local tragedy that involved three marginal individuals who collided one fateful autumn day during the 1870s. As the subsequent trial demonstrated, however, this seemingly idiosyncratic incident contained far-reaching national and historical implications.[38]

Trial

● ● ● ● ● ● ● ● ● ● ● ●

County coroners and sheriffs truly wrote the first drafts of homicide history. In late nineteenth-century New Jersey, under the authority of the 1844 state constitution, both officials stood for election annually. They were limited to serving three consecutive terms, though they were permitted to run for office again after a three-year hiatus. Essex County voters placed both offices firmly in the hands of patrician civic leaders who moved easily in elite circles and had achieved considerable local notoriety by the late 1870s. Frederick Baille Mandeville, the coroner, traced his colonial lineage directly to Peter Stuyvesant. A native Newarker, the thirty-nine-year-old physician had been privileged from birth. As a young man, he had been tutored by several prominent local educators prior to attending two of the most prestigious institutions in the state: Newark Academy and Rutgers College. Mandeville eventually decided to pursue a career in medicine, graduating from the New York Homeopathic College in 1861 and then electing to matriculate at the New York Medical College in order to master other more "regular" approaches to his profession. After a brief period in which he partnered with a homeopathic colleague, Mandeville struck out on his own in the 1870s, developing what one biographer described as a "long and successful" practice out of his Broad Street home. By the late 1870s, he had helped found the New Jersey State Homeopathic Society, served several terms on the Newark Board of Education, and contributed numerous articles to professional journals. His civic engagements included membership in the elite New Jersey Club as well as eventual election to the Holland Society of America. Mandeville personified the character, reputation, and sense of noblesse oblige that motivated many Gilded Age elected officials to seek public office for seemingly beneficent, rather than purely mercenary, purposes.[1]

Sheriff Stephen Van Courtlandt Van Rensselaer shared several common traits with his coroner colleague. Born in the pleasant suburban Essex County hamlet of Belleville in 1836, Van Rensselaer included among his ancestors some of the oldest and most prestigious names in the colonies: Bayards, Schuylers, Livingstons, and Van Courtlandts. In fact, he literally had been "to the manor born." His father resided in an "old historic mansion" occupied by his eighteenth-century forebears in Belleville, and he owned extensive tracts of surrounding land, all of which Stephen inherited. As with Mandeville, good breeding led to good education. Van Rensselaer matriculated at solid preparatory academies, graduated from Rutgers College in 1854, and received his legal training at Albany Law School. The Civil War interrupted his legal practice, but Van Rensselaer earned considerable notoriety during the sectional conflict. He rose to the rank of major in the Third New Jersey Cavalry, serving with distinction at some of the bloodiest battles in the Civil War: Antietam, Chancellorsville, and Gettysburg. After retiring from the service, he resumed his lucrative law practice and also proved to be a successful politician throughout the 1870s. Van Rensselaer served two terms in the state assembly, achieved election to the Newark Common Council, and in 1877 won his race for county sheriff. Throughout his career, the personable attorney always knew how to parlay his political connections, professional acquaintances, and social prestige into a formula that guaranteed his success. Both Mandeville and Van Rensselaer lived well-documented lives. They received favorable mention in standard county histories. Numerous public records, church registers, and society proceedings tracked their careers. In death, they were celebrated by their colleagues, mourned by their loved ones, entombed after well-attended funerals at important citadels of urban religiosity, and became the recipients of generous obituaries in the public press. The contrast with the lives and deaths of John Meierhofer, Margaret Klem, and Frank Lammens could not have been more vivid or stark.[2]

Frederick Mandeville bore the burden of initiating the Meierhofer murder investigation. New Jersey statutes mandated that, in any case of violent

FIG. 4.1 "View of Rutgers College and Grounds at New Brunswick, N.J., 1879." Rutgers continued to serve as a center of Dutch Reformed influence in New Jersey into the late nineteenth century. Many members of the Essex County legal fraternity counted both a Dutch Reformed background and a Rutgers degree among their credentials. Frederick T. Frelinghuysen, perhaps the most prominent citizen of Newark, personally trained and mentored several key figures in the Meierhofer/Lammens trial. Courtesy of Special Collections and University Archives, Rutgers University Libraries.

or sudden death, coroners had a responsibility "immediately to proceed and view the body; and make all proper inquiry respecting the cause and manner of death." When murder or manslaughter appeared to cause the death, the coroner needed to "make out a precept, directed to any constable of the county where the dead body is found or lying, requiring him to summon a jury of not less than nine nor more than fifteen of good and lawful men of the same county." This jury would be charged with determining the cause of death, ascertaining the means and manner by which the deceased had expired, and identifying "if by murder, who were principals and who were accessories." Coroners also had the power to summon witnesses and control the judicial proceedings of the inquest. They delivered the accused to jail, provided written reports and evidentiary summaries to the trial courts, and set the stage for the next step in the judicial process. The coroner's inquest functioned effectively as a grand jury, handing down indictments and determining how the trial might play out. Mandeville acted without delay. Van Rensselaer had already visited the Meierhofer farm with the county prosecutor on Friday, October 10, whereupon they decided to bring John's body out of the cellar, after which it "was put on ice by an undertaker until the post-mortem examination could be made." The postmortem, conducted on Saturday at 3:00 p.m., contained no surprises as the cause of death indeed could be traced to the bullet wound in the back of the head. Mandeville immediately convened the jury, which began its work on Monday the thirteenth. The character of the nine-man jury can be discerned simply by listing their occupations: attorney, newspaper editor, flour and feed merchant, furniture dealer, coal dealer, mason, retail druggist, auctioneer, and harness manufacturer. Merchants, professionals, and businessmen dominated the list, with eight of the nine members residing in Orange. As stipulated in the statute, these "good and lawful men" constituted prominent local worthies, mainly in their thirties and forties and all native-born. Once again, their lives and careers bore no relationship to the hardscrabble existence of the immigrant farmwoman and transient drifter whose fate they would now decide.[3]

The inquest took less than two days to complete. Jurors first visited the Meierhofer farmstead, then adjourned to the funeral parlor where they viewed John's body, after which they assembled in the afternoon at the Essex County Courthouse to hear testimony. For spectators who packed the galleries, as well as readers who combed the dailies for information about the sensational proceedings, this offered the first opportunity to form some opinion of Margaret and Frank. The *Newark Daily Advertiser* aptly captured the drama as Margaret made her appearance: "There was a stir in the audience, people stood up and strained their necks to get a better view, the door of the little jury room on the south side of the Court room opened, and a tall, well-dressed woman, with downcast head and tottering steps, was led by a Constable to a chair in front of the Coroner." Both Newark dailies portrayed Mrs. Meierhofer as a sinister, menacing, and duplicitous woman. The *Newark Daily Journal* described her as "a repulsive looking woman of about fifty," though she was actually thirty-eight years old at the time. The *Daily Advertiser* preferred to focus on her alien appearance and formidable countenance: "She was dark-featured, dark-haired, remarkably tall and muscular." Clearly, she failed to meet the standards of American beauty and femininity that might garner sympathy and empathy from light-skinned, native-born Victorians. Both newspapers also suggested that her nervousness and mannerisms suggested untrustworthiness. The *Daily Journal* claimed that "she trembled as she gave her testimony." The *Daily Advertiser* reported that "she said that she was very ill" but qualified this observation with the comment that "several thought she was playing possum." Rather than confidently telling her story, the newspaper noted that "her answers were made in a low tone, and several times she paused and called for water." Margaret, of course, possessed a limited command of English, found herself accused of murder, faced a formidable jury, and had never been involved in a judicial proceeding. Reporters and spectators, however, derided her for not performing her role with more polish and style. Her dress also occasioned commentary, with a suggestion that she attempted to influence the jury by falsely presenting a more cultured and sophisticated veneer than befitted her low station in life: she arrived in court "with a gray blanket shawl over a dark dress, a white hat trimmed with black velvet and some red ribbons and a black feather." This seemingly ostentatious display from a woman whose husband had been murdered only a few days before suggested in the minds of some that she lacked remorse and failed to observe customary mourning rituals.[4]

Frank Lammens, on the other hand, received a different reception from the press. The *Daily Journal* approvingly noted that he seemed to be "a good-natured, big-whiskered, talkative Hollander." The *Daily Advertiser* described his demeanor as "mild; and he looked like the last man who would commit a cold-blooded murder." Both dailies praised his rapid-fire delivery, his occasional asides and jokes directed at the jury, and the engaging manner in which he told his story. The notion that he had been victimized by a ruthless temptress who manipulated him for his own purposes also began to take hold in the public mind. Indeed, the *Daily Journal* drew a biblical parallel, suggesting that Lammens bore some resemblance to Jacob's son in Genesis 39. This famous and oft-repeated Bible story involved Joseph, a "handsome and good looking" young man who had been taken as a slave to one of Pharaoh's officers. The Egyptian's wife desired Joseph, grabbing his garment and asking him to "lie with me." Joseph refused temptation, remained faithful to the Lord, left the garment in her hand, and ran out of the house. He subsequently was imprisoned for insulting his master's wife, but ultimately his resistance to the woman's unholy advances won the Lord's favor. Lammens, according to the *Daily Journal*, "was a Joseph in this case without Joseph's power to resist temptation." His principal crime, in this reading, involved succumbing to Margaret's seductive wiles and physical charms, despite the fact that the same newspaper previously had characterized her appearance as "repulsive." Frank eagerly took on this narrative, vigorously maintaining his innocence and ignorance of the murder throughout the proceedings while casting Margaret as a villainous temptress who exploited him for her own evil purposes. Indeed, from the moment that the police had escorted them from the farmhouse to the Orange Police Station, Lammens had engaged in an outpouring of venom directed at Mrs. Meierhofer. Marshal Conroy recalled him scream-ing, "You bitch; you did it yourself, and are trying to put it on me" dur-ing the ride down the mountain, also muttering, "Well, my throat is now cut." Of course, Lammens in other ways made a poor appearance. The *Daily Advertiser* noted that "he was shabbily dressed, and with unkempt hair and beard looked like a tramp." The police also recovered a number of Frank's belongings at the scene that possibly constituted stolen prop-erty from a variety of robberies and break-ins. And there was the matter of his Victor Number One revolver. When the Orange police initially arrived on the scene, their shockingly shoddy investigation did uncover the firearm. They determined, however, that all the chambers remained filled with cartridges. When the county prosecutor and Sheriff Van Rensselaer examined the same weapon on the following day, however, they mysteri-ously discovered that one chamber had in fact been discharged, consistent with the .22-caliber slug found in John Meierhofer's head. This apparently tied Lammens directly to the murder despite his denials. Incredibly, no one questioned the discrepancy between the two investigations. Still, though viewed suspiciously as an outsider and a tramp, Lammens received more initial public and press sympathy than Margaret.[5]

The appearances of the accused constituted the dramatic high points of the inquest. The remainder of the hearings progressed in a more rou-tine manner. Marshal Conroy, who had taken so little interest in investigat-ing the incident, recounted his role in making the arrests and transporting Margaret and Frank to jail. John Pierson, the schoolteacher who boarded at the farm, reviewed his experiences in living with the Meierhofers and also chronicled his actions on the day of the murder. Various neighbors and visitors to the house on October 9 testified about their impressions, which varied considerably. Many noticed nothing unusual in the behavior or the demeanor of Margaret or Frank. Some detected heightened ner-vousness in Lammens and suspected that he might have been drinking. Fanny Taylor, a Saint Cloud resident who had stopped in to buy some lima beans and check on the price of grapes during the afternoon, told a dif-ferent story. She noticed that "Mrs. M's face was red; she appeared much excited; asked her what was the matter; she said she couldn't tell; saw no one but her around the place at that time; live near their place but did not hear any noise from it that day." She drew no conclusions. Jurors, how-ever, might decide from her testimony that Margaret had been shocked by the murder of her husband and feared retribution by Lammens if she said anything or signaled a problem. Alternately, they could conclude that she herself feared discovery and that her meeting with Taylor would have been the perfect opportunity to reveal her husband's murder and seek assistance, since Frank appeared absent from the scene. Yet she said nothing. Finally, the jury received testimony from the county physician, who confirmed the cause of death, adding the grizzly detail that John's "skull was fractured, either from falling or kicks from a heavy boot" after the shooting. Deliberations then began, and the jurors barely took one hour to reach their conclusions and render their official verdict: "We find that John Meierhofer came to his death in the township of West Orange on the 9th day of October, 1879, from the effects of a pistol-shot wound, received at the hands of Margaret Meierhofer and Frank Lammens, and that the said Margaret Meierhofer and Frank Lammens are guilty of murder." With that decision, Coroner Mandeville concluded his part in the Meierhofer drama. It remained for Sheriff Van Rensselaer to commit the indicted defendants to the county jail where they would await their trials.[6]

Charles Hopkins Hartshorne (1851–1918), a Jersey City attorney and Montclair resident who fashioned himself as a progressive legal reformer, asserted in 1905 that the Garden State's "system of courts at present is the most antiquated and intricate that exists in any considerable community of English-speaking people." His principal scholarly contribution to legal literature, *Courts and Procedure in England and New Jersey*, argued that the state had fallen behind in adapting rational reforms to its system of jurisprudence. Hartshorne traced the procedural peculiarities and confusing labyrinth of courts and appeal processes to English common law in the fourteenth and fifteenth centuries. He tellingly observed that New Jersey's legal system had been designed to meet "the needs of a rural community of Eighteenth Century colonists" rather than the complex urban society of the nineteenth century. Similar to many turn-of-the-century progressives, Hartshorne argued for the benefits of centralization, consolidation, expert administration, and professionalization in transforming the legal system. He decried the influence of party bosses in treating judicial appointments as mere patronage opportunities. Hartshorne reserved special scorn for local justices of the peace and police courts, such as the ones who failed to take Margaret Meierhofer's abuse charges against her husband seriously. He disdainfully viewed many local judges as unqualified hacks who should occupy no place in a rationally constructed court system. New Jersey suffered from confused overlapping jurisdictions, frustrating procedural delays, and piecemeal reforms that left a bloated bureaucracy largely intact. Many contemporaries would agree and, in fact, moved much further than Hartshorne. Progressive reformers embraced such tools as probation, domestic and juvenile courts, social worker interventions, and psychiatric testing for defendants. Gilded Age jurists, however, paid little mind to extenuating circumstances, mental debility, or sociological explanations for criminal behavior. Guilt and innocence in their view appeared more straightforward and tied to individual moral character. In New Jersey, not until the state called a constitutional convention in 1947 would the judicial system receive a much-needed overhaul.[7]

The Meierhofer/Lammens trial took place within the obsolete and arcane structure criticized by Hartshorne. Once the coroner's inquest concluded, the next step involved a formal indictment by a grand jury followed by a trial in the court of oyer and terminer. The phrase "oyer and terminer," which literally means to hear and determine, first appeared in the colony in 1699 when the Province of West Jersey established this court to try cases involving capital offenses and treason. The court of oyer and terminer persisted into the twentieth century, however, and essentially constituted a county circuit court. The New Jersey Supreme Court appointed one of its justices to preside over each county's oyer and terminer proceedings. The court maintained jurisdiction over county crimes of an indictable or presentable nature and also retained responsibility for confining criminals to jail. These circuit courts met infrequently, however, and even though the Meierhofer coroner's inquest had been concluded in mid-October, the actual indictment was not presented by the grand jury until mid-December, and the trial itself did not commence until January 1880. In the interim, the defendants remained confined to the Essex County Jail, anxiously awaiting further developments in their respective cases.[8]

David Ayres Depue (1826–1902), the supreme court justice who had been assigned responsibility for the Essex and Union County circuits, exerted considerable control over this next phase of the judicial proceedings. Depue constituted a formidable presence. At fifty-four years old, he looked the part of a seasoned and distinguished jurist. Depue stood at 5 feet, 10 inches; had piercing blue eyes and a prominent nose; boasted a thick shock of flowing gray hair that he parted on the side and combed back; and maintained a well-trimmed beard. His personal background and career trajectory illustrated the advantages of good breeding, superior education, and personal connections. He had been born in Mount Bethel near Northampton, Pennsylvania, and he could trace his French Huguenot forebears to the earliest days of settlement in seventeenth-century New Jersey and Pennsylvania. Depue's ancestors fought in the American Revolution and the War of 1812, several siblings sought and obtained membership in the Sons of the Revolution, and one branch of the family had occupied settlements on the west bank of the Delaware River prior to the arrival of William Penn. David's father, Benjamin, relocated from Mount Bethel to Belvidere in rural Warren County, New Jersey, at some point in the late 1830s. Benjamin made his money in lumbering, taking advantage of the surrounding forests and the power provided by the Pequest River to run his sawmills and support his six children. Belvidere served as a significant shipping point for goods to Trenton and Philadelphia owing to its easy access to the Delaware River and, after 1854, the opening of the Delaware Belvidere Railroad. Given these transportation advantages, Benjamin managed to accumulate a substantial fortune. As one memorialist noted, "The elder Depue gave his son, David, every possible advantage of preliminary education." Benjamin sent David first to the prestigious boarding school in Easton, Pennsylvania, that had been established by the Presbyterian minister John Vanderveer. Shortly thereafter, David began attending Princeton College. He graduated from Princeton in 1846 whereupon he began studying law under John Maxwell Sherrerd, a prominent fifty-two-year-old attorney in Belvidere. They developed a warm friendship and an amiable partnership, with Depue eventually naming his only son after his mentor. Since the town served as the county seat, a bustling legal business existed in the community, and once David was admitted to the bar, he quickly developed a "large clientage."⁹

Education, upbringing, and personal connections launched Depue's legal career, but politics held the key to his advancement. Depue originally had affiliated with the Whig Party, but like many of his political allies, he gravitated toward Republicanism in the 1850s. A eulogist at his funeral noted that David "held decided views on all public questions and did not hesitate to express them when occasion required." His Republican Party commitments, political outspokenness, and legal success likely brought him to the attention of the Republican Marcus L. Ward, who had been elected governor of New Jersey in 1866. Ward appointed Depue to the supreme court, thus catapulting him into new statewide prominence. The New Jersey Supreme Court consisted of a chief justice and four

FIG. 4.2 David Depue, the formidable judge who presided over the Meierhofer and Lammens trial. This engraving appeared in William H. Shaw, *History of Essex and Hudson Counties, New Jersey*, vol. 1 (Philadelphia: Evarts & Peck, 1884). Courtesy of Special Collections and University Archives, Rutgers University Libraries.

associate justices, all of whom served seven-year terms with the possibility of multiple reappointments. As a Republican, Depue occupied political minority status on the court, but he appeared popular with leaders of both parties. Ward's successor, the Democrat Joel Parker, reappointed him to a second term in 1873, perhaps as part of his electoral pledge and subsequent commitment to support a nonpartisan judiciary. When that term expired, Democratic governor George McClellan again reappointed him in 1880. Depue rapidly earned the respect of his colleagues on the high court. They immediately assigned him to the Essex and Union County circuits, which tried some of the highest-profile cases in the state. Further, when the state legislature appointed a three-person special commission in

1873 to propose amendments to the state constitution in response to a corruption scandal in Jersey City, Depue was named as one of the members. He clearly appeared to be a man on the rise in judicial and political circles. The supreme court appointment also necessitated an important change in David's personal life. He moved from the comfortable confines of the country town of Belvidere to the industrial metropolis of Newark. By 1880, he had purchased a downtown home at 21 Park Street, one of the most fashionable addresses in the city. Depue resided there with his second wife, Adelaide, four children ranging in age from ten to twenty-seven, and two Irish immigrant women who worked as servants. Depue had achieved status and respect within his chosen field, financial security that enabled him to maintain a comfortable urban lifestyle, and a broad range of prominent friends and acquaintances.[10]

Depue also had presided over numerous capital crime cases by 1879. The Dutch Reformed minister who presided at his 1902 funeral spent a bit of time reflecting on this aspect of the late jurist's career. The Reverend James Vance claimed that "I have heard him tell of the hard struggle he had with himself the first time it became his duty to pronounce the death sentence on a condemned criminal." Vance meant this as a testimonial to his subject's basic humanity. Yet the reverend also made clear that despite any private misgivings and sympathies that Depue might have harbored, "when he believed that right and duty demanded a certain course, he never wavered." The minister remembered him as "liberal without being weak," incorruptible and fair, courteous "but never when courtesy meant compromise," and someone who "hated shams and frauds, and was impatient of disingenuousness of any kind." Although posthumous tributes necessarily gloss over flaws and lionize their subjects, this description of Depue focuses especially on his hard-nosed pragmatism and his ability to control his courtroom by taking a firm hand. Inflexibility and single-mindedness might, though, generate injustice. Strong convictions could easily produce a cavalier attitude toward basic human rights. Decisiveness too often served as a cover to gloss over ambiguity and gray lines. One Depue memorialist noted that "especially in the trial of a capital offense, he impresses everyone present, by his manner and tone, that he means simply to act as a judge, and that in his eyes the right of the accused are just as precious as the rights of the accuser." Thieves and murderers who appeared before him, in the words of this chronicler, left "his Court-room with no bitter feelings against the Judge." The Meierhofer and Lammens trial ultimately would test his patience, raise legitimate questions concerning his reputation for fairness and evenhandedness, and offer insight into the tight-knit legal fraternity that dominated the late nineteenth century New Jersey court system. If Depue viewed himself as a neutral arbiter who could reach his decisions in a calm and impartial manner, the confused and chaotic lives of Frank Lammens and Margaret Meierhofer, as well as the contradictions that lay at the heart of their stories, would challenge those very values.[11]

Depue received some indication of the difficulties that he faced on December 16, when he first met Margaret Meierhofer and Frank Lammens in court. Six days previously, the grand jury had presented murder indictments against the accused parties, essentially confirming the findings of the coroner's jury. The twenty-one other indictments that the grand jury handed down that day reflected the more routine matters that typically preoccupied Essex County courts: four for breaking and entering, nine for assault and battery, five for larceny and receiving stolen goods, one misdemeanor, one charge of embezzlement, and one bigamy case. When the court of oyer and terminer convened on the sixteenth, however, the proceedings appeared far from normal. Reporters characterized Margaret Meierhofer as "pale and cool," someone who "exhibited little or no emotion." Throughout the hearing, she "remained cool and reserved, apparently unconscious of what was going on." The newspaper narrative, which implied that Mrs. Meierhofer constituted a cold and cunning character who icily planned the murder to further her own financial and sexual ambitions, thus received reinforcement by her supposedly calm demeanor. Frank Lammens's behavior at the arraignment took on another dimension. When Depue asked him how he intended to plead, Lammens "acted like a lunatic," in the words of the *Daily Journal*. He "grew desperately excited, and in quick succession pounded his clenched fist upon the railing of the bar on the side of the Judge's bench." Lammens could not be restrained, screaming, "Let me speak," and informing Depue that "I will make you wash your hands clean in my blood. Let me speak. I will tell you something. Let me speak." Depue repeatedly pounded his gavel, calling for order to little effect. The judge finally took matters into his own hands, stipulating that a plea of not guilty should be entered on Lammens's behalf. He then cleared the courtroom, remanding both Lammens and Meierhofer back to their prison cells. Depue tentatively set Monday, 19 January 1880, as the trial date before moving on to other more routine business. This first encounter with the defendants had not gone smoothly and proved an accurate harbinger of the subsequent proceedings.[12]

The arraignment also introduced the principal attorneys who would try the case. Gustav Abeel served as the Essex County prosecutor. He already had played a significant role in the proceedings, mysteriously locating the open chamber in Lammens's pistol that supposedly had eluded the police when they visited the scene of the crime. Born in 1839, the son of a Dutch Reformed minister, Gustav moved to New Jersey with his family from Geneva, New York, around 1850 when his father became the pastor of the Second Reformed Church in Newark. Dutch Reformed connections proved instrumental in launching his career. He graduated from Rutgers College, which retained strong Dutch Reformed ties into the twentieth century and where his father served as a trustee, in 1859. He then studied law under Frederick T. Frelinghuysen, a leading Reformed layman and perhaps the most prominent attorney in New Jersey, gaining admittance to the bar in 1862. Military service intervened, delaying the start of his legal career. Unlike the modest contribution rendered by John Meierhofer, who entered the war as a lowly private, Abeel immediately was commissioned as a second lieutenant in Company D of the First Regiment of New Jersey Volunteers in October of 1862. He quickly rose through the ranks, eventually being promoted to brevet lieutenant colonel before resigning from the army at the conclusion of hostilities. By 1865, the twenty-six-year-old attorney already had forged important legal connections, achieved a prestigious rank in the Union forces, and appeared ready to launch a distinguished practice. He next cemented an alliance with the influential Runyon family in Newark, beginning a postwar partnership that lasted into the early 1870s. Their Broad Street practice apparently generated a good income, as the 1870 census noted that Abeel owned twenty-five thousand dollars in real estate and employed three domestic servants to tend to his small family. Governor Joel Parker initially appointed Abeel to the post of Essex County prosecutor in 1872, and he held that position for ten years until the New Jersey state senate refused to confirm him for a third five-year term in 1882. His sudden death in 1884 prompted a series of saccharine eulogies from fellow bar members, but a few hinted at darker elements of his personality. Judge Ludlow McCarter noted that "he had faults—who has not—and grievously has he suffered for them. . . . He was false to no man, but he was not always true to himself." Others emphasized his outspokenness and ambition, bordering on inflexibility and arrogance: "He was full of individuality . . . nor did he truckle one whit to anyone. . . . What he wished, he wished, and went for it. . . . What he thought, he thought, and was very apt to say it." Abeel appeared to personify a vigorous, argumentative, and intense prosecutorial style. Colleagues praised his ability to confront the leading lawyers of the day, and they nodded toward his commitment to fairness, but everyone agreed that this tenacious attorney pursued his prey with vigor and stealth. He would prove to be a formidable and highly effective prosecutorial advocate, as well as a skilled cross-examiner, throughout the Meierhofer/Lammens proceedings.[13]

Margaret Meierhofer selected an attorney who seemingly provided a sharp contrast with the serious and hard-driving prosecutor. William B. Guild, in the words of one colleague, "was always genial, liked a jest, and enjoyed a pun." It remains unclear how Margaret came into contact with Guild or who paid his retainer, but it appeared to be a shrewd choice on many levels. As with many other principals in the case, Guild traced his familial connections back several generations in New Jersey and Pennsylvania. His father served as the publisher and editor of the *Newark Daily Journal*, offering the hopes that Margaret might receive favorable attention in the daily press. Further, he contained the appropriate mix of educational and personal connections that placed him at the center of public culture in Newark. Guild had been born in rural Denville in 1829, sharing similar small-town roots with many other legal professionals connected to the trial. His father, who served as a lay judge in the Essex County court of common pleas in addition to his publishing projects, relocated the family to Newark at some point in the 1840s. William briefly attended Lafayette College but left after his freshman year and completed his studies at Princeton in 1851, five years after Judge Depue had graduated from the same institution. He then studied under Frederick T. Frelinghuysen, the same patrician mentor who would train Gustav Abeel later in the decade. Admission to the New Jersey bar occurred in 1854, and before long, Guild thoroughly integrated himself into Newark politics. He succeeded Theodore Runyon as city attorney in 1860, gained election to the Newark City Council in 1865 and 1875, and served on the board of health for several years. Interestingly enough, and perhaps hinting at his ethnic roots, he also organized the German Savings Bank in 1871, toiling as trustee and counsel for that organization until his death. Before taking on responsibility for the Meierhofer case, Guild had defended many high-profile clients, including alleged safe-crackers, revenue swindlers, insurance fraud perpetrators, and murderers. He recently had gained considerable acclaim when he won an October 1879 acquittal for Joseph Blair, the wealthy Montclair resident who had been on trial for murdering his Irish-born servant. One observer noted that he excelled at trying "a large number of important cases, especially of a criminal character, and whenever he has failed to win, it has not been for lack of diligence, or learning or eloquent advocacy of his client's case." Indeed, he enjoyed an "extensive and lucrative practice" that allowed him to support his wife, mother-in-law, and six children in fine style by 1880. The family employed two servants and a cook at their comfortable Lagrange Place residence, only a short walk from the law offices of Guild & Lum. In selecting the fifty-year-old Guild, Margaret had acquired the services of a quintessential Essex County legal insider who offered the promise of mounting a vigorous and effective defense.[14]

Frank Lammens necessarily pursued a different course. At the arraignment, Sheriff Van Rensselaer testified that Lammens "had neither counsel nor money," with all his assets having been confiscated as evidence. Judge Depue thereupon assigned Charles Borcherling to serve as pro bono defense attorney for the impoverished drifter. Borcherling differed from the other principal legal actors in the case in several respects. First, he was an immigrant, albeit one from a wealthy background. Borcherling had been born in Berlin in 1827 and emigrated from Germany with his family as a young man. His father, a land agent, soon sent Charles back to his native country to complete his classical education. Charles returned to America in 1854, at which point he decided to pursue the law. He never attended Princeton or Rutgers, the institutions that provided basic educational training for most of his colleagues, but he did apprentice with Cortlandt Parker, a prominent Newark attorney and close personal friend of David Depue. Borcherling began practicing law in 1860, eventually establishing a partnership with William Hagaman (1850–1883) in the early 1870s. Hagaman ultimately bore much of the burden for defending Lammens after Borcherling took ill early in the proceedings. He also had been a Cortlandt Parker protégé, clerking with his law firm after graduating from the Newton Collegiate Institute. Both attorneys remained somewhat on the margins of Newark's clubby legal fraternity. They had not graduated from the same elite prep schools and colleges as their colleagues, nor did these two Episcopalians move in the same social and Dutch Reformed ecclesiastical circles. Borcherling in particular took no role in municipal affairs, never seeking public office and apparently eschewing most civic engagements. Rather than recalling any unique personality quirks, Borcherling's memorialists focused on such stolid character traits as rectitude, honor, and "strict observance of legal ethics" in describing the German-born barrister. Lammens could likely count on receiving competent representation from his assigned attorney, and perhaps someone with the language skills to shepherd him through his testimony. Yet the selection appeared problematic in other ways. Neither Borcherling nor the inexperienced Hagaman had presided over high-profile criminal trials in the past. And Lammens's own erratic behavior and penchant for wild exaggeration might well prove a poor fit for one lawyer who conducted his practice "never by chicanery" and another who was remembered fondly as a man of strict integrity who lived "a pure and blameless life." In any event, with the attorneys set and the trial date established, Meierhofer and Lammens were about ready to have their days in court as the fateful year of 1879 came to a close.[15]

Perhaps the most significant moment in the proceedings occurred during a pretrial hearing. On the snowy and sleety Tuesday morning of January 13, Borcherling and Guild appeared before Judge Depue to request separate trials for their clients. Borcherling mounted a careful legal defense, citing statutes and precedents that supported his call for two trials when multiple parties had been charged with the same offense. Guild cut more quickly to the heart of the matter. He simply stated that if Meierhofer and Lammens were tried together, "one party would become a prosecutor of the other, and the State having the assistance of the parties would claim both guilty." Each defendant thus would face what amounted to two prosecutors. The joint trial itself, Guild argued, "would present a spectacle unseen and unheard of, and would be attended with embarrassments that must deprive the defendants of such a trial as is contemplated by law." Guild further urged Depue to carefully consider the coroner's inquest testimony, which pointed toward radically different accounts by each accused murderer. He felt that jurors ultimately would need to make a judgment based on these contradictory stories, "since either nothing or murder was committed" by each of the individual defendants. Abeel, of course, vigorously opposed the motion, since a single trial clearly benefited the prosecution. Each defense attorney would assist in the cross-examination of the other defendant, thereby considerably easing his burden and magnifying the adversarial relationship between Margaret and Frank. Depue ruled on the motion on Friday the sixteenth, denying the request for separate trials. His legal rationale centered on the fact that separate trials would create a problematic situation whereby the prosecution "would have to select which one would be tried first, and that party would be placed at an unfair disadvantage." He stipulated that the defense attorneys could have the same number of jury challenges in a joint trial as each would have in an individual trial, but this hardly compensated for his denial of the motion. Based on this ruling, Borcherling and Guild now faced significant uphill battles as they plotted their respective strategies. Depue, for his part, ordered the attorneys, their clients, and all impaneled jurors to report for trial duty on the following Monday.[16]

The Essex County Courthouse, which had been built in 1838, provided an imposing and formidable setting for the proceedings. John Haviland (1792–1852), a British-born architect who worked primarily out of Philadelphia in the early nineteenth century, had designed the structure in keeping with the numerous public commissions that he received during his career. Haviland specialized in prison and institutional architecture, having been responsible for the Eastern State Penitentiary in Philadelphia (1821), the New York City House of Detention—also known as the "Tombs"— (1835–1838), and the New Jersey State Prison in Trenton (1833–1836), as well as various places of incarceration in Missouri, Rhode Island, and Arkansas. Though especially drawn to neoclassical designs, Haviland also incorporated into his buildings elements of the Egyptian Revival movement, which had achieved considerable popularity in early Federal and Jacksonian America. The Essex County Courthouse, a beautifully proportioned brownstone structure that sat outside the downtown area and bordered on the German "Hill" section of the city, reflected these influences. Its massive central columns, smooth exterior, window frames that narrowed upward, and Egyptian iconography that was embedded throughout the structure made it a fine example of the genre, which was nearing the end of its popularity in the late 1830s. Egyptian Revival, similar to other classical architectural expressions, attempted to convey a sense of permanence, timelessness, and eternity, in this case tinged with foreign exoticism. The style proved especially popular for mausoleums, cemeteries, memorial structures, and prisons that sought to impress upon inmates a sense of deadly foreboding as they contemplated their future fate. It also became identified with banks, insurance companies, and public institutions, owing to its association with power, authority, authenticity, stability, and

Old Court House, Newark, N. J.

FIG. 4.3 The Essex County Courthouse, an Egyptian Revival building that had been designed by prominent architect John Haviland and opened in 1838, served as the setting for the Meierhofer and Lammens trial. Courtesy of the author.

monumentality. Essex County officials no doubt hoped that the prisoners and jurors who climbed the stairs and opened the heavy courthouse doors would do so in a spirit of reverence accompanied by a sense of awe.[17]

Jury selection for the Meierhofer/Lammens trial took place on January 19. Sheriff Van Rensselaer remained responsible for compiling a list of qualified jurors at the beginning of each year and delivering it to the court at the commencement of each term. New Jersey statutes stipulated only that jurors must be citizens of New Jersey, residents of the particular county in which they would serve, and between the ages of twenty-one and sixty-five. Although they technically met these statutory qualifications, no women served on any New Jersey jury until after 1920, when they had achieved suffrage. The twelve White men who were selected to decide the fates of Margaret Meierhofer and Frank Lammens proved to be a relatively homogenous lot, somewhat more plebian than the elite coroner's inquest group but hardly reflecting Essex County's diverse population. Ten of the twelve resided in Newark, with the other two living in Orange. Only two immigrants had been empaneled, and both were successful businessmen: Jacob Hammacher, a hat manufacturer who had been born in Prussia, and William Ridler, a retired Englishman who had owned a paperhanging firm with his son. The other ten jurists had been born in New Jersey and were

Trial • 103

the sons of native-born parents as well, far removed from their immigrant forebears. Virtually all of the men operated their own businesses or worked in skilled artisanal trades: carriage trimmer, painter, grocer, mason, merchant in a leather and findings store, hat manufacturer, mason and builder, owner of a paperhanging firm, hatter, builder, produce dealer, and worker in a hat factory. Every juror owned his own home, lived with his wife and children, and in a few instances had taken on boarders often connected with the family business. They skewed older, ranging from forty-three through sixty-five, with the average and median ages both being fifty-one. In sum, based on their demographic profile, the jurors overwhelmingly constituted a group of respectable middle-aged family men who lived in good neighborhoods, pursued urban occupations, and had achieved stability and success throughout their careers. Once again, their lives offered a marked contrast to the two individuals over whom they would stand in judgment. Ultimately, these jurors would receive two completely conflicting sets of testimony concerning the events that resulted in John Meierhofer's murder. The prosecution had no witnesses to the actual shooting, so the entire case rested purely on circumstantial evidence. Jurors would necessarily draw on their life experiences and prejudices in gauging the credibility and reliability of the accused parties and making the requisite judgments.[18]

And so began the trial that Prosecutor Abeel characterized as "one of the most important, one of the most extraordinary, and one of the most dreadful cases that any jury of Essex County has ever been called upon to try." The key testimony centered on the conflicting stories told by Margaret and Frank. Margaret Meierhofer faced the jury first on January 23 amid "a little flutter of excitement in the court room as she went forward, and all strained their necks to get a glimpse of her." Margaret claimed that she had no trouble with Lammens until the Sunday before the murder. On that day, he entered her room through a window in the parlor, refused to leave, confessed his desire "to take possession [of my body] in the worst way he could of a female," and lingered about an hour. On Monday, when she retired for the evening, she again "found him in her room." Since Lammens refused to move, she decided to sleep in the schoolteacher's bed, as Pierson had gone home for the weekend and would not return until Tuesday. Shortly thereafter, Lammens entered the schoolteacher's bedroom and unsuccessfully "tried to take improper liberties." On Tuesday morning, Lammens "picked me up in the kitchen and carried me to my room and said he must have me alive or dead. I told him to leave me alone or it would be a sorry thing." That same evening, he entered her room through an unlocked window, but she "compelled him to go out." Finally, on the morning of the murder, he burst into her room once more and "said he was bound to have her dead or alive, and would kill a thousand to have her." Under cross-examination, Margaret described living in fear of sexual assault and physical attack for the week before the murder. Still, she kept all these incidents to herself, failing to seek help from the schoolteacher, a laborer who had been boarding at the farm, or any of her neighbors. Pierson, she claimed, had also grown fearful of Lammens, and she did not want to place him in danger. Neighbors had not offered her help of any kind in years. And the boarder, an unmarried Irish laborer from Orange, appeared unlikely to provide support. For several days prior to the murder, Margaret remained convinced that Lammens had not been capable of violence. Her views changed, however, as his behavior grew more unhinged, as he neglected his chores, and as he "kept lingering around the house like a tramp and a loafer would." Finally, on the morning of the murder, when he told Margaret that "if he had a knife he would cut my throat from ear to ear" and she replied "Kill me if you want me; my body is only clay," she decided to take action and summon the police.[19]

After Theodore's failed errand to obtain help from constables in Orange on the morning of October 9, things deteriorated around the farm. At approximately 11:00 a.m., as Frank occupied himself raking leaves and John Meierhofer tended to the cows, Margaret heard an argument break out. John bitterly scolded Frank, telling him that "if you don't want to do any work, clear out." Margaret tried to calm her husband, telling him that she planned to have police escort the hired hand off the premises. Shortly thereafter, around 11:30 a.m., Lammens emerged from his room with a pistol. After briefly threatening Margaret, Lammens turned his rage on John, who had dug up some potatoes that he intended to deposit in the cellar for storage. Margaret ran out the front of the house to intercept and warn her husband, but Lammens caught up with John first near the cellar stairs. When Margaret reached the back door, she "saw Frank shoot and kick him down stairs." Lammens then leeringly pursued Margaret into the kitchen, telling her "you're mine and I will do with you as I like" and proudly proclaiming "that's the nicest job I ever done." He demanded some money so that he could buy whiskey at Jaillette's tavern down the road, though she thought that he only "pretended to go, but he was gone only a short time."

Frank concocted an alibi upon his return. He ordered Margaret to tell everyone else in the household that her husband had gone to Newark to buy a suit of clothes. The body would remain in the cellar overnight, and the following day Lammens planned to "cut off the head and burn it; the body he would cart away in a load of hay, and put into the Passaic river" near Bloomfield. Frank also took care to head down to the basement, clean up the blood, purloin a bag of money that he found downstairs, and burn John's hat and handkerchief in the stove. He next presented Margaret with the box of now blood-soaked potatoes that John had carried into the house, perversely asking her "if she did not want to use them." For the rest of the day, Margaret testified that she remained fearful of her increasingly maniacal hired hand, hoping that either Pierson or Theodore might complete their mission to obtain assistance from the authorities.

Throughout the afternoon, several individuals stopped by the Meierhofer farm. An Orange grocer arrived shortly after the murder to pick up the household's usual shopping orders, but Margaret quickly sent him away without purchasing anything. The grocery clerk claimed that she "was composed and there was nothing about her actions or anything else to indicate that a terrible crime had been committed." Margaret insisted that her demeanor owed to the fact that Lammens was lurking in the hallway and carefully monitoring her behavior. Shortly thereafter, three other men arrived on the scene: Herman Zwinscher, a forty-five-year-old German-born saloon-keeper from Orange; his son; and his friend John Krumm, a forty-three-year-old fellow Wurttemberg native who also owned a bar in Orange. The three had taken advantage of the warm autumn day to go on a hunting expedition on the mountain. They spent the morning "shooting birds" and drinking from a canteen full of bitters in the woods across the street from the Meierhofer farm. Several Northfield Road residents noticed the threesome, all of whom appeared drunk according to multiple reports. The hunters denied that fact, though John Krumm cast some doubt on their sobriety when he testified that "I think a man is drunk [only] when he can't stand up." In any case, they decided to refresh themselves at the Meierhofer house by purchasing either some cider or milk before continuing the hunt. Upon entering the kitchen, they found Frank sitting alone at the table and Margaret nowhere to be seen. Lammens claimed that he had nothing for the hunters to drink, but Krumm knew from previous visits that the family kept milk in the cellar and offered to retrieve it himself. Frank insisted that Krumm stay in the kitchen and quickly ran down to the basement. When Lammens returned, "he came up much excited and trembling; he trembled so much that he spilled the milk, and we asked him if he was sick." Zwinscher then gave him one dollar to pay for the milk, which cost twenty-five cents, and Lammens first gave them only fifty cents in change. When Zwinscher complained, he gave them one dollar and fifty cents from John Meierhofer's money bag and appeared anxious for them to be on their way. The trio gave him a drink of bitters to calm him down and left. Margaret claimed that she had been hiding in the water closet during this exchange and did not try to enlist the armed hunters to subdue Frank because they all "seemed drunk," she herself "was exhausted and afraid," and she thought that "Lammens might kill us all." Fanny Taylor arrived midafternoon, as she testified at the coroner's inquest, but Frank surveyed that encounter from the cellar stairs, and Margaret had no opportunity to escape with her. Another young woman from nearby Edgewood Avenue stopped in later in the day because Margaret had failed to send her the butter and eggs that she had promised, but Mrs. Meierhofer claimed that "she was sick," and the visitor acknowledged that "she looked pale."

The situation escalated further when Pierson and Theodore returned home from school. After Margaret informed Pierson of the murder and convinced him to make a trip to the Orange Police Station, she again attempted to ward off Lammens until the schoolteacher arrived with help. She kept Theodore awake well into the night doing his homework, hoping that this would stabilize matters until the authorities arrived. After Theodore fell asleep on the couch, however, Frank woke him and took him upstairs where the two shared sleeping quarters. He made sure to inform Margaret, however, that "'I want you to go to bed'; his eyes rolled and I was afraid." Margaret then "went into the kitchen and wound up my clock" before retiring to her room. A short time later, "Frank came into my window, he was undressed." Margaret, fearing for her life, let him in and he climbed into bed with her. She "was partly undressed; he said I must go to bed and he threatened me so that I did not dare hesitate any longer." He also informed her that he had left his pistol upstairs in his satchel. At approximately 11:00 p.m., shortly after Frank fell asleep and Margaret slipped out of the bed, they both heard a banging at the door. She told Frank that Pierson had stepped out for a while and that she would let him in. At that point, the police entered the house, discovered John's body in the basement, found Frank in the bedroom, and handcuffed both parties before taking them to the station house. Margaret concluded her testimony by claiming that she had been somewhat naïve about Lammens's motives until it was too late: "She did not know that he was going to shoot her husband and did not think he would have the heart to do so after the way she had treated him."

Frank Lammens related a far different version of the events when he took the stand on February 3. His style also offered a marked contrast to his codefendant's. When Margaret testified, observers noted that she "gave her answers in a clear, strong voice, audible all over the court room" and "with perfect composure." At a few moments during cross-examination she needed to retire to an anteroom, complaining once of "a pain in her heart." At another time, she found herself "being overcome with emotion" when she described the murder. Generally, however, she appeared calm and serious throughout the proceedings, displaying in the words of one reporter "a pale, sallow and almost bloodless face that showed absolutely no trace of emotion." Lammens, on the other hand, at times did not appear cognizant of the seriousness of the proceedings. He arrived at the trial "neatly dressed in a new suit of dark clothes" that had been purchased for him by Borcherling and Hagaman. When called upon to swear on the Bible, he added a few phrases of his own to the amusement of the audience. He frequently referred to Prosecutor Abeel as "my noble Lord," addressed Judge Depue as "my noble brother," and informed William Guild that he was "respected and beloved by me as a very learned man and a good natured man." He offered his testimony "in a frank, simple way, speaking very rapidly and in a low husky tone." At times he sounded incomprehensible, thus motivating Depue to offer the services of a translator, which Lammens refused. He first sat back leisurely in his chair while addressing the court but eventually leaned forward, placing a pillow on the railing in front of him to rest his arms. Generally, he seemed comfortable relating his tale in an informal, even "complaisant," manner according to some observers. All of the nervousness that characterized his appearance at the arraignment appeared to have vanished, and he enjoyed his moment in the spotlight.[20]

Lammens claimed that, at the outset, he viewed Margaret as a "pleasant country woman" and "respected Mrs. M. as an industrious woman, &c." He soon discovered, however, that the farmhouse constituted a scene of debauchery and sexual profligacy. For weeks prior to the murder, Margaret carried on with a variety of boarders and other suitors. One day he caught Margaret with a painter, who Lammens described as "a monstrous brutal seductor," engaged in a sexual act. Another night she partied with the schoolteacher until after midnight, disturbing Frank's sleep and forcing a confrontation. A fifty-year-old French laborer named Deodome Ple, who worked nearby for a merchant on Walker Road, regularly climbed through Margaret's window at night and spent the evening with her, despite his having a wife and child in Europe. Ple, according to Lammens, became her steadiest suitor. He took her to the Centennial Exposition in Philadelphia, as well as on a series of excursions to theatres and museums, eventually even presenting her with a gold ring. Lammens considered him "only a brute," however, and told Margaret that "if anyone saw him come in or out of her window it would rob her of her character." But she continued her flirtations with other men as well. One carpenter bragged to Lammens that he "frolicked with Mrs. Meierhofer" whenever possible. A "fat man" who kept a livery stable nearby took her on regular jaunts to Bound Brook and Springfield in Central New Jersey. Lammens admitted to growing increasingly drawn to his employer and desirous of a sexual relationship. He claimed that Margaret "told him she was called a devil when only eighteen years old," which apparently made her even more attractive. On the Saturday before the murder, with Pierson away for the weekend, "they arranged that he should enter her window at night." On Wednesday, the day before the murder, "Mrs. M. asked him to come to her room that night, and he did so." They planned another liaison for Thursday with Margaret asking him "to come in the window as the door made a noise" and the sound might wake Theodore. In Lammens's account, Margaret always assumed the role of sexual aggressor and manipulator. At one point, he excitedly proclaimed to the jury that she had been "a wasted nature from birth, would never be any better" before Judge Depue order him to refrain from such comments.

Lammens described the day of the murder as routine. He rose with the sun around 6:00 a.m., walked to the nearby Rock Spring in order to get a pail of water, ground some coffee in the kitchen, milked the cows, chopped wood, raked leaves, and ate breakfast. He spent the rest of the morning raking leaves until around 11:00 a.m., when Margaret asked him to run an errand and get some whiskey at Jaillette's tavern. They both sat down and had a few drinks at the kitchen table, after which time he continued raking leaves. At one point he saw Margaret "come running out in a kind of a wild way" and motioning to him to come into the kitchen. The hunters had just arrived, and Margaret did not want to deal with them, since she considered Krumm "a bad man." Lammens went down to the basement to fetch some milk off of a hanging shelf in the cellar. Given the location of the milk near the top of the stairs, he claimed that he never saw John's body in the cellar. He also now recalled that he "heard a shot" prior to the hunters' arrival, though he never mentioned this fact in any other accounts of the day that he previously provided. After the hunters left, Margaret informed Frank that her husband had "gone to Newark to get a suit of clothes," and she asked him to feed the horse. Lammens worked around the farm for the rest of the day. When Pierson and Theodore arrived home from school, "Mrs. Meierhofer acted very jolly," and the foursome had a pleasant dinner. Lammens then went out on the stoop to smoke his pipe, came inside to help Theodore with his arithmetic homework, and spent some time playing dominos with Margaret. After Theodore finally went to sleep upstairs, Lammens entered Margaret's quarters through the bedroom window as previously arranged, and they climbed into bed together. The next thing he knew, he saw lantern lights shining in his eyes, police officers ordering him to lie still and be quiet, and Conroy restraining him with handcuffs. For the first time, Lammens learned that John Meierhofer lay dead in the cellar.

The proceedings confirmed the central significance of Depue's decision to hold a joint trial for both defendants. The *Daily Journal* observed that "the contest has been principally between the counsel for the two defendants, whose interests are conflicting. Prosecutor Abeel takes things easily. He has a zealous assistant in each of the other counsel." Each defense attorney spent most of his cross-examination attempting to prove that the other defendant had both intent and motive to murder Meierhofer. Borcherling and Hagaman claimed that Margaret had grown weary of her husband's abuse and deteriorating mental condition. They focused especially on a remark that she made to Pierson in the days leading up to the murder when, in his words, "she asked me what she would give [John] that would make him sick; I replied that salt and water would do it, thinking that she was jesting; afterwards I suggested calomel." Marshal Conroy recalled that, based on his interviews, Margaret had asked Pierson "to get poison to put the old man out of the way." The attorneys chronicled the troubled marriage, recounted previous attempts to institutionalize John and place him in an insane asylum, and highlighted the constant household arguments. They produced one neighbor who claimed that John arrived at her house one day begging for food, "very cold and almost frozen." John claimed that Margaret "had thrown some hot lard at him and burned his neck . . . said he was ugly and hit him with a pan on the head." Prosecutor Abeel took this argument to its logical conclusion, observing that "her husband was disgusting to her, she being in the prime of life." The defense attorneys portrayed Margaret as a desperate woman who wanted release from her marriage and conceived a sinister plot to implicate the gullible and dim-witted hired hand in her endeavors. She gained Lammens's confidence by sexually seducing him, sent him on an errand to purchase whiskey on the morning of the ninth, retrieved his pistol from a satchel that he kept in his room, fatally shot her husband, and returned the pistol to its original location. She then concocted a fake story about her husband heading to Newark to buy clothes, duped the hapless schoolteacher into thinking that Lammens had committed the murder, kept the hired hand occupied throughout the evening until the police could arrive, and told a fantastical story that, in the words of the prosecutor, "is too absurd to be believed by a child." In the final analysis, Defense Attorney Hagaman claimed, the entire case came down to the fact that Lammens had been victimized by "a designing and wicked woman."[21]

Defense Attorney Guild, however, assembled a considerable body of evidence to counter this claim. Margaret informed the court that she had long ago made peace with her husband's deteriorating mental condition. When John threatened at one point to cut her throat, she had "the charge drawn back, as he was behaving himself and she thought that between man and wife there should be no trouble." She claimed that John himself insisted on sleeping in the barn and that their sexual relationship had ceased primarily owing to a series of illnesses that she suffered from rather than from any anger on his part concerning her alleged extramarital affairs. Margaret further insisted that they behaved amicably toward each other in the weeks directly leading up to the murder. Both Meierhofer children staunchly defended their mother, claiming that she treated John with kindness, even on the many occasions when he scolded her or acted in a strange manner. Former boarders viewed the household as reasonably peaceable. One East Orange carpenter recalled that Mrs. Meierhofer "always treated her husband kindly; he did just as he liked." Another carpenter who spent time at the residence claimed that "Mrs. Meierhofer treated her husband as a wife should." James Osborne, a painter who rented a room at the farm for some time, testified that he "never saw any quarrel between Mr. and Mrs. Meierhofer but once and that could not be called a quarrel; Mr. Meierhofer jawed about something she had done." Schoolteacher Pierson denied that he ever told Marshal Conroy that Margaret intended to poison her husband. At best, the claim that their deteriorating marital relationship made Mrs. Meierhofer intent on murdering John seemed ambiguous and inconclusive. Lammens's defense attorneys and the prosecutor, however, also pursued two other strategies to besmirch her character, demonstrate motive, and convince the jury that she masterminded the crime.[22]

First and foremost, they portrayed Margaret as a sexually voracious and promiscuous woman who carried out a series of well-publicized affairs throughout the 1860s and 1870s. Lammens, of course, provided fuel for this fire when he named numerous boarders, neighborhood residents, and casual acquaintances as sexual partners for Margaret. From his first encounter with the police, Lammens especially directed attention toward Deodome Ple, the laborer who he described as "the old Frenchman," as a potential suspect in the murder. Ple, according to Lammens, owned a pistol, showered Margaret with money and attention, and had made vague promises to run away with her. Borcherling, Hagaman, and Abeel also produced other neighbors who provided evidence along these lines. Henry Richey, the alleged father of Theodore, confirmed that he had a long-term affair with Margaret, regularly sneaking in and out of her window at night during the Civil War. Eugene LeClare, a thirty-six-year-old carpenter who lived nearby on Northfield Road, testified that he witnessed Ple sneaking "out of the house by means of a window in Pierson's room seven or eight times before 5 o'clock in the morning; had seen him go in in the evening; this was about two years ago last summer." Other witnesses claimed that Margaret and Ple regularly attended dances at a German saloon on Canfield Street in Orange. Christianna Weinman, an elderly German woman from Wurttemberg who lived approximately one mile from Margaret, provided perhaps the most damning testimony. She briefly lived at the Meierhofer house in 1873, as she "attended Mrs. M. when the latter had a miscarriage." At the time, a mason named Archie Day also boarded on the farm. Weinman found that "the talk there was too filthy" and refused to remain in the household. She implied that Day and Margaret had been engaged in a sexual relationship, possibly resulting in the miscarriage, and further identified a photograph that had been recovered by police at the crime scene as a portrait of Archie Day with Mrs. Meierhofer. For the prosecution, these stories supported the narrative that Margaret behaved in a reckless and irresponsible manner, taking on lovers at will and flaunting her promiscuous behavior in front of community members as well as her own husband.[23]

Defense Attorney Guild strongly refuted these charges. Margaret, not surprisingly, denied engaging in any so-called improprieties. And the men who boarded at the farm during the 1870s backed up her version of events, with James Osborne observing that during the evenings his painting crew "passed the time in reading and playing dominos." Ple vigorously challenged Lammens, insisting that he never stayed overnight at the farm, did not accompany Margaret to the Centennial, never offered her a ring, and maintained only a business relationship with her. He brought his dirty laundry to the farm on Saturdays and would retrieve the clean clothes the following day, occasionally lingering to play dominos with some local German men as he did the Sunday before the murder. Guild also attacked the credibility of the three main witnesses who questioned Margaret's morality. Richey and his wife, who both bore long-standing grudges against Mrs. Meierhofer that dated back to the alleged affair during the Civil War years, wanted revenge. A laborer who boarded at the Jaillette tavern testified that Richey gleefully told him, "'Wait till I get up [to the witness stand] and I will give her a shot and make her hang her head.'" Guild noted that the Richeys happily attended the trial every day "looking for a verdict which shall consign her to death, with a desire born of the hatred in his heart." Eugene LeClare, on the other hand, had an unsavory reputation throughout the community. Two neighbors claimed that "his reputation for truthfulness is not very good," while Claude Jaillette recalled that LeClare boasted in the tavern that "'the time has come and I will have revenge'" on Margaret. William J. Fuller, the prominent Saint Cloud attorney, testified that LeClare "was a notorious thief and a liar" who had stolen lumber from him and a ring from another neighbor: "His reputation for truth and veracity is bad," and Fuller "would not hang a dog on his testimony." Guild ridiculed Christianna Weinman as a moralistic busybody "who thought it was improper for Mrs. Meierhofer to be pulled on a sled by a man" and a "wideawake woman, who readily sees the faults rather than the virtues of other people." By casting doubt on witness credibility, Guild hoped to counter the disdain that many community members felt toward Margaret and to rehabilitate her sordid reputation.

But the prosecution also played a second gender-based card. Borcherling, Hagaman, and Abeel regularly returned to the issue of Margaret's physical appearance as they argued their respective cases. Hagaman ridiculed the notion that Lammens had the ability to carry Margaret from the kitchen to the bedroom against her protestations on the Tuesday before the murder.

He asked his diminutive defendant to stand before the court, noting that "Lammens is not very strongly made" in contrast to Margaret's powerful, even unwomanly, build. He labeled as ludicrous fantasy the notion that "this little man picked up that giant of a woman and carried her all over the house." In his final summation, Hagaman built upon the theme of physical power to discredit the notion that Margaret feared Lammens and could not seek help from neighbors and visitors. He described her as "a large and strong woman, almost a giantess in strength, and of strong passion and excessive sexual desire." Prosecutor Abeel also disparaged the notion that Margaret lived in fear of Lammens throughout October 9: "She could have pitched him into the brook . . . or when he was about to shoot her husband she could have seized Lammens and broken his neck." Both attorneys chronicled the numerous visitors to the farm, the opportunities that presented themselves for Margaret to escape, and her failure to subdue Lammens at several possible points during the day. Ultimately, despite the specific evidence and testimony that unfolded over three weeks, the case against Margaret Meierhofer hinged on gender, class, and ethnicity. She did not look the part of a proper Victorian woman, violated middle-class sexual norms by not sleeping with her husband and carrying on serial affairs with multiple men, and constituted a potentially dangerous outsider whose actions threatened the respectable reputation of her own community. Guild recognized the difficulty that he faced in countering these impressions. He first asked the all-male jury to reject a gender-based double standard. Even, he asserted, if we "admit, for argument, that she did all they say she did, does it follow that because she committed adultery she would commit murder? Apply this rule to men and does it hold?" He then completely shifted gears and made a plea based on female essentialism: "Though Mrs. M. has not the accomplishments which education and wealth gives, it will not do to say she hasn't the instincts and nature of a woman." On one level, therefore, the case rested on circumstantial suppositions concerning the murder of John Meierhofer. As the attorneys framed their arguments, however, other issues came into play. Jurors ultimately would need to decide the case on factors that transcended merely physical evidence. Margaret, by virtue of her foreignness, her menacing physical appearance, and the accusations that she acted in a manly fashion by pursuing adulterous sexual gratification, clearly constituted a significant threat to Victorian cultural values. It remained to be seen whether her supposed cultural transgressions would result in a guilty verdict.[24]

Frank Lammens presented his defense attorneys with entirely different challenges. First, his courtroom demeanor became impossible to manage. He rambled, proved difficult to understand, changed important elements of his testimony during cross-examination, and contradicted more reliable witnesses. He could not account for large gaps in his personal history. No credible supporters appeared who could vouch for his character. And his account of the day of the murder contained numerous inconsistencies. For example, one key piece of information that he provided concerned his midday trip to Jaillette's tavern to procure rye whiskey, which would have placed him away from the farmhouse at the time of the murder. Susan Jaillette, who managed the establishment with her husband, recalled a different chronology. She testified that Lammens arrived at the bar shortly after 6:00 a.m. to purchase alcohol "but was not there in the afternoon or any other time of the day." Andrew J. Hopkins, a laborer who boarded at the tavern and had arisen around the same time, since "on that day he was to help load hay for a man at 6:30," confirmed her account. He saw Lammens leaving the premises, looked at the clock, and noticed that it read 6:40 a.m. Hopkins also returned to the tavern around 10:00 a.m., stayed there until the early afternoon, and "was sure Lammens was not there between those hours," thus destroying his alibi. Similarly, the drifter's account of his trip to the Meierhofer basement to fetch milk for the Zwinschers and Krumm came under scrutiny. Lammens claimed that he grabbed the milk off a shelf near the top of the stairs and therefore did not notice the dead body. Unfortunately for his story, the shelf apparently did not exist. Theodore Meierhofer testified that "there was no shelf where Lammens said he got the milk for the hunters" and that a table in the basement had been removed several weeks prior to the murder and placed in the kitchen. Constable Rendell and Marshal Conroy confirmed that no such bench or shelf existed in the basement. Henry Hoffman, an Orange fish dealer who police placed in charge of the farmhouse to secure its contents following the murder, observed that "the milk was on hanging shelves in the back part of the cellar," where the body would have been visible. Essentially, it would have been impossible for Lammens to retrieve the milk without virtually stepping over John's corpse.[25]

During the trial, the defendant also exhibited signs of erratic behavior that sometimes suggested mental illness. He often dozed off in the courtroom, appearing remarkably disinterested in the proceedings. On January 26, Lammens arrived at court in "a wretched condition," suffering from erysipelas in the face and running a fever of 103 degrees. His swollen and discolored face, as well as his general poor health that doctors attributed to anxiety, rendered him unable to stand up. One reporter found him "sleeping on the floor, with his head resting on his soft felt hat . . . a most pitiable sight." His physical debility forced an eight-day recess in the trial until he gradually recovered his strength. Essex County Jail officials worried even more about his mental condition during this period and effectively placed him under suicide watch. Lammens's comments and conduct immediately prior to the murder also cast suspicion in his direction and raised questions concerning his state of mind. Even if they chose to discount Margaret's testimony, jurors heard a variety of other acquaintances describe him as a sinister and potentially dangerous figure. James Osborne, the painter and former farmhouse boarder, testified that Lammens proudly flaunted his status as a "professional tramp," frequently reminiscing about the time that he spent in German prisons and explaining why those facilities proved far superior to American penitentiaries in Albany and Clinton. "When I read in the papers about the murder I thought more than likely he had committed the deed," Osborne observed. James Conover confirmed this account, agreeing with Osborne's assessment "that [the] tramp is going to show this family a trick before he goes away from here." Minard Magie, another carpenter who boarded at the house, mentioned that Lammens once told him that he would shoot Meierhofer "for a paper of tobacco." Schoolteacher Pierson recounted several arguments between Frank and John in the week before the murder. All in all, witnesses documented a series of hot-headed and intemperate remarks by Lammens that easily could be construed as intent to harm his employer. In the final analysis, Lammens's status as an unreliable and curious community outsider undermined his defense. As Prosecutor Abeel argued in his final summation to the jury, Lammens should be viewed above all "as a tramp, a burglar, and a man who carried a deadly weapon. If there is one more criminal than another who is careless about the property and life of other men, it is the tramp who enters the house at night to rob, and prepared to shoot down anyone who interferes with him."[26]

From the time of his arrest, Lammens had to explain how he managed to possess the diverse objects that police had seized from his room. The court of oyer and terminer logged in the following pieces of evidence that had been procured from Lammens: a nickel-plated clock, various overcoats, one bag of money, a piano cover, various silk handkerchiefs, one pair of spectacles, one chemise, a black stiff hat, some silverware, a tobacco pouch, and even a sign warning trespassers to stay away. Newspapers printed rumors that he had been responsible for shooting a night watchman near South Orange in another attempted burglary. He further admitted to breaking into the home of Theodore Morgan, a Caldwell attorney, and to storing the goods that he had pilfered there in Jersey City. Many items that the police recovered from his room had been traced to the robbery that had occurred in August at the "Eyrie" mansion in West Orange, suggesting that he played a role in the crime spree that plagued the community in late summer. Lammens fully acknowledged his guilt in this heist during the trial, describing at one point how he climbed into the "Eyrie" window at night looking for something to eat, at which time "I took those coats; don't know whose they were; they are mine at present; I got that clock in a barn; I took it because it looked pretty; I got those handkerchiefs in the coat pocket." He denied "stealing" the chemise, however, since he "got that off the grass" and "picked it up" rather than removing it from the house. And he attempted to demonstrate his peculiar sense of honesty by noting that "when he stole the silver-knife and fork, he might have taken more, but he simply wanted one of each kind for his own use." Earlier in the decade, during the height of the depression, many middle-class Americans expressed some empathy for homeless tramps who took to the road looking for work. Even Allan Pinkerton, the hard-boiled founder of the famous detective agency that bore his name, urged his fellow countrymen to look kindly on this "brotherhood of strollers" and remember the "keen needs of thousands of our fellows who have fought the fight against persistent and relentless misfortune, and fallen." Pinkerton argued that tramps deserved more public sympathy, since they "are made up of people often as good as we." By 1880, however, the term *tramp* had taken on a severely negative connotation, typically associated with robbery, rape, and murder. Lammens, a self-confessed burglar and thief who proudly proclaimed himself a tramp, could expect little sympathy from the respectable men who would determine his fate. It became quite easy for Guild to caricature him in his final argument as a "cool and desperate" character, the type of man "who enters your house at night to steal, armed with a revolver to protect his life if necessary." All attorneys in the case believed that playing to heightened public anxieties concerning both gender and class served as an effective way to sway jurors.[27]

One other element of the trial, however, proved difficult to contain and generated considerable hand-wringing. Newspapers struggled with reporting the salacious details that emerged during the testimony. On the one hand, they knew that sex sold. Daily coverage kept the case firmly in the public mind and stimulated excitement among the readership. Prurient interest in Margaret's alleged affairs and domestic relations remained at the heart of the ongoing fascination. On the other hand, reporters and editors feared that they might cross a gray line and diminish their standing as guardians of public morality. They needed both to titillate readers and to present themselves as responsible news outlets. The three major local newspapers that provided coverage took somewhat different approaches. The *Orange Journal*, an avowedly boosterist weekly that always aimed to present a positive image of its hometown, offered relatively sparse and succinct stories. Once the trial concluded, it provided a self-congratulatory justification for this approach, observing that "we have purposely avoided a repetition in these columns of the disgusting detail." The *Journal* referred to the murder as "one of the most uncalled-for, brutal, and dastardly crimes ever committed," something that reflected poorly on personal ethics and local culture. By publishing merely minimal accounts, the newspaper believed that it best served community interests. The *Newark Daily Advertiser*, befitting its middle-class Republican leanings, took a more centrist approach. The Meierhofer murder trial served as the lead local story every day, and the newspaper often printed virtually verbatim excerpts from the trial. Yet the newspaper noted that "a large portion [of the testimony] is unfit for publication," and it consciously played the role of public censor by summarizing some details and only vaguely referencing others. The *Newark Daily Journal*, a more freewheeling Democratic publication that provided more extensive coverage of the city's immigrant population, proved less restrained. Its reporters offered more detail and first-person accounts than the *Advertiser*'s correspondents, discussing more extensively such sensitive topics as Theodore's alleged illegitimacy, Margaret's supposed miscarriage, and sleeping arrangements in the farmhouse. Though its editorialists agreed that the trial contained "many revolting features," the *Journal* justified its approach by asserting that "a case more difficult, more dramatic . . . more interesting, has not been presented before in the courts of this county." For the *Journal*, at least, public interest trumped propriety.[28]

Newspapers might take different approaches to reporting on the trial, but all agreed that one of the most disturbing features of the proceedings involved the spectators who daily crowded the courtroom. From the start of testimony, visitors poured into the galleries, with interest gradually increasing as newspaper coverage intensified. On peak days, such as when Margaret and Frank took the stand, crowds swelled to over five hundred. Curiosity seekers occupied every seat and stood in the aisles hoping to catch a glimpse of the accused and take in their shocking testimony. The fact that proved most disconcerting to reporters and courtroom officials, however, involved the growing numbers of women who appeared at the courthouse. On the second day of the trial, the *Daily Journal* nervously noted that "this morning were observed about fifty ladies, some of whom had to stand." On the following day, the same paper reported that public interest had exceeded expectations and "not only were the seats occupied, many of them by women, but the aisles were also crowded with men standing." Perhaps even more distressing, "not only men but their wives and children" were also present as the Frenchman Deodome Ple testified about his relationship with Margaret. For some Newark residents, the trial apparently had become transformed into family entertainment. On the day that Lammens took ill and Margaret had been expected to face cross-examination, the *Daily Advertiser* sneered that "a large and motley throng" had arrived, with the number of women estimated as exceeding one hundred. By January 28, the newspaper critically informed readers that "a large number of well-dressed women, the majority of whom have no connection with the case in any way, has excited much unfavorable comment among court officials and others." These women appeared to take an excessive interest in the proceedings: "They come early in the morning to get good seats and are about the last to leave in the afternoon." The newspaper reserved special scorn for one "well-dressed woman" who arrived with her sixteen-year-old daughter to imbibe Margaret's testimony concerning her relationship with Lammens "and apparently enjoyed the disgusting recital." The press preferred to interpret this female presence as a simpleminded fascination with the trial's sexually explicit content. At this historical distance, with no corroborating first-person testimony, motives appear difficult to entangle. Yet another possibility also exists. Perhaps these "well-dressed women" found Mrs. Meierhofer's story compelling and relevant in other ways. Margaret, a strong and independent woman who emerged from poverty to achieve some level of financial success and control over her life in a new land, had been abused by her husband and shunned by her neighbors as she struggled to raise her children. Rather than viewing her life story as a threat to social norms, these "well-dressed" women may well have been captivated by the ways in which her story reflected the burdens placed on their less fortunate sisters by the Victorian gender code. In any case, their presence quickly became too much for civil authorities to tolerate. By February 6, Judge Depue and Sheriff Van Rensselaer stationed officers "at the doors of the court room with instructions to give a decided hint to the women who attempt to enter that this is not a proper case for them to hear." Female attendance declined thereafter. Order and gender propriety had been restored by the civil authorities.[29]

Judge Depue had the final word as the trial closed on February 13. His charge to the jury, which lasted over one hour, recited the basic facts of the case. Yet a close reading reveals that he also guided the deliberations in subtle ways. He first declared that murder in the first degree would be the only appropriate guilty finding for both defendants, since "the killing clearly indicates a purpose to take life" and the act had been premeditated. He urged the jury, when considering Margaret's testimony, to "weigh it in the light of the situation in which this witness is placed, interested as she is in fixing guilt exclusively on the other prisoner in order to discharge herself." He warned the jurors that, even if they accepted Margaret's account of the actual events, they should consider the possibility that "she may have done the deed herself and put [Lammens] in her place as the guilty actor." Further, he observed, "though you may accept the description given by Mrs. Meierhofer of the scene of her husband's murder" and the fact that the deed had been carried out by Lammens, "it by no means follows that she will be entitled to an acquittal." Depue spent considerable time discussing the ways in which Margaret might constitute an aider and abettor by virtue of her witnessing the attack and being "willing that her husband be killed." This made her a "principal in the second degree" who should still be convicted of first-degree murder. He focused on her "most extraordinary conduct." Despite the fact that "seven dwelling-houses are in sight, two of which are a stone's throw" from the farm, she failed to seek help from neighbors. Further, she "made no effort to induce" Lammens to cease his wild behavior and "no entreaty that the life of her husband should be spared." When a laborer named Calvin Clayton passed the house shortly following the homicide, he observed that "she was peeling potatos for dinner" in a calm manner. Seven other visitors arrived through the course of the early afternoon and Margaret "made no effort to put herself under their protection or to denounce the murderer of her husband." In seemingly impartial judicial language, Depue thus raised serious questions concerning Mrs. Meierhofer's behavior on the day of the murder and steered the jury toward a guilty verdict.[30]

Depue's supposedly "impartial" charge damaged her credibility in other ways as well. He acknowledged that Margaret claimed to be in fear for most of the day but then informed the jury that "in no one of these statements is she confirmed by the testimony of any other witness." When reviewing the letter that she had drafted for John Philip Jacqui, he reminded jurors to consider whether this might constitute "a device contrived by her to shield herself from suspicion of a crime she meditated." The judge questioned why Margaret sent the letter to Orange "instead of to officers and magistrates whom Mrs. Meierhofer knew in the neighborhood," underscoring the fact that "she made no other effort to save herself and her husband from death except to direct Theodore to go and hunt Jacqui up." He reviewed the Meierhofers' marital history, accepting as fact "testimony which, I believe, shows that she had lived in adultery." Describing John Meierhofer as "decrepit beyond his years," Depue noted that although the deceased was only in his fifties, the postmortem examination revealed that "he appeared to be sixty-five or seventy, perhaps a little older." He contrasted this fact with Margaret's relative youthfulness at age thirty-nine, describing in detail the contentiousness surrounding their marriage. Given these factors and the way in which John carried on in a "querulous, exacting and unreasonable manner," the judge concluded that the "relations between husband and wife were not such as were conducive to conjugal harmony." He acknowledged that "the evidence is that in the altercations between husband and wife she was the submissive party, endeavoring to pacify him and avoid difficulty" but then deemed these considerations irrelevant. Marital discord itself provided a convincing motive for murder. Margaret may have felt trapped in a dysfunctional relationship and eager to find some way to free herself from a deteriorating situation. Depue spent far less time parsing Lammens's testimony, likely concluding that his story lacked basic credibility and appeal. His final charge, however, went a long way toward discrediting Margaret Meierhofer. Even a sympathetic audience might have paused as the judge systematically poked holes in her testimony.

Jurors deliberated for approximately eight hours and returned their verdict on the evening of the thirteenth. Stephen Simonson, the foreman, announced the results at 7:00 p.m. Both prisoners had been found guilty of murder in the first degree. Margaret, "pale, rigid, and seemingly paralyzed, continued to stand, staring at the jury, until two constables pressed her down into her chair." Her son Joseph and her brother ran to comfort her and both broke into tears. Theodore did not attend the proceedings, remaining instead at his uncle's home in East Newark. Lammens, for his part, initially "gave no sign of the feeling which filled his mind" and "with his usual shuffling gait he passed to his room." Reporters subsequently discovered that the vote to convict Lammens had been unanimous from the start, but that jurors disagreed somewhat about Mrs. Meierhofer. The initial ballot contained ten paper slips marked "guilty" and two blanks. After some discussion, however, unanimity had been achieved by the third ballot. Outside the courtroom, both prisoners continued to assert their innocence. Lammens recovered some of his characteristic mannerisms. He gestured wildly, loudly proclaimed his honesty, and responded "'all right, my noble sir; I'm perfectly satisfied'" when informed that he would be returning to his jail cell. Margaret, for her part, negotiated the courthouse steps haltingly and with some difficulty. She parted from Joseph in a scene that "was painful to witness" by reporters. Jurors primarily expressed relief that the four-week trial, exceptionally long in the late nineteenth century, had finally ended and that they could return home. Attorneys plotted their next moves, as Borcherling and Hagaman already hinted that they might file an appeal on behalf of Lammens. Judge Depue returned to his comfortable Park Place residence after announcing that he planned to sentence the pair in the near future. Colonel Ebenezer Davis, one of the undersheriffs, performed the final official act of the trial as he escorted the prisoners to the carriages that would carry them to the Essex County Jail, where the next phase of this protracted drama would play out.[31]

5

Prison

● ● ● ● ● ● ● ● ● ● ● ●

Margaret Meierhofer and Frank Lammens were fated to spend nearly eleven months in the Essex County Jail. The facility had opened in 1837, near the onset of the greatest depression in American history until it was eclipsed by the financial downturn that dominated the 1870s. A formidable and foreboding structure, the lockup occupied a site near the Morris Canal on the outskirts of the city, only a short walking distance from the courthouse. John Haviland, the architect who had conceptualized the Egyptian Revival court building, received the commission to design the jail as well. It contained few of the architectural amenities and none of the classical iconography that characterized the courthouse and his other prison commissions. Still, public officials viewed it as a significant improvement over the previous places of incarceration in Newark. A twelve-foot perimeter wall, constructed of brownstone that had been procured from the plentiful sandstone quarries in northern New Jersey, meant that prisoners would be housed aboveground. Prior to 1837, they had languished in dark and dank basements that had no light, minimal ventilation, and plentiful filth. Now they occupied small individual cells built of brick that offered some air circulation and benefited from natural sunlight. Newark leather manufactories and tanneries, however, existed in close proximity to the prison creating a fetid atmosphere that somewhat nullified the advantages of being aboveground. The jail afforded prisoners the ability to mingle during

FIG. 5.1 The Essex County Jail, which opened in 1837, is depicted in this 1934 sketch by Rowland C. Ellis. Courtesy of Special Collections, Newark Public Library, Newark, N.J.

the day, though they returned to their solitary quarters at night. A central courtyard offered additional ventilation and space to exercise, but it also doubled as the site for executions. Each environmental improvement contained its downside.[1]

Historians generally agree that by the time the Essex County Jail began its operations, the public zeal to create more effective and humane prisons had faded. During the early nineteenth century, reformers hoped to design institutions that might rehabilitate inmates and transform criminals into law-abiding citizens. They embraced such tools as religious instruction, educational training, good hygienic practices, strict personal discipline, and architectural innovations that produced highly controlled environments. By the late 1830s, however, disillusionment had become widespread and social attitudes toward criminals hardened. Increasingly, inmates became associated with immigrants and the urban poor, two groups that received little public sympathy from fearful and morally judgmental natives. Corporal punishment, solitary confinement, and forced labor now characterized many penitentiaries. A fundamental long-term ambivalence concerning the purpose of prisons played out over the course of the nineteenth century. Some reformers continued to embrace the notion of rehabilitation and pushed for more humane treatment of prisoners. Others abandoned these hopes and viewed harsh punishment as the primary purpose of such institutions and the most effective deterrent for criminality. Parsimonious public allotments and incompetent administration typically led to overcrowding, disease, security lapses, and cruelty. And governmental officials sometimes considered prisons to be potentially profitable sources of income for the state, using convict labor on lucrative public works projects. Unfortunately, no records or firsthand accounts exist to document the Essex County Jail, making it impossible to reconstruct the attitudes that shaped its administration or the policies that determined the quality of life for inmates. A few clues from the 1870s do indicate that, by the time Margaret and Frank arrived at the facility, the typically confusing mix of motivations appeared in play.

Adolphus J. Johnson served as the prison warden in 1880. A native Newarker, he had been born in 1815 when the city existed as a preindustrial village on the banks of the Passaic River with a population that barely exceeded seven thousand. Johnson came of age during a period when Newark experienced significant growth and emerged as one of the most productive artisanal and manufacturing centers in the republic. He found employment in the growing and thriving hatting industry. Johnson quickly achieved business success as a young man, operating a wholesale and retail hat manufacturing establishment downtown on Broad Street. In 1837, he married Susan Meeson, the daughter of an English-born saddler who had arrived in the United States early in the nineteenth century. Their rapidly growing family included four children by the early 1850s, and Adolphus appeared destined to live out his life as a steady and successful businessman. The Civil War intervened, however, and altered the course of his life. Johnson eagerly enlisted in 1861, despite his family commitments and the fact that he recently had celebrated his forty-sixth birthday. He joined the military at the rank of colonel, reflecting his social stature, and initially commanded the First Regiment of New Jersey Volunteers. Johnson saw considerable action during the war. Most notably, he led New Jersey troops during the difficult Battle of Williamsburg in May 1862, part of General George McClellan's ill-fated and aborted attempt to capture Richmond. Local historians portrayed Johnson as a tough and unforgiving commander during this heated battle who "had some misgivings as to the mettle of a few of his command, and he resolved to shoot the first man who blanched in action." The Jersey troops, suffering from exhaustion and ammunition shortages, eventually were forced to retreat through a muddy ravine in heavy rain. Johnson suffered a serious injury during the skirmish "when a bullet entered one side and passed entirely through his body around his spinal column and out the other side." Primarily owing to this wound, though he had suffered a series of scars and minor injuries in other battles as well, Johnson resigned from the service in 1863 and returned to Newark.[2]

The Essex County Board of Freeholders named him as warden of the jail in 1866, despite the fact that the Colonel's previous career indicated no particular experience or affinity that might prepare him for this task. Perhaps his injuries made it more difficult for him to continue managing his hatting concern. Johnson's reputation as a distinguished war hero certainly would make this a popular political appointment. And the fact that he was "always an ardent Republican," according to his 1893 obituary, certainly helped him in a county that politically leaned heavily in that direction. In any event, Johnson soon relocated to the two-story warden's house that adjoined the jail where he would spend the next twenty years. Prison management soon became a family enterprise. Susan worked at housekeeping, cooking, and cleaning for the prisoners as well as for her own family, helping out with jail-related chores. George H. Johnson, one of the children, had turned twenty-six years old when Adolphus was appointed to his position. George became the assistant warden and moved his wife and infant daughter into the house. Indeed, the existence of the house itself, a small brownstone structure also designed by John Haviland, constituted an attempt at prison reform. Officials hoped that the warden and his family might model good domestic behavior for the inmates and that proximity to the prisoners would encourage more humane relationships. Several additional public policy initiatives also modified the character of the jail during the late 1860s and 1870s. New Jersey opened a new juvenile detention facility at Jamesburg in 1867 that removed children from county jails, intentionally isolating them from the influence of more hardened adult criminals who might encourage lawless behavior among the young. Essex County prisoners found themselves "employed in the manufacture of Skate & Straps, Dog Collars & Muzzles" by 1870, part of a state-sponsored attempt both to profit from convict labor and to train them for industrial pursuits. Overcrowded conditions also stimulated Essex County to open a second jail on a hilltop overlooking rural Caldwell in 1873. Public officials viewed this as an opportunity to separate inmates awaiting trial, who would be housed at Newark, from convicted criminals, who would be transferred to Caldwell where they would be employed in such pursuits as agriculture and "cracking stone for county roads." All of these changes seemed designed to help Johnson more efficiently and effectively manage the prison population.[3]

The warden, however, did not have a smooth administrative tenure during the late 1870s. Gustav Abeel, the hard-charging prosecutor who tried Margaret Meierhofer and Frank Lammens, launched a particularly blistering public attack on police and prison administrators in November 1879. Abeel informed the *Newark Daily Journal* "that the work done by police detectives is almost worthless and that jail officials frequently embarrass the State in its prosecution of important prisoners." The prosecutor claimed that police officers conducted sloppy work at crime scenes, a charge at least partially borne out by the Meierhofer/Lammens trial. Officers had responded slowly and reluctantly to that scene, mishandled evidence, and failed to find an empty cartridge in the murder weapon. During the trial itself, Marshal Conroy had to amend his testimony after first claiming that Margaret could not possibly have seen Lammens shoot her husband from her position near the back window. When jurors made a field trip to visit the farmhouse, they discovered that her location would have offered a clear and unimpeded view of the crime. Conroy recanted on the stand. Abeel also claimed that policemen held a vendetta toward the prosecutor's office: "They have sometimes been against us, and most of the work which they do has to be done over again at the Court House." He reserved special contempt for Newark police chief William Meldrum. The top constable's office constituted a revolving door, with most officials serving for only two or three years before moving on. The forty-eight-year-old Meldrum, who had worked as a hatter until he joined the force in the mid-1870s, rapidly ascended through the ranks and received his appointment as chief in 1878. Abeel dismissed him as "like so much putty. He doesn't know his business, and amounts to nothing as the head of the police." Needless to say, Meldrum vigorously denied all charges, claimed that his detectives fully collaborated with attorneys at every step of an investigation, and magnanimously asserted that he would never "sacrifice his official position to vent out any spite" on the prosecutor.[4]

Abeel proved equally dismissive of Essex County Jail administrators. He claimed that Adolphus and George H. Johnson treated prisoners too leniently, allowed them to communicate with each other even when kept in separate cells as a security measure, and intervened inappropriately in criminal cases. He also asserted that "they sympathize with almost every important prisoner and work up public sentiment in their favor." Further, Abeel accused prison staff of routinely working behind the scenes to obtain pardons for dangerous offenders. The warden and his son responded with anger, describing the prosecutor as a haughty and arrogant tyrant whose main problem "was that the jail authorities did not fall upon their knees and indorse Col. Abeel's views in all cases." Adolphus Johnson revealed that he had been subjected to insults and tirades for years, ignoring Abeel's condescending behavior primarily because he did not want to develop an adversarial relationship with the court system. He also defended his attitude toward detainees, emphasizing that he firmly believed "the all important fact that an accused citizen is guaranteed some rights that I am bound by law to respect." Abeel apparently wanted all prisoners to experience severe punishment and remain confined to solitary cells where they could not communicate with fellow inmates. This both violated the philosophy that guided the construction of the jail and would prove impossible to execute without a dramatic expansion of the facility. Similar to the response by Chief Meldrum, Johnson documented a long history of personal and professional cooperation with law enforcement authorities. He dismissed the prosecutor's charges as false and "without the slightest shadow for their foundation." Rather than pursue a constructive dialogue with the Johnsons, every time that Abeel requested some extraordinary favor that could not be satisfied or demanded information that could not be provided immediately, he fell back on his assertion that "the jail always works against me" and bombarded the staff with insults. Johnson presented himself as a patient and diligent civil servant who finally had grown frustrated after years of unprofessional abuse and needed to speak out. At the very least, this public controversy indicated that fundamental disagreements existed within Essex County concerning prison management. Johnson, who by this point had served in his position for over thirteen years, supported a looser and more generous approach to inmates that took at least some cognizance of the need for humane treatment. Abeel viewed both prison and police as part of his prosecutorial empire. He exhibited scant sympathy for the men and women who languished in their small cells.[5]

Unfortunately for the warden, within two weeks of his response to Abeel appearing in the newspapers, an incident transpired that again cast serious doubts on Adolphus Johnson's administrative abilities. On the morning of December 4, Johnson accompanied one of his prisoners, Edward Lindner, to Trenton. The latter had received a writ of habeas corpus to appear before the United States District Court in the state capitol on the grounds that he had been improperly detained in the Essex County Jail since May, with no attempt to bring him to trial. Lindner, described as a "man of large size and great strength," operated under an alias and had been arrested on suspicion of forgery. He allegedly served as the brains behind a gang that passed bad checks and swindled naïve marks all along the Atlantic seaboard from Boston to Richmond. Lindner shrewdly used his time behind bars to plot an escape. He asked Warden Johnson to take the New Jersey Central Railroad rather than the Pennsylvania Railroad to Trenton, supposedly because he planned to meet his attorney on board. This travel adjustment meant that the prisoner and the warden would need to change trains in Elizabeth. In fact, Lindner's attorney never boarded the train. Once in Trenton, the court refused to hear arguments in the case and postponed consideration of the matter. After the dismissal, Lindner claimed that he needed to spend more time in the state capital to confer with his counsel. He thus managed to delay his return to Newark until nightfall, even though the prisoner and the warden might easily have caught a train back as early as noon. Instead, they boarded a passenger car after 4:00 p.m. as darkness descended on New Jersey. After they changed trains in Elizabeth to complete the final leg of their journey, "the car in which they took passage was imperfectly lighted." As the train left Elizabeth, Lindner feigned illness and asked permission to go the bathroom, which was "located in the forward part of the car and immediately adjoining the door leading on to the platform." The locomotive then slowly approached the small and insignificant station of Elizabethport where it backed onto a sidetrack, allowing a few passengers to exit and enter before proceeding to Newark. When the train approached Ferry Street in Newark, Johnson attempted to retrieve Lindner from the bathroom. He quickly discovered, however, that his charge had either jumped out of the bathroom window or disappeared into the crowd at the Elizabethport station. Public outrage ensued, and Johnson bore the humiliating burden of recounting the story to Abeel.[6]

Essex County convened a grand jury to investigate the matter. Jurors issued their report to the court of oyer and terminer on 15 January 1880, three days before the start of the Meierhofer/Lammens trial. The report, no doubt skillfully shaped and gleefully guided by Abeel, offered a scathing indictment of the warden's behavior on the day of the escape. Johnson failed to take even minimal precautions to control and secure the prisoner. He made the trip from Newark to Trenton alone and unarmed. He never handcuffed Lindner, "nor had the warden handcuffs in his possession." Johnson seemed to treat Lindner more as a valued acquaintance than a dangerous criminal. Once in Trenton, the pair "proceeded in a leisurely way towards the Court House stopping on the way at a hotel where the prisoner was shaved." Johnson referred to Lindner as "my friend" when introducing him to court personnel, prison officials, and railroad conductors. He "failed to disclose to anyone in charge that his companion was a prisoner and in his custody." In midafternoon, the pair stopped at the opulent Trenton House Hotel, which had hosted dignitaries ranging from Abraham Lincoln to a bevy of state and local politicians, for a sumptuous dinner. Johnson allowed Lindner to dictate the terms of the entire outing. The prisoner wished to visit the state prison and the warden complied. Lindner prolonged the day by claiming that he needed to have a midafternoon meeting with his attorney "although ample opportunity was afforded for the full conference before the departure of the noon train." Careless behavior persisted on the ride home. Even after the conductor made a comment to Johnson indicating that the bathroom was unoccupied after Lindner faked his illness, "the Keeper did not think it necessary to make an immediate investigation." Johnson paid no attention to the passengers who departed at Elizabethport. After he discovered the escape, "he gave no alarm. He advised no one upon the train of the escape." Not surprisingly, the jurors concluded that "Warden Johnson wholly failed in his duty" to vigilantly guard the inmate, and "we find that under the circumstances he was guilty of culpable negligence." The grand jury elected not to indict Johnson based on a legal technicality: the actual escape occurred as the train progressed through Union County, which would have made prosecution in Essex County more complicated and less likely to succeed. The deliberations and conclusions, however, clearly cast an indelible black mark on the warden's reputation.[7]

And the grand jurors went even further. They ended their report to the court with several general comments concerning Essex County Jail management, finding the institution "exceedingly blameworthy" on many levels. Perhaps most seriously, the report concluded that "a mere semblance of discipline and authority exists therein." The jury uncovered evidence that the warden and his staff routinely allowed prisoners to conduct unsupervised interviews with newspaper reporters, family members, and casual acquaintances. Indeed, "so little precaution has been used that weapons or means of effecting escape might have been freely placed in the hands of criminals charged with the higher grades of crime." Jail officials regularly withheld information from prosecutorial staff, hindering their ability to achieve convictions. Unlimited correspondence existed between prisoners without any restrictions. Standard rules and regulations received "lax and inefficient" enforcement. David C. Dodd Jr., a wealthy Newark jewelry manufacturer who served as foreman, concluded with a flourish that, "in our opinion, the interests of Justice and the public good demand the removal of the officials in charge, especially the subordinates." The proceedings seemingly constituted a clear victory for Abeel and a humiliating rebuke to Johnson. Yet for whatever reason, the report served only as a temporary triumph for the prosecutor. Warden Johnson remained in charge of the jail until his retirement at the age of seventy in 1886. His son George continued as assistant deputy warden for several years after that. Abeel, on the other hand, courted controversy for the remainder of his career. Although Democratic governor George C. Ludlow nominated him for Essex County prosecutor for another five-year term in 1882, the state senate refused to confirm his reappointment. Shortly thereafter, Abeel retired from the bar, citing ill health. Perhaps appropriately, given his volatile temperament, he died of apoplexy in 1884. The Essex County Jail, however, remained a site of suspicion and contention. Margaret Meierhofer and Frank Lammens entered the facility at a moment where considerable pressure existed on Warden Adolphus Johnson to tighten discipline, enforce regulations, and take a less forgiving stance toward his charges.[8]

The Newark jail contained by far the largest number of incarcerated individuals in the state during the late 1870s and early 1880s. Demographic details concerning the inmates offer some insight into the challenges that faced administrators and the population that greeted Margaret and Frank upon their arrival. The New Jersey Bureau of Labor Statistics conducted an extensive survey of county prisons between May and October of 1882, providing useful data. Essex County committed 1,844 people to Newark during this period, with average daily numbers varying from a low of 95 in May to a high of 164 in September. Adult males accounted for nearly 79 percent of the inmates with less than 14 percent consisting of adult females. The state defined over 89 percent of the prisoners as White, though considerable ethnic diversity existed within this group: 57 percent had been born in the United States, 22 percent hailed from Ireland, 11 percent emigrated from one of the German states, and 6 percent traced their roots to either England or Scotland. Most prisoners possessed minimal job skills. Three hundred and fifty-six (22 percent) reported no trade at all and another 301 (18 percent) worked as common laborers. Hatters were the largest group of incarcerated skilled workers. The prison population tended to be temporary and transient. Three-quarters of the inmates had been sentenced to terms of one month or less, and 90 percent served for less than five months. Approximately 61 percent identified their religious heritage as Roman Catholic, the overwhelming majority had no education beyond common school training, and many lacked the ability to write. Most prison occupants were being held for relatively minor infractions. Over 60 percent had been charged with crimes against public order and decency, primarily drunkenness, disorderly conduct, and vagrancy. Another 18 percent allegedly committed assault and battery, while 17 percent were arrested for such crimes as larceny, breaking and entering, and malicious mischief. Only three prisoners had been accused of murder, manslaughter, or homicide, and an additional two faced rape charges.[9]

When Wolcott C. Gray arrived at the Essex County Jail to officially enumerate the prisoners for the U.S. census on 15 June 1880, his findings essentially mirrored those of the state survey with a few variations. Including Frank Lammens and Margaret Meierhofer, eighty-eight prisoners occupied the facility that day. Gray classified eighty-five of the eighty-eight as White. Seventy-two males and sixteen females composed the prison population. The gender breakdown, however, contained an interesting ethnic contrast. For the male prisoners, 61 percent were native-born, though the census taker failed to ask about their parents' birthplaces, thereby making it impossible to determine their immediate ancestry. Approximately 19 percent had been born in Ireland, and less than 2 percent hailed from Germany. Not surprisingly, Frank Lammens constituted the only Hollander on the list. Of the sixteen females, however, twelve had been born in Ireland and two hailed from Germany (Margaret Meierhofer and a thirty-year-old named Catherine Muller). Only two native-born women had been confined to the jail, one White and one African American. Margaret and Frank thus appeared as anomalies within the jail for a variety of reasons. They became relatively long-term residents in a facility designed primarily for transients and those awaiting trial. The Caldwell penitentiary, which held ninety prisoners according to the 1880 census, supposedly housed all criminals following their convictions. For some unstated reason, however, Lammens and Meierhofer remained in Newark. They also possessed immigrant backgrounds that differed considerably from their fellow inmates, with language skills alone likely serving as a significant communication barrier. The median age of the prisoners was less than thirty-two, considerably younger than the two convicted murderers. As celebrity criminals who had emerged from a high-profile trial that dominated the media, Margaret and Frank seemed a world apart from the younger drunks, sneak thieves, and vagrants who occupied adjoining cells. Warden Adolphus Johnson, whose reputation and competence had been questioned by the recent grand jury investigation, would need to take careful precautions to ensure that these two outliers remained in careful custody and received no special favors.[10]

Johnson immediately took steps to secure the prisoners and minimize potential problems. He claimed that since Frank Lammens had once been confined to the mental hospital in Auburn and Margaret Meierhofer's sister, Catherine, recently had been committed to the Essex County Hospital for the Insane on Camden Street in Newark, both convicts should be placed on "death watch." The warden expressed his fear to reporters that "they may lose their reason at any moment" and decided that they required constant surveillance. He assigned two constables to watch over Lammens, who would be placed in isolation in cell block number four. A special closed wire porch had been constructed in front of this cell so that Lammens would remain isolated and could not communicate with other prisoners or possible visitors. Such extraordinary precautions, which normally occurred only after sentencing and prior to execution, reflected the heightened tension that greeted the arrival of the new inmates. Margaret, on the other hand, spent her first few days of posttrial incarceration in the prison hospital. The warden had hired two women, including one professional nurse, to attend to her since the beginning of the trial, and they would remain on staff for the duration of her stay at Essex County Jail. Both prisoners exhibited signs of exhaustion and illness during their first days at the facility, though they predictably reacted differently to the guilty verdict. Margaret remained in her hospital bed, repeatedly asserting her innocence and "filling in the brief intervals between these declarations with heart-rending groans." Lammens, on the other hand, "showed considerable bad temper" when constables attempted to rouse him from his cot in the morning following the trial, displaying "a manner quite different

from the easy and polite demeanor which characterized him in court."
Each prisoner sought to plead with the other to confess. Frank asked
Adolphus Johnson to intercede with Margaret and beg her to save his life.
Mrs. Meierhofer enlisted George H. Johnson for a similar errand, request-
ing him to "at once go to Lammens and entreat him to acknowledge his
guilt and proclaim her innocence." Both convicts held fast to their stories,
but each would experience incarceration in their own unique ways during
their respective confinements.[11]

Frank Lammens had high hopes over the next several months that his
conviction might be overturned and that he would be set free. The morning
after the trial concluded, his attorneys informed Depue that they reserved
the right to ask for an appeal, and they moved again to quash the original
indictment. Borcherling and Hagaman claimed that the entire procedure
should be invalidated on the grounds "that it is defective in alleging that
both of the accused committed the assault and fired the revolver." Though
that motion went nowhere, the defense requested permission to argue
two additional points. Given the extraordinary length of the trial and the
general exhaustion of all parties, however, Depue delayed hearing their
motions until March 13. The defense attorneys made two principal arguments on that date. First, they claimed juror bias. Borcherling produced an
affidavit from a mason contractor named James McMenemin, a colleague
of one of the jurors, Cyrus C. Williams, who worked in the same trade.
McMenemin described an encounter that they had in a Newark plumbing
store, where Williams began railing against accused murderers who previously had been found innocent. He then told McMenemin that "he would
like to be one of the jurors to try Mrs. Meierhofer and Lammens so that he
could hang those devils." Since Williams already had been called as a juror
but not yet assigned to any trial, McMenemin warned him against expressing such bias. Williams responded again, however, "that he hoped to God
he would be called upon to be a juror to hang the devils." Borcherling
viewed these declamations as clear evidence of bias that made Williams
unfit to serve, noting that he would have challenged and dismissed the juror
if he had known about these prior statements. Prosecutor Abeel trivialized
the remarks, arguing that once Williams took his solemn oath as a juror, "it
counter-balanced all idle expressions made outside. With that oath the law
bars out the past." Characterizing McMenemin as "a liar" who should have
come forth during the trial if he had such evidence, Abeel also observed
that "every citizen probably expressed some opinion about the homicide,

for the matter was in all the newspapers, and such declarations are of no consequence." Preexisting bias, according to this view, would be impossible to eradicate under any circumstances and certainly did not serve as a reason to overturn the verdict. Depue ruled quickly and decisively in favor of the prosecution, stating that "the law in this State is clear—when a juror is sworn the question of his competency is settled. No new trial, therefore, can be granted because of the alleged declarations of Williams."[12]

The defense attorneys proved more successful with their second contention. They produced a new witness named William Crosby, a fifty-year-old shoemaker from Ireland who lived on Northfield Road in Livingston with his wife, five children, and nine boarders who worked in a nearby hat shop. Crosby claimed that on the day of the murder, he had been traveling down the Northfield Road and back to conduct some business in Orange. When he passed the Meierhofer barn around 11:00 a.m., he became startled by a pistol shot that seemed to emanate from the rear of the premises. Crosby did not bother to investigate, "thinking that possibly Meierhofer, whom he knew to be queer, had shot himself." A short way down the road, as he passed the Rock Spring, "he met a man small in stature, poorly clad, with full and long whiskers, carrying a light-colored glass bottle containing liquor" and heading toward the Meierhofer farm. After "they exchanged the time of day," each went about his appointed rounds. Crosby learned of the murder the following day and began thinking over the entire situation. He now recalled that "he had before seen the man" who he met on the road working at the Meierhofer farm. The earlier pistol shot, coupled with his encounter with the man who appeared to be Frank Lammens, convinced him that the hired hand did not commit the murder, and he "expected to be subpoenaed." Nothing further happened until after the verdict, however, when Borcherling requested an interview and brought Crosby to the jail to examine Lammens. At that time, Crosby "became satisfied that he was the man whom he met at Rock Spring." Borcherling presented this as new evidence that mandated a second trial for his client. Abeel countered that the Crosby testimony proved inconsistent with Lammens's former remarks about his location at the time of the murder. He also observed that Crosby never mentioned a milk pail that Lammens supposedly was carrying. He excoriated the witness for failing to come forward during the trial, claiming that his entire "story is made up" and that nothing "could be more cruel than that committed by a man who has facts which would save another and never comes forward to relate them." The prosecutor

FIG. 5.2 The Rock Spring, an iconic local landmark, was located roughly midway between the Meierhofer farm and Jaillette's tavern. It played an important role in Frank Lammens's appeal when witnesses offered conflicting evidence over whether the defendant had been spotted fetching water there during the time of the murder. Courtesy of the author.

then presented affidavits from additional individuals who had traversed Northfield Road on the day of the murder that contradicted Crosby's testimony and placed Lammens on the farm at the time of the shooting. In this instance, Depue issued a temporary ruling in favor of Borcherling and Hagaman, requiring all witnesses to appear before him on the following Saturday, March 20, for examination.[13]

Crosby reiterated his story on the stand, but in some ways, he proved an unreliable witness. Under cross-examination from Prosecutor Abeel, he admitted that "he keeps a beer saloon in his house" while working as a shoemaker. Indeed, his purpose for traveling to Orange on October 9 had been to obtain more beer in the valley. He carefully testified that "he drank beer that morning, but no spirits." He also acknowledged that his morning routine involved drinking "about a pint, with ginger in it, before breakfast, and more after breakfast." After arriving in Orange and purchasing beer from a Ballantine wagon, he had a few more beers but denied "he was roaring drunk when he went back up the mountain." He also stated that he had not been aware that he attracted the attention of occupants at the Saint Cloud Hotel by his raucous behavior and at that point "couldn't say whether he was full or not" when heading back up the hill. Crosby proudly informed the court, however, that upon arrival in Livingston, he managed "to take a barrel of beer off the wagon and put it into the cellar without incident." Under pressure from Abeel, he also "admitted that he gets drunk some time." Abeel then produced an Orange stagecoach driver who had overheard Eugene LeClare, a neighbor who testified at the trial and who bore a grudge against Margaret Meierhofer, helping Crosby to cook up his testimony on his way to Borcherling's office. He further implied that Henry Richey, Margaret's alleged former lover, had assisted in this effort to exonerate Lammens in order to cast all blame on Mrs. Meierhofer. Abeel produced three additional witnesses who had been traveling up the hill at the time of the murder, none of whom saw Crosby and all of whom witnessed Lammens raking leaves about the property shortly after the murder.[14]

Abeel next produced several witnesses who had testified at the original trial. The hunter and saloonkeeper Herman Zwinscher offered little support, testifying that he "could not remember seeing Crosby . . . or any man in a wagon" on the Northfield Road. His son confirmed the fact that the hunters "did not see Crosby on the road" and also stated that the three men had spent about an hour and a half in Susan Jaillette's tavern prior to returning to the woods and firing some shots reasonably close to the Meierhofer farm. Calvin Clayton, who had seen Lammens washing windows on the farm around the time of the murder, told the judge that he had met Crosby in downtown Orange around ten o'clock in the morning on October 9, meaning that he had passed the Meierhofer homestead on his way down the hill well before the tragedy occurred, and "he is sure that he did not meet Crosby that day on the Northfield road." Other witnesses also contradicted Crosby, ascertaining that he had mixed up the time and perhaps even the day that he encountered Lammens. Elias Meeker, for example, a portly fifty-eight-year-old farmer who lived a few houses down from Crosby in Livingston and who described his occupation as "'settin' around the house," claimed that Crosby had left for Orange around ten o'clock on the morning of the murder, which would have placed him far from the scene when the shooting took place. Charles E. Bertram, a seaman who had just returned from a month-long voyage to Charleston, offered some new testimony. He had been walking up the hill with a companion around the time of the murder, "and as they approached the house he heard a shot, which seemed to come from some confined place." Shortly thereafter, he "saw this man come from the house, pick up a rake, and begin raking. He was a short man, with a high forehead, small nose and full whiskers."

Bertram identified him as Frank Lammens, who "seemed to be trembling" in court when Abeel presented this evidence. All in all, the Crosby testimony contained considerable ambiguity and several contradictions.[15]

Borcherling produced two more witnesses, however, to support his request for a new trial. His strategy involved discrediting Susan Jaillette, the tavern keeper who had destroyed Lammens's alibi during the original trial. Anthony Coleman and Charles Johnson—a shoemaker and a mechanic, respectively—who both lived on Northfield Road in Livingston, testified that they had discussed the murder with Susan two days after it occurred. Both claimed that she told them Lammens actually came to the saloon to buy whiskey between eleven o'clock and noon, not at 6:00 a.m. as she had told the jury. They had read about the trial and "knew that Madame Jaillette testified untruly" but waited until it was over before informing anyone "that she had made a mistake or told a lie." Borcherling placed his hopes on the fact that this new uncertainty concerning the timeline constituted enough evidence to justify a new proceeding. Abeel, of course, dismissed all this testimony. He characterized Crosby as a habitual drunkard who could not be relied on and charged that Coleman and Johnson had concocted their stories "for the sake of notoriety or some other cause." Further, he underscored Lammens's suspicious behavior when the hunters arrived at the farm, refusing to let them enter the cellar to retrieve milk and trembling nervously when he returned upstairs, evidence in his view that confirmed "Meierhofer was lying there dead" in the basement. Depue concluded the hearing on April 16 but took over three months to make a decision, since he remained occupied in the interim with the business of New Jersey's court of errors and appeals.[16]

Perhaps surprisingly, Depue ruled on July 19 that "there ought to be a new trial granted on the ground of newly discovered evidence." Lammens would receive a completely new trial before a new jury panel, which would be added to the docket for the September term of the court of oyer and terminer. Always conscious of burnishing his reputation for evenhandedness, Depue stated that it would be improper for the court to "enter upon any discussion of the evidence in the case," since the proper venue for that would be at the trial. He then promptly proceeded to violate that principle through his additional remarks. He noted his agreement with Abeel that Crosby's behavior and failure to come forward during the trial "deserves criticism and rebuke." He underscored the fact that his ruling did not mean "that the Court disapproves of the verdict of the former jury."

Rather, he confirmed that, in his view, "the verdict they rendered was justifiable." Depue also dissuaded legal practitioners and the public from thinking, "from the granting of this motion, that the Court is of the opinion that on the presentation of this testimony—the testimony of this man—a different result ought to be reached." Rather, he based his ruling on the limited ground that newly discovered evidence had appeared relating to a vital point in the case. If Lammens had indeed purchased whiskey at the tavern and greeted various strangers near the Rock Spring at the time of the murder, he could not have participated in the shooting. Given the seriousness of the crime and the potential sentencing for murder in the first degree, Depue reluctantly agreed to the new trial "simply on the grounds that have been mentioned." Similar to his charge to the jury following final arguments in the first trial, the judge attempted to preserve his reputation for neutrality but also subtly guide the new proceedings in a direction that he found acceptable. Even so, the decision left Lammens hopeful that his conviction might be overturned and that freedom loomed.[17]

Margaret, on the other hand, spent the spring and summer of 1880 largely tending to spiritual matters. William Guild apparently never contemplated filing an appeal for his client, and extant accounts suggest that she stoically accepted her conviction. Though she continued to proclaim her innocence, Mrs. Meierhofer had no hope of release unless Lammens recanted his story and admitted to the crime. Johnson informed the press that she regularly read her Bible, peacefully finding comfort in Christian teachings. The prison did provide religious counsel for inmates, but this service proved problematic for Margaret throughout the early days of her confinement. The Reverend William Wynkoop McNair, a Presbyterian clergyman, served as the prison chaplain. The fifty-five-year-old minister had professed his faith while teaching school at Pennington, New Jersey, in the early 1840s, thereafter graduating from the Presbyterian bastions of the College of New Jersey (1844) and Princeton Theological Seminary (1849). Since he did not receive a call from a congregation, McNair was ordained as an evangelist and sent by the Presbyterian Board of Home Missions to establish missions in Wisconsin. He proved successful, founding several churches in the central part of that state before joining the Union troops as a chaplain during the Civil War. McNair seemed to lose his footing after the war. His official seminary biography noted only that he "resided in Philadelphia" from 1866 through 1869, after which time he served as a supply priest in Atlantic City for a few years and held a short-term pastorate at Cedarville in rural Cumberland County, New Jersey, from 1872 until 1875. McNair then moved from unincorporated Cedarville with a population numbering in the hundreds to Newark, the largest city in the state, seeking work as an urban missionary with no specific pastoral charge. The Essex County Jail soon became part of his pastoral responsibility, and he first met Margaret there on the day after her conviction. When McNair arrived at her cell, "he found Mrs. Meierhofer in bed, reading her Bible." She eagerly greeted the chaplain, informing him that "she was a Christian and had given herself to God five or six years ago." Margaret likely hoped for some empathy and constructive conversation. She received a strong rebuke instead. McNair shut down her story, clearly establishing his ministerial and manly authority: "'I don't want you to talk that way. A woman who has led the life you are said by others to have been leading, whether you are guilty of the crime of murder or not, should not talk of having given herself to God.'" He then demanded that she repent her sins, ordered her to place her hopes in divine forgiveness, and promised, or perhaps more accurately threatened, to return again. McNair had an equally unproductive meeting with Lammens, refusing to engage in theological discussions and agreeing only to pray over the convict for the salvation of his soul, whereupon he left both prisoners likely dissatisfied and confused by the encounter. McNair himself left Newark in 1881 and spent the rest of his life in the Philadelphia area constructing a ministry designed to convert the rising tide of Italian immigrants to the United States. Like most Protestants, the minister viewed these Catholics as perhaps worse than complete heathens. McNair condescendingly described his mission as giving them "that gospel of God's grace and love of which they have known little or nothing, but which is the one supreme power which can fit them for American citizenship and citizenship in God's everlasting Kingdom." Presbyterians crowned him "the Apostle to the Italians" for his efforts, though the heavy-handed approach and severely judgmental arrogance that he demonstrated in the Essex County Jail would repeatedly evidence itself in his future missionary endeavors.[18]

Margaret's next encounter with the prison ministry proved even more disastrous. In March, Warden Johnson asked Rev. Frederick Kern, who pastored the West Newark Dutch Reformed Church on nearby Blum Street, to replace McNair as Margaret's spiritual advisor. Kern had been born in 1846 at Eisenbach in Lower Saxony and graduated from Leipzig University, so Johnson perhaps felt that their German roots and common language might foster a connection. After arriving in America during the 1860s, he attended the seminary in Dubuque and pastored Presbyterian churches in Wisconsin and Carlstadt, New Jersey. The West Newark church, which constituted his first Dutch Reformed assignment, maintained an active ministry. In addition to his regular congregational responsibilities, Kern administered a small foundling hospital that housed ten abandoned children in 1880 with a staff of three nurses. Kern proved to be a relentless publicity seeker who displayed an imperious attitude toward Margaret that even exceeded that of McNair. In one interview with a *Daily Journal* reporter, he described his purpose as "moving her to confession." Kern refused to pray with her "for he does not think her fit now, he says, to address God, and he does not want to make a hypocrite of her." He viewed his role as attempting "to excite penitence in her soul." Kern then moved further and cavalierly violated the substance of what most observers would agree constituted priest-penitent privilege. Kern titillated the reporter by claiming that he had been on the verge of extracting new revelations from the murderess: "I am sure from her admissions . . . that she is guilty, and I am equally sure that Lammens is innocent, but I want to have it in black and white before making the matter public. She is tricky and might deny all she has said to me. I believe she will confess in a day or two." The Reformed minister portrayed her as a cold-hearted and calculating woman who displayed no emotion, even on her wedding anniversary: "Her eyes were not moistened once. She prides herself on this and said to me once 'I never shed a tear and never will.'" He viewed her as a master of deceit, acting insane when it suited her purposes, reserving a stash of poison to end her own life should she ever truly face the gallows, and fabricating wild stories to support her innocence. Perhaps the most disturbing fact of all, in the minister's mind, was that "she knows the Bible by heart and claims to be a child of God." Kern could not reconcile her appropriately feminine religiosity with his conviction that she had committed cold-blooded murder and lacked basic womanly virtues. Both Margaret and her defense attorney expressed outrage over Kern's public comments. William Guild "directed her by letter not to receive the clergyman again." Margaret denied making any incriminating statements, claimed that Kern "had given her assurances of his interest in her . . . and proposed to be her friend," and hypothesized that the minister might have been paid to aid Lammens. In a final rebuke, Margaret concisely commented that if Kern's remarks "had been correctly reported, he had neither religion nor sense." She refused to see him again. Her experience with Protestant prison chaplains ended. "'I have my Bible,'" she told reporters in a statement that many evangelicals might consider a perfect encapsulation of *sola scriptura*, "'and I don't want any minister.'" Kern, for his part, left Newark in 1882 and resigned from the Dutch Reformed Church, moving to rural Pennsylvania and joining the Lutherans, an odd transition away from his strict Calvinist education and denominational affiliation.[19]

Frank Lammens's appeal got underway on 11 October 1880, almost precisely one year after the murder. The trial lasted only ten days, a far cry from the four-week marathon that occupied the court throughout January and early February. For the most part, the testimony replicated evidence that had been introduced both in the earlier trial and at the July hearing overseen by Depue. Newspapers continued their daily coverage, though the crowds appeared smaller and the stories sometimes became relegated to less prominent local events columns. Still, the proceedings differed from the earlier trial in several respects. The cast of characters had shifted somewhat. William Guild played no role, excepting his presence in court when Margaret Meierhofer appeared as a witness. William Hagaman, who argued his case vehemently for Lammens when Charles Borcherling took ill in January, had moved to Colorado in an attempt to recuperate from his own declining health. Within three years, he would die of a severe bronchial infection at the age of thirty. Borcherling instead engaged a twenty-one-year-old Newark attorney of German ancestry—John G. Rose, who lived in Short Hills—to assist him. A new jury had been empaneled for the trial, but it contained the same mix of primarily native-born small businessmen and skilled artisans who had convicted Lammens at the original trial. Their deliberations may have been enlivened, however, by the presence of one juror, William E. Ketcham of Newark, who listed his occupation as "illusionist." Several new witnesses had been summoned to court, either to support or contradict Lammens's claims that he had been away from the farm at the time of the murder. The defense also employed a surveyor, Herman Lehlbach, and a photographer, Theodore Crane, who provided detailed documentation concerning the Meierhofer basement in an effort to prove that a stand might have been located near the front steps.

This would support Lammens's contention that he retrieved milk for the hunters from the basement without noticing John Meierhofer lying dead under the stairs.[20]

Other elements remained consistent. Police incompetence again came to the fore. Law enforcement authorities somehow managed to lose the murder weapon. Ebenezer W. Davis, the deputy sheriff, nervously testified that the pistol had been sent to the jury room during the previous trial, and "the next morning everything in the jury-room, as was then supposed, was gathered up and placed in the janitor's room. Recently it was discovered that the pistol was not among these things." Subsequent searches proved fruitless. This careless violation in the chain of custody for a key piece of evidence, however, shockingly had no consequences. Abeel procured another pistol, supposedly similar to the lost Victor Number Two, and simply substituted it as a facsimile during the trial. Depue went along, agreeing that since Lammens had testified at the first trial that he owned a similar pistol, the substitute would be fine. The press also attempted to maintain the circus atmosphere that surrounded the initial proceedings. Reporters continued to provide colorful physical descriptions of defendants and witnesses. The *Daily Journal* noted that "Lammens was decently clothed, his face whiter than when he was in court early in the year, and his long hair and bushy blonde beard were less tangled; in a word, he was a more respectable looking man." Margaret Meierhofer testified briefly for the prosecution on October 13, "dressed in deep black," and her appearance "caused considerable excitement" as onlookers hoped for a witness-stand confession. She stuck to her earlier story, however, relating her account "with more energy" and passion than before. She chastised Lammens as a "beast and a murderer," exhibiting intense contempt for the defendant. And Lammens continued engaging in the occasionally bizarre behavior that previously subverted his case. One day he arrived at court "pale and half sick," asking the county clerk to provide him with some opiates. During prosecutorial cross-examination, he shook his fist at Abeel, garbled his sentences, at first denied and then admitted to various thefts in the West Orange area, and had to be restrained by constables. When prodded about how he obtained so many diverse possessions, he responded, "'I don't know nothing about that,'" and "'ask me about that after this trial is over and I will tell you.'" He remained a defense attorney's worst nightmare throughout the ten days.[21]

Lammens's demeanor on the day of the murder also proved problematic for his case. Prosecutor Abeel produced two new witnesses, Gustavus Hirtz and his friend Charles Bertram, who passed by the Meierhofer house around the time of the murder on their way to visit a local farmer, Bernhard Hirt. After hearing a shot that emanated from the farmhouse, Hirtz noticed a man, who he subsequently identified as Lammens, "raking in front of the house. . . . He hung his head, appeared to be excited, and raked where there were no leaves." Bertram confirmed this account. In his telling, Lammens "came from the side of the house, seized the rake and began raking. Though in the hot sun, he had no hat on. He trembled and perspired and yet was not working hard." Lammens demonstrated similar anxiety to the three hunters who asked him to retrieve milk from the basement. He "trembled so much that he spilled the milk" and "shook fearfully," unable to even correctly count change. All observers agreed that the defendant behaved irrationally, exhibiting the type of nervousness that suggested fear and guilt. Borcherling did attempt to refute this testimony by summoning Peter Van Pelt Hewlett, the highly respected county physician. Hewlett had examined Lammens shortly after his arrest and determined that the defendant suffered from *paralysis agitans*, essentially a form of Parkinson's disease. Hewlett explained that the condition caused severe trembling and also "prevents a man from holding his hands still." Further, in Hewlett's words, it affected the "motor and sometimes the intellectual power of the brain, and weakens a man's physical condition." This medical defense contained some explanatory power, but the jurors also witnessed the raucous laughter that permeated the courtroom when Lammens had acted strangely on the stand and was reduced to babbling incoherence as he jousted with Abeel. Whether jurors would judge his actions as emanating from physical debility or mental illness might determine their conclusion concerning his role in the murder.[22]

Character assassination and gender continued to play a significant role throughout the proceedings. Phoebe LeClare, the Northfield Road resident who bore a long-standing grudge against Margaret, relished her time on the stand. She portrayed her neighbor as a ruthless and reckless murderess who possessed the tools and the temperament to intimidate anyone. LeClare claimed that "Mrs. Meierhofer came to her house seven years ago, and drawing a revolver from her bosom said she wasn't afraid to stay in the house alone while she had that; with that she wasn't afraid of God or man;

she thought she could make five out of the seven bullets tell." Another defense witness, who did not appear, owing to confusion in the sheriff's office over serving him with a subpoena, had worked for the Meierhofers prior to accepting another position in Montclair. He stood ready to claim that he had been "solicited by Mrs. Meierhofer to cut her husband's throat and leave the knife beside the old man, that suicide might be inferred." Defense Attorney Borcherling especially pursued the gender line of argument. Although claiming that he "would not speak of the unfortunate woman in harsher terms than were actually necessary," he spent much of his closing statement to the jury focusing on her reputation and raising the specter of evil women who conspired against their spouses. Margaret, he claimed, "departed from the path of virtue" shortly after her marriage, and "what a terrible realization is there here of the fate of a woman who does this!" Infidelity itself constituted a cause for indictment. Further, women inherently acted with acute maliciousness once they no longer lovingly fulfilled their marital obligations: "There is no stopping place when a woman begins going downward, and we have seen in the case of Mrs. Meierhofer what a woman may do once she starts on the descent." Strong women, in this reading, required weak men to do their bidding. Schoolteacher Pierson became the special focus for Borcherling. In the previous trial, he mocked Pierson as "an inoffensive, milk and water man, with no salt and pepper in his composition." Borcherling sneeringly dismissed the schoolteacher's testimony that he had attempted to shield Mrs. Meierhofer from harm: "God pity any woman whom Pierson would be called upon to protect!" He returned to the theme in his summary, describing the young man as "a natural born fool," noting that the crafty Margaret Meierhofer "soon saw of what material he was" and used him to her advantage. As for Lammens, Borcherling dismissed him as "a good-natured, kind-hearted man" ripe for exploitation. The murder reflected the depths to which a fallen woman might descend. But it also owed much to the failures of men to exercise their masculine virtues of strength, decisiveness, and rational clearheadedness. The entire episode ultimately exposed broader tensions that tore at the fabric of male-female relations and threatened familial harmony in the Gilded Age.[23]

David Depue, however, based his charge to the jury on more mundane matters. He acknowledged that the case rested on circumstantial evidence but urged jurors not to shy away from a guilty verdict only owing to that fact. He cited Lammens's claim to have multiple sexual encounters with

Margaret and the sharp words that John had directed toward him on the morning of the murder as instances that might act "on a temper excitable and a mind weak in moral sentiments" to provide a powerful motive. Depue meticulously reviewed witness testimony concerning the time of the murder, concluding that it must have occurred between 11:00 and 11:40 a.m. He urged jurors to deliberate carefully the question of Lammens's whereabouts during those forty minutes and thoroughly interrogate his alibi concerning Jaillette's tavern based on the recollection of several witnesses who passed by the farm around that time. Depue then read from the stenographer's notes. They indicated that Crosby, who claimed to have encountered Lammens near the Rock Spring, responded with considerable vagueness and little exactitude when asked about time. Crosby also indicated that he heard a shot coming from the farm before he met Lammens on the road, thus supporting the alibi, but Depue urged jurors to discount this as "boys were playing in the woods," hunters had been stalking birds, "and there was shooting all around that day." Further, the condition and removal of the body pointed toward Lammens at least as an accomplice. County Physician Hewlett noted that John's blood flowed down his face and none appeared on his back. He clearly had lain in a headlong position for at least fifteen to thirty minutes following the murder until it congealed. This made it highly improbable that Margaret had time to remove the body from the stairs and into the back of the cellar before the hunters arrived. Further, the lack of blood on John's clothing meant that the corpse had been carried, rather than dragged, across the cellar, a fact "that may throw some light on the number of persons engaged in the removal." If jurors did not receive the appropriate message, Depue underscored the fact that if Lammens "stepped over the dead body his silence as to the horrible sight he had witnessed is only explainable on the theory of a guilty knowledge of the crime." The judge considered this "of the utmost importance" and something that "deserves careful consideration." In final remarks, Depue noted that "if convinced of his guilt, the jury should so find without regard to consequences." Once again, the judge provided a clear road map to guide the deliberations.[24]

The jurors remained sequestered overnight and did not deliver a verdict for nearly twenty-four hours, quite a bit longer than those at the original trial. One juryman subsequently informed the press that considerable disagreement marked the early deliberations. The first ballot indicated eight in favor of a guilty verdict and four who supported acquittal. Eventually, the tally widened to ten to two. Still, a hung jury appeared a real possibility until the jurors asked to meet with David Depue about the timing issue. The judge pointed them toward the testimony of Abraham Messler, a sixty-year-old farmer who testified that he passed the Meierhofer house accompanied by his son on the morning of the murder on his way to Orange. The Messlers saw Lammens raking leaves and Meierhofer picking potatoes, at which time they bowed to the elderly farmer. The pair arrived in Orange at noon, the same time that Crosby claimed to be there. Depue urged them to consider the chronology and to determine whether "Crosby passed the house first and saw Lammens at the spring, then the Messlers saw him afterwards at the house when the old man was alive." After the judge's instructions, the jury retired, and within twenty minutes, they reached a unanimous verdict of guilty of murder in the first degree. Once again, Depue had helped bring matters to a speedy conclusion. Lammens, who never completely understood the American legal system, appeared composed after the verdict. He simply turned to Borcherling and asked, "'Can't I have a new jury?'" Afterward, he returned to his second-floor cell, where he laid on his cot and refused meals for the next two days. Margaret, on the other hand, expressed relief at the verdict. Also misunderstanding the nature of the proceedings, she turned to a prison employee and said, "'Then, I suppose, I can pack up my things and go home.'" After being informed that this would not happen, she also fell into silence. One of the jurors expressed some remorse, stating that "I carried Lammens as long as I could . . . but as I heard the evidence I had to throw him off. He undoubtedly was on the ground when the murder was done." He eventually came around to the prosecution theory that Margaret masterminded the event and Lammens served as a useful tool, shaking his head and commenting that "it's a terrible thing to stand between a man and death." With the final appeal exhausted, the only remaining duties for Depue involved dismissing a few pro forma motions by Borcherling and sentencing the pair.[25]

The judge determined to conduct this final act on November 6, but he kept the date secret in order to discourage crowds and curiosity seekers. Depue personally contacted a few reporters, but the solemn event offered a marked contrast to the atmosphere that surrounded the trial and appeal. Neither convict appeared resigned to receiving the death penalty. From the moment of her conviction, Margaret believed that she would escape the gallows and serve out a life sentence at the New Jersey State

Prison in Trenton. She told reporters that "she does not wish to return to the outside world, and would be quite willing to live the rest of her days in the seclusion of a prison." On the day of sentencing, William Guild tried to both steel her for the probable outcome and also "buoy her up by giving her slight hope of a commutation of sentence to imprisonment." She dressed in black for the occasion, "looking pale and weak" and constantly pressing her left hand against her heart as though she suffered from chest pain. Lammens "entered the court with a steady tread" and cheerfully greeted William Hagaman, who had returned from Colorado and attended the sentencing of his former client along with Borcherling and Rose. He continued to proclaim his innocence and claimed he had not had a fair trial, but Borcherling urged him to remain quiet during this procedure. Depue sentenced both convicts to "be hanged by the neck until your body be dead" and he also took the opportunity to deliver one final lecture. The judge first praised all four defense attorneys, "who displayed a zeal, earnestness, and ability on your behalf, which reflected credit on the bar of which they are members." He then commended the jurors as "men of intelligence and probity" who patiently and fairly considered all evidence. Speaking to Margaret and Frank, Depue underscored the "crime of extraordinary atrocity" that they had committed. The judge admonished the pair "not to permit any hope that you may escape the judgment we are about to pronounce to induce you to postpone preparation for the dread event to which the sentence of the law leads." And he concluded his harangue with the classic statement "And may God have mercy on your souls."[26]

Attorneys made a few last-minute attempts to save their clients. Both defense teams petitioned the court of pardons to commute the sentences, but their requests were denied on December 13. Governor George McClellan might have been expected to intervene, but he exhibited no inclination to exert his gubernatorial authority to stay the executions. He even refused requests from Roman Catholic and Episcopal clergymen to delay the hangings until after the selected date of January 6, since the executions were scheduled to coincide with the Feast of the Epiphany. The McClellan mansion on Mountain Ridge stood less than two miles from where the Meierhofer murder took place. The crime clearly constituted the talk of the neighborhood, but McClellan surprisingly never mentioned the case, the verdict, or the pleas for clemency in his public or private correspondence. No documentation exists to explain his motivations, but political considerations might have played a role. McClellan still hoped to revive his presidential ambitions, calculating that the New Jersey governorship would provide a new springboard for national exposure. Ex-Union soldiers, many of whom fondly recalled his generalship and bore unstinting loyalty to "Little Mac," constituted a principal source of support. He may well have shied away from exhibiting mercy toward two disreputable defendants accused of murdering a damaged Civil War veteran. A pardon might also alienate the politically shrewd New Jersey Supreme Court justice that he recently had reappointed. Respectable community opinion already had weighed in on the side of the death penalty. Even the ethnic German press viewed Margaret as receiving her just deserts for her crimes against the family patriarch. Clemency contained little political upside. McClellan's only concession involved his providing Abeel with two possible pardons that could be used at the execution in the event one of the parties confessed before heading to the gallows.

Borcherling carried matters one step further. He applied for a writ of error and presented his case on December 22 before Theodore Runyon (1822–1896), the New Jersey chancellor, who constituted the highest judicial authority in the state and who chaired the court of errors and appeals. Runyon, a former law partner of William B. Guild who had also served as the city attorney in Newark, agreed to hear the appeal. Borcherling made three points. First, he argued that the prosecution never established who actually committed the murder and who served as an accessory, which resulted in "a legal absurdity" whereupon both suspects had been indicted for the same shooting. Second, he objected to the loss of the pistol between the first and the second trial. Finally, he observed that "one of the jurors who convicted Lammens is now in jail for attempting to bribe jurors in another case." Abeel dismissed the arguments as inconsequential, claiming that the court had the discretion to try both defendants as shooters and that Depue had admitted the second pistol "as he would admit a model of steps or a house, or photographs of premises." He argued that Lammens had received two fair trials and that even though "a defendant is rarely convicted on a second trial . . . the State's case was strengthened tenfold and the jury had no doubt." Runyon tersely delivered his decision in favor of the prosecution on December 29, thereby ending Lammens's final hope to escape the gallows.[27]

Margaret Meierhofer, on the other hand, received some public support and sympathy from unlikely sources. John Laurie Blake (1831–1899), the Republican congressman who represented the Sixth District that

FIG. 5.3 General George B. McClellan, who served as governor of New Jersey and also resided in the exclusive Mountain Ridge section of West Orange during the trial. Courtesy of Special Collections and University Archives, Rutgers University Libraries.

encompassed all of Essex County, drafted a petition that he circulated "among the influential citizens of Orange" asking the court of pardons to commute her sentence. As an attorney and an Orange resident, he had followed the trial closely and considered it a miscarriage of justice. Blake drew up a thirteen-point plea. He asked several pertinent questions about the day of the murder, including the key issue of why Margaret might have attempted to summon the police that morning if her entire purpose had been to commit the crime. He also noted that her story remained remarkably consistent when officers arrived at her home, at the coroner's inquest, throughout the trial, and during the appeal. In fact, her testimony alone convicted Lammens twice. Blake indirectly criticized Depue for downplaying the lack of direct evidence and instructing the jury to cavalierly accept circumstantial evidence that the congressman deemed "inconclusive." No motive had been established, since Margaret had not quarreled recently with John and, even if her supporters conceded that she committed adultery, "nor did the husband stand in the way of any illicit love." Blake also felt that jurors failed to take into account the fact that Lammens inspired terror. His out-of-control courtroom behavior and occasional reversion to violence supported her contention that she spent the day living in fear. In concluding, Blake urged a commutation of the sentence to life in the New Jersey State Prison, "believing that there are serious doubts of her guilt and that human life should not be sacrificed except upon clear testimony." Remarkably, Blake approached all the jurors in the case and eleven of the twelve signed his petition asking for the change of sentence. Only William Ridler, the retired owner of the paperhanging business, "says she should hang." Seemingly, the jurors did not recognize the implications of their guilty verdict and the harsh justice that Depue would mete out when they rendered their decision. Their petition, however, ultimately fell on deaf ears.[28]

Margaret Meierhofer increasingly resigned herself to her fate. Reporters described her return to prison after the sentencing as "the picture of woe" as "the shadows of her awful doom seemed to gather around her." She required assistance to walk from the carriage to her second-floor hospital room at the Essex County Jail. Warden Johnson continued to assign two experienced nurses to watch over her in alternating shifts, fearing that she might attempt suicide. She clearly experienced moments of extreme depression and continued to profess her innocence. Yet as the days passed, observers described her most often as "very composed," acting "with the utmost calm," and speaking "in tones that expressed resignation." When she received the devastating news that Governor McClellan refused any request for a pardon and would not even postpone the execution owing to the Feast of the Epiphany, "no tears moistened her eyes and not a sigh escaped her." Her new spiritual advisor may well have contributed to her peaceful state of mind. Father Gerard Pilz, a Benedictine who had been assigned to the Newark priory, had been born in Margaret's home state of Bavaria. An accomplished artist, he had received formal training at the Royal Art School in Munich. Pilz also translated several Biblical commentaries into English and published a book of his own sermons. The forty-six-year-old monk had arrived in Newark via Saint Vincent's Abbey in Latrobe, Pennsylvania (established 1846), the oldest Benedictine monastery in the United States and the center for training German-speaking priests who labored throughout the nation. Father Pilz, along with his colleague Father James Zilliox, who attempted to minister to Frank Lammens, took a far different approach than the Protestant ministers who had infuriated Margaret Meierhofer earlier in the year. Although they typically did not engage in prison ministry, concentrating their efforts instead on following the Rule of Saint Benedict and administering educational institutions that they had established in Newark, the monks took an interest in the two prisoners and obtained permission to counsel them. Father Gerard had learned that Margaret received the sacraments of baptism and confirmation in her native town of Bavaria and subsequently discovered that she baptized both of her children at Saint Mary's in Newark. He felt it his mission to attend to her and visited her frequently following the sentencing procedure. He also respected her confidentiality. Unlike Rev. Kern, he refused to discuss the case with reporters. The press frustratingly noted that even though Fathers Zilliox and Pilz lived together in the monastery, "the two priests do not speak even to each other about the murder or their relations to the prisoners." In Father Gerard, Margaret finally found the religious mentor that she sought as she returned to her own Roman Catholic faith.[29]

Another source of Catholic comfort during these final months came from the De Vallerot family. Louis De Vallerot had sailed for the United States from France in 1846 with his wife, Aimee, and four children. He listed his occupation aboard the ship as "Gentleman" and made the journey as a cabin passenger. After arriving in America, the family established residence in Manhattan, where Louis tutored respectable clients in music.

By 1870, the De Vallerots resided on East 21st Street, next door to the magnificent new Church of the Epiphany, which opened that year. Rev. Richard Lalor Burtsell, one of the most respected canonists in the United States and a priest with strong social justice commitments, pastored the wealthy congregation at Epiphany. By all accounts, he communicated social conscience, religious zeal, civic responsibility, and an intellectual approach to the faith. The De Vallerots, however, moved to Newark in the early 1870s. One immigrant daughter, Louisa, had relocated there, finding employment as a French teacher. Louis and Aimee, both in their seventies by 1880, soon followed along with twenty-six-year-old Marie, who had been born in the United States. They purchased a comfortable house on Hill Street, a reasonably short walk from Saint Mary's in a neighborhood populated by merchants, manufacturers, jewelers, and white-collar workers. Louis, the family patriarch, died in October 1880. Following his interment at Holy Sepulchre Cemetery in a funeral service presided over by a Benedictine father from Newark, Aimee and Marie began taking a special interest in Margaret Meierhofer. Marie became an almost constant companion, captivating the press who referred to her as "the young French religieuse" and "a ministering angel" with an "exceedingly tender and touching" manner. The women prayed together, read the Bible aloud, sometimes celebrated Mass with Father Gerard, and shared their thoughts on religious topics in conversations that at times exceeded two hours. Marie even ran some small errands for Margaret, agreeing to have her soiled white skirt washed and ironed, since she wished to wear it to the hanging. On the night before the execution, Marie read to Margaret from a nineteenth-century devotional tract, "Suffer Little Children to Come Unto Me," and prayed with her until ten o'clock. Marie remained at the prison hospital overnight and greeted Father Gerard, who arrived shortly before six o'clock in the morning "bearing with him a small bouquet of sweet-smelling flowers and some other things used in the mass." All three celebrated Mass using a miniature altar that they erected in the hospital, after which Father Gerard administered the last rites. Marie and the Benedictine then departed, and Margaret had one last cup of coffee, awaiting her fate with a "cheerful and happy" demeanor. For Marie De Vallerot, her experiences with Margaret propelled her into a lifelong work of lay missionary activity. She traveled throughout the United States with her friend and companion, Minnie Woodbridge, teaching at a Convent School on an Indian Reservation in Washington State, working at the Tonti Hospital in New Orleans, and ministering to the scattered Catholic population in rural Alabama. When she died in 1922 at a hospital in Woodhaven, Queens, Marie left behind a life of good works and caring for others.[30]

Margaret demonstrated her growing religious commitment in other ways as well. When Joseph and Theodore arrived for their final joint visit to the prison in early January, their mother presented them with identical Christmas gifts: a pocket-sized Holy Bible and a book of Catholic devotions. She instructed her younger son to pray regularly and read one chapter of the Bible every day. "'Prepare a home for your soul, Theodore, as well as look out for your body,'" constituted her last words to the child who had supported her unflinchingly through fifteen tumultuous months. Joseph returned on January 4, and Margaret delivered another religious message: "'My dear child, God will raise a friend for both of you. Don't be led astray by the vanities of this life.'" Their tear-filled meeting contained one moment of tension when Joseph urged his mother to confess if, in fact, she had committed the murder. She responded with astonishment: "'My God, is it possible you think I am guilty?'" At that point, Joseph declared himself completely convinced of her innocence, and they embraced one last time. She handed Joseph a keepsake locket along with some money, and both began sobbing uncontrollably. Similarly emotional farewells occurred with her brother, John, and her sister, Catherine Greiner, who recently had escaped from the Essex County insane asylum but who had been allowed by authorities to remain free as long as she lived with her brother in East Newark and refrained from getting into trouble. Margaret grew more stoic in early January, declaring her "willingness to die if it is God's will." During one last interview with her attorney, William Guild, she again insisted upon her innocence and speculated about how the wives of her accusers and jurors might have behaved on the day of the murder under similar circumstances. Margaret affirmed that she had made peace with her executioners: "There are those who will not believe it, but I know, and God knows, that it is true, and I am satisfied." Father William Walter, the prior of the Benedictine Abbey, visited Margaret two days before her death and left convinced that "her faith was strong as a rock." Warden Johnson broke his vow of silence on the day of the murder, remarking that Margaret "was either an innocent woman or a Lucretia Borgia in the way of nerve and ability." Her attitude, resignation, calmness, and rectitude reminded the warden "of the picture of the Christian martyrs as they neared the hour when they were to be burned at the stake." But perhaps the truest and most appropriate eulogy of all had been provided by her sister, Catherine, who had been incarcerated in the insane asylum: "'She was a dear sister, and was a good woman, but she had a crazy husband.'"[31]

Frank Lammens found neither peace nor comfort during his final weeks on planet Earth. After the sentencing, two officers handcuffed the unruly prisoner and brought him to Warden Johnson, who conducted a full-body search. Johnson then escorted Lammens to cell number four, which had been outfitted with a wire screen to prevent any conversation with prisoners in the corridor. The condemned man remained prone to wild mood swings. At times he would remain silent and refuse food for three or four days at a time. During other intervals, he ate voraciously and talked nonstop, spewing out hatred for Margaret Meierhofer and denying any knowledge of the crime. The only constant seemed to be that he smoked incessantly throughout late December and early January. Rev. James Zilliox, the Benedictine who began visiting Lammens around the end of November, found him to be irascible and difficult to deal with. He often refused to communicate at all. During one visit, he paced up and down the cell in a frenzy, muttering to himself. He finally "began to gesticulate wildly, stamp his foot, and scream 'Go away from me, don't bother me; go away from me.'" On another occasion, "he ran around the room with only his shirt on, abused the constables watching him, and made grimaces at the window, though no one was in sight without." He quickly dismissed Father Zilliox and Rev. William Walter and proved equally rude to Marie De Vallerot when she attempted to visit. Some jail personnel believed that Lammens had been feigning insanity throughout the Christmas season, but others judged his behavior authentic. An exasperated Father Zilliox finally determined that he could not in good conscience perform the sacrament of last rites "if Lammens continues in his present state." The Benedictine provided the prisoner with some written instructions concerning how he might prepare for death, but Frank promptly tore up the paper. Lammens proved obstreperous almost until the end. On the day before the execution, he remained "excited and unruly," refusing to discuss religion with Father Zilliox, declining to confess his sins, and dashing off three incoherent letters to Margaret who he referred to as "that black devil." On the morning of the execution, however, he finally "agreed to conform to the requirements of the Catholic Church." He made a confession, received the last rites, and then ravenously downed a breakfast that consisted of a porterhouse steak, rolls, mince pie, and coffee. His behavior offered some solace to the Benedictines, who might now make an arrangement to provide the prisoner with a Christian burial in consecrated ground.[32]

For the most part, Frank Lammens spent the last two months of his life in complete isolation, his only visitors being the Benedictine monks, some Benedictine sisters from Saint Scholastica's Convent in Newark, and his attending constables. That changed on December 28, when a short and stout woman in her early fifties arrived at Sheriff Van Rensselaer's office. She identified herself as Bridget Lammens, the long-lost wife of Frank who had not seen her husband since 1865. She bore with her a letter of introduction from Linus Pierpont Brockett (1820–1893), a graduate of Yale Medical College and prominent Brooklynite who edited and authored myriad articles concerning medicine and social work for various cyclopedias, magazines, newspapers, and monthly reviews. Brockett testified that Bridget was a "worthy and honest woman" who spent several years in his employ and "thinks, but is not certain" that Lammens "was, before his imprisonment in the Auburn State Prison, her husband." Van Rensselaer directed her to the Essex County Jail, where Adolphus Johnson received Bridget and listened to her story. The Irish-born woman informed him that she had read about the murder in the newspapers but remained skeptical that he was "her Frank." Lately, however, "she saw her husband in her dreams," and neighbors in Brooklyn encouraged her to visit Newark to determine whether the prisoner indeed was the same man who disappeared in 1865. Someone claiming to be her husband, after all, had been seen around the neighborhood in 1879 attempting to locate Bridget. She confirmed many details that Frank provided at the trial, including the fact that their children died during the war and that Frank then "lost his mind" and left for Ohio. Upon his return to New York, he had been sentenced to jail at Sing Sing and subsequently been transferred to the Auburn Asylum for the Insane. Bridget told the warden that an attending physician at Auburn had informed her that Frank had died in the asylum. Johnson found the story sufficiently convincing that he brought Lammens from his cell and found a private spot for them to meet. After a brief period of confusion, Lammens blurted out, "'Hallo, Bridget, is that you? My God, Johnson, this is my wife.'" Bridget initially did not recognize him, Frank having been transformed from a sturdy, broad-shouldered, and clean-shaven man into a slender and decrepit "wreck" with a full-flowing beard. She finally admitted that he was her former husband, and they shared a long conversation. Bridget urged him to admit to the murder and confess the truth, chastised

Lammens for making little effort to find her, upbraided him for his relations with Margaret Meierhofer, and criticized the condemned man for seeking guidance from Protestant ministers. Lammens countered by reiterating his innocence, describing his efforts to locate her before arriving at the Meierhofer residence in September 1879, and stressing that he only had spoken with Catholic priests. The meeting ended in a somewhat unsatisfactory manner. A weeping Frank kissed his former wife, but she refused to return the sentiment. She recalled Frank as a "good, kind, tender hearted husband, so much so that if he saw a splinter sticking out of your finger, he would not pull it out for fear of hurting you." But the brief reunion produced only sadness. Bridget turned to George Johnson and proclaimed that "'my life is ruined now. I will go from Brooklyn to some place where I am not known; and, oh, that poor lunatic.'" The *Brooklyn Daily Eagle* confirmed Bridget's assessment that her reputation had been destroyed. Her hometown newspaper viewed the encounter as a cynical attempt by her to gain notoriety and save the convicted killer. An editorialist blamed Bridget for neglecting her womanly responsibilities, disdainfully remarking that "a wife who could bear the thought of her husband's death in an insane asylum, without expressing a sufficiently strong desire to learn the truth, ought not to be so much distressed many years afterward, at the prospect of his dying suddenly, in a jail yard."[33]

One final strange and desperate attempt to save Lammens's life occurred shortly before the execution. Theodore F. Crane, the thirty-five-year-old photographer who had been hired by Borcherling to document the Meierhofer home during the appeal, excitedly demanded a meeting with David Depue in early January. Crane operated a successful photography business on Broad Street in Newark. His carte de visites and cabinet cards documenting nineteenth-century urban life remain popular collectibles to this day. His real passion, however, concerned evangelical religion. Crane regularly attended camp meetings, ran for state office on the Prohibition Party ticket, and eventually moved to Mount Tabor in Morris County, which had been incorporated by the Newark Methodist Conference as a religious community and retreat center in 1869. The photographer proved especially subject to receiving prophetic visions and premonitions throughout his life. On the night before the scheduled 1877 execution of Charles Oschwald and Thomas Ryan, who had been convicted of killing a Newark policeman, Crane dreamed that the latter prisoner would commit suicide: "Ryan swallowed poison that minute." Now he wished to produce new evidence.

Crane informed Depue that "he had learned in dreams that Lammens was innocent." His nocturnal visions taught him that "Mrs. Meierhofer alone did the deed," and he urged the judge to grant another trial. Depue quickly dismissed the enthusiastic photographer, explaining that "his dreams would not be testimony" and that another trial would prove useless. Crane then visited the prison in a last-ditch attempt to provide some comfort for Lammens but "being refused went away with a heavy heart." Indeed, the only other individuals who expressed any interest in Frank Lammens were members of the Essex County medical community. Physicians had debated whether Lammens truly could be classified as insane. The court ordered doctors to examine him daily over the course of several weeks "to determine whether he was crazy or not." The examiners finally concluded, "after the use of the most delicate instruments known to medical science," in the words of the *New York Sun*, that Lammens suffered from an obstruction or disease of the brain, likely emanating from some area above the eyes. The physicians eagerly awaited his execution so that they might scientifically examine his brain. As one public official informed *New York Sun* reporters, "Those doctors are waiting for it and would not let the opportunity pass for $1,000 if the man is hanged." The poor tramp's sad and tragic life had been reduced to a medical curiosity.[34]

6

Memory

• • • • • • • • • • • •

On New Year's Eve 1881, the *Newark Daily Advertiser* printed its annual review of the most significant news stories from the previous year. The Margaret Meierhofer and Frank Lammens executions received prominent mentions. Other less deadly local events also took center stage. The Newark city auditor admitted in December to pilfering approximately $125,000 in municipal funds. The Mechanics' National Bank, a seemingly solid business concern, failed and went into receivership earlier in the year, leaving many depositors penniless. A few more uplifting events also characterized the previous twelve months. Perhaps most notably, and a harbinger of things to come, the first electrical streetlight appeared in downtown Newark. Business had indeed picked up as the nation seemed in recovery from the depression decade of the 1870s: "Ordinary trade has been as prosperous as usual throughout the county." The *Advertiser* further expressed excitement over the appearance of a new translation of the Scriptures into English, the *Revised New Testament*, which excited considerable controversy in the Protestant world and infuriated staunch adherents of the *King James Version*. All in all, however, the look back at 1881 produced more angst than optimism. For the Republican-leaning newspaper, the election of Democrat George Ludlow to the New Jersey governorship necessarily generated some concern. Partisan intraparty infighting on the national level also had led to a split between the Stalwart and Half-Breed

Republican factions, resulting in the resignation of powerful political boss Roscoe Conkling from the Senate. In the final analysis, the *Daily Advertiser* concluded, the year "will stand prominent in history and especially in the memory of Newark as generally one of sadness." Indeed, one particularly sad incident overshadowed all these events and seemed to ensure that 1882 would not start on a happy note.[1]

On July 2, Charles Guiteau walked into the waiting room of the Baltimore and Potomac Railroad Station in Washington, D.C., and fired a bullet into the back of the head of President James A. Garfield, who had intended to board a train for the New Jersey shore where he would join his wife, Lucretia. Guiteau, an unpredictable and delusional fanatic, had wandered the nation throughout the 1870s, moving from one unsuccessful venture to another. He had failed at everything he attempted, from living in a utopian commune to practicing law to preaching as a traveling evangelist. Charles's father attempted to institutionalize his son in an insane asylum but lacked the money to confine him. As he grew increasingly unhinged, Guiteau became convinced that he had played a major role in electing Garfield and that he was owed at least an ambassadorship to France for his efforts. Eventually, God sent Guiteau a message, commanding that he assassinate the president. The impoverished Guiteau borrowed some money, walked into a sporting goods store in the District of Columbia where he purchased a revolver and a box of cartridges without any questions being asked, and calmly undertook his divinely inspired mission. The president lingered throughout the summer, as the nation endured a protracted death watch that finally ended near Long Branch when he expired on September 19. Garfield had entered office with a reputation as an ardent abolitionist during the 1850s and had served the Union with distinction during the Civil War. A skilled orator and resourceful politician as well as a gifted and versatile intellectual, he generated hope in those who sought justice for former slaves and a return to a more ethical and honest government. Garfield's death inspired a new wave of patriotism and an outpouring of vitriolic vengeance directed at his assassin.[2]

Americans especially feared that Guiteau would get away with murder by utilizing the newly created and broadly despised "insanity defense." The concept had reached the United States from England, where defense attorneys employed it twice in recent memory to save the lives of the assassins who unsuccessfully attempted to kill British prime minister Robert Peel and Queen Victoria. Guiteau, who largely managed his own defense and berated his own attorneys, pleaded insanity and claimed that he could not be held responsible for his actions at the time of the shooting, since he had been acting under divine guidance. His trial, which began on November 14, turned into a long-running farce and circus. Guiteau remained prone to incoherent rants, regularly made lengthy and idiosyncratic speeches justifying his behavior, and tried the patience of both judge and jury. The *Daily Advertiser* conveyed the prevailing popular mood in its year-end roundup, lamenting that if only "the murderer had been put on sharp and speedy trial, conviction, and hanging, there would have been something manly in the year." Instead of exacting quick and unsparing "manly" retribution, the newspaper criticized "judicial imbecility" for creating a situation where "the prisoner is now still howling at the Court and will keep on as long as his throat can outbellow the mild rap of the gavel from the bench." Justice, in this view, demanded bold, decisive, and rapid action. Femininity, empathy, and psychosocial behavioral analyses had no place in legal proceedings. The Guiteau trial dragged on until 26 January 1882, whereupon the jury took less than one hour to deliberate and find him guilty. The judge pronounced his death sentence, appeals for clemency proved fruitless, and the deranged killer was hanged on June 30. As the historian Candice Millard cogently commented, however, "The death of Charles Guiteau, which was greeted by a triumphant shout that echoed through the courtyard and was picked up and carried by the crowd pressed against the prison walls, accomplished nothing." His execution failed to prevent future political assassinations, offered no solace or comfort to the grieving family, and ultimately could not satisfy the desire for bloodthirsty revenge among the American public. Both the Garfield presidency and the gunshot that ended it remained brief blips on the historical radar.[3]

Frank Lammens certainly differed dramatically in most ways from Charles Guiteau. He never attempted to claim an insanity defense, insisting instead on his complete innocence. He certainly never harbored Guiteau's grandiose ambitions. The two loners shared some common characteristics, however, that contributed to their tragic life stories. Both spent the 1870s largely on the road, attempting to find some measure of economic security in dark times by engaging in highly unconventional and occasionally illegal pursuits. Lammens also turned his trial and appeal into dark comedy with his asides to the jury, his excessively formal speaking style, and his complete lack of understanding about the American judicial system. Both appeared delusional throughout their confinement. Guiteau expected either General

William Tecumseh Sherman or a grateful nation to forcibly free him from prison. Lammens continued to insist that he should have yet another trial and an additional chance to address jurors who had long since dispersed. Guiteau's family attempted to place him in an insane asylum while Lammens actually spent time in the Auburn facility for the mentally ill. Their behavior generated deep public and juridical skepticism. Prosecutor Abeel persistently argued that Lammens methodically and cold-bloodedly murdered John Meierhofer and that his insane-like behavior constituted a dodge and a scam. He even questioned whether Lammens ever had been married or if his children had actually died during the war, claiming that his entire autobiographical account was just another con job perpetrated by a master manipulator. Medical professionals found both men fascinating subjects for dissection and study. The physicians who regularly examined Lammens during his confinement certainly concluded that he suffered from some mental illness and suspected a physiological cause. His conviction, however, depended on the jury viewing him as a rational and cynical actor, shooting the household head as part of a well-conceived master plan to take up with his wife and secure a stable livelihood on the farm. American culture lacked a solid infrastructure for addressing mental illness or determining fitness to stand trial. Execution became a convenient revenge-based social solution for much more intractable problems.

Public memory concerning the Meierhofer murder faded as quickly as the Garfield presidency. The executions soon passed into forgotten history. Only one subsequent nineteenth-century newspaper article has been located that substantially featured the events. In May 1881, the *Newark Sunday Call* ran a ghoulish story titled "Murderers' Graves: The Places of Interment of Those Who Have Paid the Dread Penalty of the Law in Newark." The newspaper invited readers on a tour of local cemeteries that held the remains of infamous criminals "who paid the penalty of Mosaic law" in New Jersey's largest city. Reporters tracked Margaret down in the extreme eastern end of Holy Sepulchre Cemetery, where "there is only a plain mound of light-colored earth like scores around it." Excepting the "withered remnants of a bouquet of flowers" that had been placed there during the burial ceremony, no marker identified her final resting place. Frank Lammens, however, whose grave existed "all alone in the extreme northeast end" of Saint Mary's Cemetery, fared somewhat better. The Benedictines carefully tended to his plot, having planted lilies, verbenas, and other flowers on the site. They also erected a wood-painted white cross at the head of the grave, which contained a German inscription in black letters: "Heir Ruht [Here Lies the Body of] Frank Lammens, 47 yra alt [years old], Jan. 1881." John Meierhofer, on the other hand, perhaps surprisingly had the most enduring presence on the memorial landscape. After the autopsy, he had been interred in an unmarked grave in the old "single grave" section of Rosedale Cemetery in Orange, in effect a "potter's field." In February 1879, however, the U.S. Congress had passed legislation extending the privilege of free government-provided gravestones to all honorably discharged Civil War veterans who had been buried in private cemeteries. Federal authorities contracted with private companies, typically quarries in Vermont and Massachusetts, to cut and carve standard stones that measured four inches thick, ten inches wide, and twelve inches tall. In June 1888, the Gross Brothers firm in Lee, Massachusetts, received the commission to prepare the marble monument for John Meierhofer. Unfortunately, virtually every fact inscribed on the stone proved to be erroneous. His first name had been carved as "Jonathan" rather than "John," and his last name had been misspelled as "Meirhoefer" instead of the correct "Meierhofer." The Gross Brothers listed him as having served in Company K of the 37th Regiment, New Jersey Infantry, when he actually served in Company H of the 39th Regiment. In a final mistake, John's date of death appeared as September 10 rather than October 9 in the Gross Brothers' company records. Perhaps his error-laden headstone constitutes the most fitting epitaph of all for a man whose disorderly existence had been marked by so much confusion and whose chaotic life ended so suddenly with a bullet to the back of the head.[+]

Margaret Meierhofer would have been only fifty-nine years old had she lived to welcome in the twentieth century. She would have found certain things quite familiar in 1900. Her farmhouse still stood on Northfield Road, though her son Joseph and his family now occupied the weather-beaten structure. The Kirstens, who had provided shelter for her during the 1870s but who initially had refused to accompany John Pierson down the hill to summon police on the night of the murder, remained prominent hilltop residents. The LeClare and Richey families, who undermined her defense through gossip and innuendo, still labored on the mountain as farmers, teamsters, and carpenters. Michael Klem, who originally copurchased the farm with John Meierhofer, continued to work his own land near the intersection of Northfield Road and Cherry Lane despite his advanced age of seventy-four. Balthazar Klem, who owned the

FIG. 6.1 The grave of John Meierhofer at Rosedale Cemetery in Montclair, N.J. Courtesy of John Celardo.

home in East Newark where Margaret's body lay in state following the execution, had grown infirm owing to a Civil War injury and would live out the remainder of his life at the New Jersey Home for Disabled Soldiers in Kearny. Margaret's brother John, whose Livingston farmhouse served as the Meierhofer wedding site, apparently passed away prior to 1900. John's son, however, never married, and he continued to labor on the family farm, maintaining the operation until well into the twentieth century. Margaret would have recognized other aspects of West Orange life as well. German-born and second-generation farmers remained a substantial presence on the mountain. Hatting continued to be an important-if-shrinking industry in the valley, where Margaret first met John. Llewellyn Park still attracted wealthy urban businessmen seeking solitude and comfortable country living. Saint Cloud had not fully developed, but lawyers, brokers, real estate agents, and publishers occupied its substantial homes. Mountain Ridge still sheltered the wealthiest town elites, though Browns, Delanos, and Kruegers had replaced McClellans, Marcys, and Adamses as the most prominent property holders.[5]

This apparent continuity masked radical change. Thomas Edison personified the transformation. The "Wizard of Menlo Park" had married Mina Miller in 1886, two years after the sudden and unexpected death of his first wife. Neither Thomas nor Mina found New York City congenial, preferring relaxed country living to urban congestion. Thomas soon procured a twenty-three-room Queen Anne-style mansion in Llewellyn Park at a bargain price, owing to the fact that the previous owner had embezzled massive amounts of money from the Arnold Constable & Company department store. "Glenmont," as the estate was known, constituted one of the largest structures in Llewellyn Park, part of the Gilded Age trend toward erecting more substantial and even gaudy homes in the prestigious development. Shortly thereafter, Edison crafted a plan to build the best equipped industrial research facility in the United States in West Orange, a true "invention factory," in the words of technology historian Andre Millard. By January 1887, Edison purchased fourteen acres on Main Street near the entrance to Llewellyn Park and convenient to a nearby train station. A three-story laboratory contained his office and a beautiful wood-paneled library as well as the powerhouse, complete with a boiler, steam engine, and dynamos that powered the enterprise. Four auxiliary buildings also existed on the site, providing room for electromagnetic experiments, chemical testing and storage, woodworking shops, and a metallurgical laboratory.

Another building, known as the Edison Phonograph Works, opened in 1889 and housed all of the inventor's experiments that attempted to perfect his beloved "talking machines." Edison also expanded into such areas as moving pictures, magnetic ore separation, and electrical traction late in the century. By February 1901, he incorporated the Edison Storage Battery Company, with plans to build another massive factory that ultimately dwarfed his original laboratories upon its completion. Constant experimentation occurred at the West Orange site, creating a vital and dynamic work culture that attracted smart and creative people.[6]

Both Edison and his inventions exerted a tremendous influence on West Orange. A glance at the 1900 census reveals that townsfolk engaged in many occupations that did not even exist in 1880: machinists, electricians, stationary engineers, typewriters, telephone operators, draftsmen, and individuals who were classified by the enumerator simply as "Eddison [sic] Phonograph." The factory complex quickly became the largest employer in town. Edison's rise coincided with the gradual decline of the hatting industry, where workers suffered from mechanization and a business slump that produced massive layoffs in the Oranges throughout the 1890s. Although his various enterprises also suffered during the economic depression in the middle of that decade, Edison always seemed to rebound with bigger and bolder plans. He became a major force in the electric streetcar industry, and in 1892, a line was laid from Newark through the Oranges. Good streetcar service allowed Edison to expand his own labor force, as commuters from throughout northeastern New Jersey could now easily work at his factories. Edison increasingly became associated with West Orange, and the town proudly branded itself as the home of this cultural icon. His presence undoubtedly stimulated other transportation ventures. Several projects during the 1880s and 1890s lessened the physical barriers that had hindered development and made life difficult during Margaret's lifetime. The Northfield Road became fully macadamized during the 1880s, easing travel between the valley and the mountainous areas of town. The Orange Mountain Cable Car Company began running regular routes from the Orange border to the vicinity of the Rock Spring in the early 1890s. Stimulated in large part by the economic boost that the Edison industries provided, the town experienced a period of sustained growth.

West Orange's population more than doubled between 1880 and 1900, numbering nearly seven thousand inhabitants in the latter year. Indeed, by far the largest percentage of that growth occurred after the Edison plant

opened in 1887. The population would increase by approximately 150 percent between 1900 and 1920, and an additional 56 percent between 1920
and 1930. The local infrastructure grew more complex. West Orange
stopped relying so heavily on neighboring Orange for services. It established its own police force (1884), opened a water company (1892), and
built a new high school (1898). Developers began purchasing farms, subdividing plots, and laying out streets near the Edison factory. Watson Whit-
tlesy, for example, created something called "Watchung Heights" near the
train lines. His suburban development featured detached three-bay, gable-
front, clapboard homes that rose two stories, contained side entrances, and
often featured some millwork ornament on cornices, porches, doors,
and windows that broke up their uniform appearance. As Edison expanded
his workforce, two-family and four-family detached homes also sprouted
up in the downtown area, creating a much more urban feel than it had during Margaret's day. On the mountain, development remained somewhat
stagnant. Margaret might have noticed that a few new shingle-style and
arts-and-crafts houses appeared in Saint Cloud, keeping the carpenters
and contractors who would have boarded at her house in earlier days busy.
But excepting improved transportation, her immediate surroundings
exhibited relatively few signs of change. The Jaillette tavern, which played
such an important role in her trial, did cease operations at some point
in the 1880s. Claude and Susan, the proprietors, had several run-ins with
the law. One notable case occurred during May of 1880 when two African American farm laborers purchased beer and malt liquor there in violation of Sunday closing laws. Both admitted to patronizing the tavern "on
account of the interest attached to it in consequence of the Meierhoefer
murder." No evidence survives, however, that the Jaillettes had managed to
turn their notoriety into a longer-term tourist attraction. Indeed, Claude
died in 1882, and Susan continued to live on the property at the corner of
Northfield and Walker Road until her death in 1898.[7]

Many individuals who played a prominent role in the Lammens
and Meierhofer trial had passed into eternity by the turn of the century.
George McClellan died suddenly in October 1885 after suffering an attack
of angina pectoris at age fifty-eight. He sought to revive his frustrated
presidential aspirations after his successful New Jersey gubernatorial run
in 1877, but the solicitation from national Democratic Party leaders never
materialized. His hopes quickly became dashed, similar to the pardons
that never arrived for Frank Lammens and Margaret Meierhofer. Unlike

the condemned prisoners, however, he spent the early 1880s traveling the world, touring the nation, enjoying the New York City social scene, and reaping substantial financial benefits from his numerous trusteeships and stock holdings. William H. Hagaman died in Boulder City, Colorado, in August 1883, where he had returned a short time after the executions in yet another attempt to regain his failing health. The *Newark Daily Advertiser* praised the fifty-six-year-old attorney for leading "a blameless life" and especially cited his work for Frank Lammens, noting that he "won high encomiums for his able conduct as associate counsel for the defense" though the newspaper claimed that "he had a hopeless task." In keeping with the general tributes accorded to all members of the bar during this period, he shouldered no blame for the verdict but reaped only accolades for his abilities. Gustav Abeel, as previously noted, expired at age forty-five in 1884, leaving behind a wife and three children. When the Essex County Bar Association appointed a committee to prepare the appropriate tributes to his memory, Sheriff Stephen Van Courtlandt Van Rensselaer stood out as a prominent member. Van Rensselaer himself died the following year, having served out his term as sheriff and transitioned to a comfortable position as general agent for the Equitable Life Assurance Society. Peter Van Pelt Hewlett, the Essex County physician who supervised the executions and conducted the postmortems on Margaret and Frank, served as the sheriff's personal physician during his final bout of bronchitis. The late nineteenth-century local legal and political network remained intricately connected through personal and professional ties.[8]

Three principal legal figures from the trial did survive into the twentieth century. Judge David Depue continued to function as a master politician. The genteel and cultured jurist earned the accolades of colleagues on all sides of the political spectrum. He received continual reappointments to the state supreme court and became chief justice in 1900. Depue's kidneys broke down shortly after his ascension to this position, however, forcing his retirement and causing his death in 1902. William Guild received newspaper mention as a close friend who attended the family during the wake. Charles Borcherling did not, but he had forged an even closer tie when his stepdaughter married Depue's son. Defense attorneys and prosecutors alike maintained a clubby relationship with the judge and his family. Demand at the funeral proved so great that North Reformed Church hosted capacity crowds, and the "massive casket, covered with somber black cloth" and liberally festooned with lilies-of-the-valley and white roses, remained open for two hours so mourners from the bench and bar could catch one final glimpse of the bewhiskered judge. Less pomp attended the funeral of William B. Guild in 1909, but he also received his due prior to his interment at Mount Pleasant Cemetery, the final destination for Newark's most elite citizenry. Charles Borcherling, who argued so vigorously for Frank Lammens and against Margaret Meierhofer during the trial, served as a pallbearer for her defense attorney. Guild had carved out a robust civic career since the trial and also established one of the most high-profile and lucrative law firms in the state: Guild, Lum & Tamblyn. The *Newark Evening News* listed the many famous cases that occupied him throughout his career, including that of Margaret Meierhofer. An earlier tribute to Guild that appeared in a county history a few years following the trial, however, took an opportunity to dismissively trivialize Margaret one last time: "As for Mrs. Meierhofer, for the murder of her husband, there was no hope except in the circumstance that her woman's gear might operate in her favor with the jury. In [this] and many other cases, Mr. Guild won for himself great applause." Once again, a trial loss and failure to save a client from the gallows proved to only burnish his reputation and enhance his career. The German-born Charles Borcherling proved to be the last survivor from the trial. Described as "one of the oldest members of the Essex County Bar," he died of apoplexy at the age of eighty-six in 1912. Borcherling transformed his practice into a family-based enterprise, partnering with his son, Frederick. By the time of Charles's death, however, the Newark newspapers took no note of Frank Lammens or of the famous trial that had captivated the city, the county, and even the nation from 1879 through 1881.[9]

The comfortable "good old boy" culture that dominated New Jersey legal affairs began to break down both physically and institutionally in the late nineteenth and early twentieth centuries. Mary Philbrook (1872–1958) served as one important change agent. New Jersey had never accepted a woman into the legal fraternity when she applied to take the bar exam in 1894. The state supreme court, with David Depue sitting as a member, rejected her application based on the notion that women had no rights to practice as attorneys despite their constitutional status as citizens. She persisted. Philbrook organized a lobbying effort that induced the legislature to pass an 1895 bill that allowed women to become lawyers. She quickly achieved admission to the bar. Philbrook moved her practice to Newark, became the first female probation officer in Essex County, helped establish the New Jersey Reformatory for Women in 1913, organized the first state-wide legal aid association, and became a tireless advocate for civil rights throughout her career. New Jersey law no longer constituted a male-only affair. Another seemingly inconsequential event that contained transformative implications occurred in 1908 when the New Jersey Law School opened its doors on the fourth floor of the Prudential Home Insurance Company in Newark. The modest institution, with only three faculty members and thirty students, eventually merged with two similar entities to form Rutgers Law School. Legal education in the state transitioned gradually from the elitist apprenticeship system to the somewhat more egalitarian province of formal academic training in designated and accredited institutions. When Charles Borcherling encouraged his son to go into law in the 1880s, the route appeared clear: preparatory school training at Newark Academy, a baccalaureate from Princeton University, and some time spent reading law with Cortlandt Parker, the same well-connected attorney that Charles himself had sought out in the 1850s. As the twentieth century progressed and graduate education formalized, such familial inbreeding at least became somewhat less common.[10]

Physical change accompanied institutional transformations. On the day of Judge Depue's funeral, Essex County draped its courthouse to honor the fallen jurist. Five years later, the Egyptian Revival building itself passed into memory. In its place, freeholders commissioned Cass Gilbert to design a magnificent five-story structure that architectural historians still consider one of the finest examples of the American Renaissance period. It contains an impressive rotunda topped by a Tiffany stained-glass skylight, an exterior portico supported by eight giant Corinthian columns, allegorical murals by master artists that adorn the interior plaster walls, and a noteworthy statue of a seated Abraham Lincoln sculpted by Gutzon Borglum, whose controversial and noted commissions included Stone Mountain and Mount Rushmore. If the Egyptian Revival courthouse where the Meierhofer trial took place suggested stability and civic engagement, the new building articulated those concepts on a massive scale and without ambiguity. The Essex County Jail also underwent substantial modifications. In 1895, administrators added a women's wing that separated females and children from adult males. A new administration building allowed for more offices and guards as the bureaucratic infrastructure increased following Warden Johnson's retirement. The Essex County Board of Freeholders approved construction of a north wing in 1904, which expanded inmate capacity by 50 percent, and extended the perimeter wall northward to the Morris Canal. An onsite powerhouse now provided heat and electricity to the facility, taking advantage of the technologies pioneered by Thomas Edison in his nearby West Orange laboratory. Indeed, Edison made his mark on the institution in another way as well. The electric chair began to replace the gallows as the preferred mode of state-sponsored execution in the late 1880s. New York bore the distinction of being the first state to electrocute a prisoner in 1889 at the Auburn correctional facility where Frank Lammens had spent time. Edison's experiments at West Orange, which involved electrocuting animals in order to prove the dangers of the alternating current technology supported by his rival George Westinghouse, became an important element in claiming regularity and rationality for the new technology. Proponents argued that the electric chair would serve as a more humane and civilized form of capital punishment than the messy and unreliable method of hanging. Fifteen states, including New Jersey (1909), adopted electrocution as the preferred mode of execution between 1888 and 1913, with many more following throughout the twentieth century. Contrary to public perception, the method often proved horrific and painful, but its adoption mirrored popular faith in science, technology, and efficiency. By the second decade of the twentieth century, Essex County executioners no longer hanged inmates in the prison yard. The Meierhofer and Lammens executions, however, did not prompt any extended debate concerning capital punishment in New Jersey, which continued to put prisoners to death at a rate of forty or fifty per decade through the 1930s. The last electrocution took place in 1963, and the state did not abolish the death penalty until 2007.[11]

Margaret would have noticed another change at the turn of the century that provoked heated discussion, heightened nativist fears, and generated widespread hatred. By 1900, new national elements had arrived in West Orange. Hungarians, Poles, Italians, Austrians, Russians, and Bohemians composed a small but growing component of the population. Ethnic diversity spread even more quickly throughout the rest of northern New Jersey, fueling religious and cultural change. Essex County contained twenty-one Roman Catholic parishes in 1880, the result of fifty years of growth. An additional seventeen churches began serving parishioners between 1880 and 1900, an increase of 44 percent in only twenty years. Many of the new churches functioned as national parishes that catered to Italians, Poles, Slovaks, and the newer ethnicities. Others penetrated into such previously

Protestant and native-dominated communities as Caldwell, Bloomfield, East Orange, and Montclair. The first Jewish synagogue appeared in Essex County in 1874, with a tiny membership that consisted of only ten families. By 1895, Temple Sharey Tefilo had grown to the point where the congregation needed a much larger building in a more prominent Orange location. On a national level, anti-immigrant agitation proved politically popular and produced new restrictions. Congress passed the Chinese Exclusion Act in 1882, one year following Margaret's death, mandating a ten-year moratorium on Chinese labor immigration and earning dubious distinction as the first federal legislation banning an entire ethnic working class from the nation. West Orange apparently had no Asian residents, though a small "Chinatown" began to develop in Newark around the Mulberry Street area, where laundry workers who left Belleville started to congregate in 1882. Immigrants soon discovered, however, that nativist hostility extended to other recent arrivals as well.[12]

Josiah Strong, an influential Congregational minister employed by the American Home Missionary Society, articulated and exemplified the new attitudes in his best-selling tract from 1884, *Our Country*. On the one hand, Strong produced a robust and optimistic book designed to convince Anglo-Saxons that they had been destined to rule the world. Their two great contributions to civilization, "civil liberty" and "a pure spiritual Christianity," made them intellectually and morally superior to the other races in the author's telling. Drawing on the works of Charles Darwin and Herbert Spencer, Strong claimed that Anglo-Saxon virility and vitality would bloodlessly destroy the inferior peoples who inhabited such places as Asia, Africa, and South America, thereby planting the glories of American civilization throughout the globe. On another level, however, *Our Country* prophesied a horribly dystopian future in which the nation faced potential doom and disaster. Immigration constituted the core of the problem. Drawing the appropriate imperial parallel, Strong described the waves of immigrants from Europe since 1880 as "a peaceful invasion by an army more than twice as vast as the estimated number of Goths and Vandals that swept over Southern Europe and overwhelmed Rome." He warned true Americans that the immigrant invaders seemed to be "coming in great numbers and rapidly increasing." Further, the typical arrival appeared particularly undesirable: "A European peasant, whose horizon has been narrow, whose moral and religious training has been meager or false, and whose ideas of life are low. Not a few belong to the pauper and criminal

172 • Murder on the Mountain

classes." The invasion threatened the United States at its most basic level. Immigrants, in the mind of this minister who traced his North American lineage to seventeenth-century Massachusetts, always seemed prone to promiscuous intermingling, which produced degenerate progeny. They drank excessively, engaged in debauchery, sowed political division, dwelled in clannish enclaves, and lived for the moment in a self-indulgent excess that soon deteriorated into pure licentiousness. Immigrants had poor work ethics, suffered from underdeveloped intellects, and more often than not became "the hoodlums and roughs of our cities." The great question of the late nineteenth century, concluded Strong, was "whether this in-sweeping immigration is to foreignize us, or we are to Americanize it."[13]

Strong reserved special contempt for the foreign ideologies that seemed to be penetrating Anglo-Saxon culture. Roman Catholicism remained at the top of his list. Stringing together a series of disembodied quotes from prominent ecclesiastical figures, he concluded that Romanists despised such core American values as liberty of conscience, free speech, public schools, and an independent press. He worried about the political power that Catholics exerted in the cities, their increasing numbers and wealth, and the successful manner in which their leaders appealed to simple minds. Even apostate Romanists posed a social threat in his view, as these deluded simpletons typically gravitated toward such un-American ideologies as socialism and nihilism rather than embracing the true religion of evangelical Protestantism. Margaret Meierhofer likely would have found such language jarring and unfamiliar. Her German background certainly proved disadvantageous during the legal proceedings. She could not read or write in English, and verbal communication proved something of a barrier when she tried to tell her story. The judge and jury consisted almost exclusively of native-born men from a superior socioeconomic caste who shared little empathy for her. Yet she also lived in an agricultural area where hardworking German and French farmers predominated. Native-born residents of Saint Cloud stopped at her farm daily to place shopping orders and obtain fruits and vegetables. Since no Roman Catholic church existed in the immediate area, she attended the North Orange Congregational Church for several years. Her husband fought for his country during the Civil War. Her children attended the local public schools. Many boarders at the Meierhofer farm had been born in the United States. Margaret no doubt considered herself a good American. She certainly did not live in a multicultural utopia, but as the nineteenth century wore on, nativists grew more overtly aggressive. They used harsher language and developed novel pseudoscientific theories to proclaim their racial and ethnic superiority. Hate groups, including the Ku Klux Klan, turned their attention to the cities and directed their vitriol against Catholics, Jews, and anyone they considered a "foreigner." Violence and overt discrimination increased throughout the early twentieth century, ultimately leading to reactionary immigration restriction legislation in the 1920s. Southern and eastern Europeans bore the brunt of anti-immigrant racism, but anti-German hysteria also flourished during World War I. Attitudes hardened, America became a more foreboding and unforgiving place, and Margaret Meierhofer would indeed have been a stranger in her own land by the 1920s.

She also remained a stranger to twentieth-century observers as her story faded from public consciousness. Margaret earned an occasional mention in academic treatises that focused on the history of the death penalty, but the Meierhofer incident soon became overshadowed by more contemporary and sensational stories. Only three professional historians wrote brief synopses of the West Orange murder, and they took a similar approach. Daniel Allen Hearn, who compiled *Legal Executions in New Jersey* (2005) as part of a series of regional studies that he published with McFarland Press, summarized the tragedy in a few pages. Hearn tended toward hyperbolic prose, relied on four contemporary newspaper accounts as his sole sources, and sacrificed complexity for a smooth and sensational narrative. For example, he described the murder as a simple "love triangle" where the "lovers conspire to do away with the cuckold." Without any particular evidence, Hearn described Margaret as living in "a crowded tenement in the slums of New York City" before arriving in the Garden State. Lammens, in this telling, becomes "a handsome hobo" whose former wife had departed "for parts unknown" before he arrived at the Meierhofer farm and provided "stud service" for Margaret. John Meierhofer had worked as a "sharecropper" before the "middle-aged bachelor" connected with Margaret Klem, who flaunted her sexuality "in a most tactless manner together with a succession of male companions." Hearn garbled chronology, played fast and loose with facts, and generally presented the murder as high comedy. David V. Baker also addressed the murder in a more recent McFarland publication, *Women and Capital Punishment in the United States* (2016). Baker's take proved similar to that of Hearn, though he added a few odd facts and assumptions. He incorrectly claimed that John Meierhofer was thirty years older than Margaret rather than the true age difference of around fifteen years and characterized Lammens as "a young wayward Dutchman" when he actually had been older than Margaret. Baker also regularly accepted prosecutorial suppositions as unvarnished facts. A similar narrative treatment can be found in Kerry Segrave, *Women and Capital Punishment in America, 1840–1899*, also published by McFarland in 2008. One local history enthusiast also directed some attention to Margaret. Joseph Fagan, the official West Orange town historian who has done valuable public history work in the community, occasionally published articles concerning the Meierhofers in his weekly township newspaper column, again based exclusively on a few contemporary press accounts.[14]

Mrs. Meierhofer has fared little better in cyberspace. She has no Wikipedia entry. Her actions have, however, been highlighted in an online blog called *Murder by Gaslight*, which was established in 2009 and describes itself as "a compendium of information, resources and discussion on notable nineteenth century American murders." Unfortunately, the blog contains no creator profile, though the compiler appears to be an independent author named Robert Wilhelm, who has written a series of popular books concerning murder and true crime. The blog promised in its initial post to focus on "greed, jealousy, revenge, and obsession," which it viewed as the "universal and timeless" motives that prompted acts of violence. The site provides a valuable compilation of primary sources concerning murders, as well as links to songs, gravesites, newspaper articles, and other online references concerning its individual stories. It also encourages discussion among individuals who wish to comment and debate the grisly cases. *Murder by Gaslight* began by relating tales of well-known national murders before branching out into regional history. Under the provocative title "Who Shot Meierhoffer?," the blog related the West Orange story in January 2019. It generally recounted the trial and execution as covered in contemporary press accounts, relying especially on the *Jersey Journal* and the *New York Herald* and referencing several other newspapers but oddly not including any of the Newark dailies. The blog proved a bit more circumspect than the writings of the print-based historians, presenting primarily direct quotations from Margaret and Frank to tell the tale. When the author ventured into interpretation, however, he or she once again confused some facts. Both convicts were described as "good Catholics" though Frank expressed nothing but disdain for formal religion prior to making his final confession. Lammens is depicted as "an intelligent man" and someone who faced death "in the most solemn manner possible," belying his general demeanor. The blogger dismissed Lammens's attorney as "a court-appointed public defender" even though Charles Borcherling actually functioned as a distinguished member of the Newark bar. The Meierhofer and Lammens legal teams received criticism for failing to "attempt a unified defense," ignoring the fact that Judge Depue's pretrial decisions negated that potential strategy. The site remains a laudable attempt to shed light on obscure cases, but once again, breadth has been sacrificed in the interest of a smooth and simple narrative. As with many such projects, the assumption that the blog might serve as a lively discussion forum unfortunately proved misplaced. In nearly two years, the Meierhofer story has received twelve "likes" and generated no comments.[15]

One might expect that an oral tradition would at least have kept the Meierhofer story alive within familial circles, but this apparently has not happened either. John and Margaret's two children pursued different paths following the execution. Joseph became extremely emotional after the jury announced its verdict, proclaiming, "I am ruined for life. I have no home and I have lost my place. And, oh, I can't believe my mother is guilty, she's been so kind to me." He had been employed most recently as a clerk and driver by James H. Gedney, a retail grocer in East Orange who allegedly became so "much annoyed by [Joseph's] enforced attendance at his mother's trial that he discharged him, and employed another man to take his place." After receiving harsh newspaper criticism, Gedney publicly denied firing Joseph for that reason and earned a retraction from the *Newark Daily Advertiser*. Still, Joseph's future fortunes appeared grim. Apparently, however, he rebounded quite rapidly from the tragedy. In 1882, Joseph married Elizabeth Jane "Jennie" Clay, the twenty-five-year-old daughter of an Orange shoemaker. Shortly after the pair set up house in East Orange, Jennie gave birth to a daughter, Lillian C., in October 1882. Joseph sold off a section of his parents' farmstead bordering on Swamp Road to the West Orange Board of Education for $150 shortly following the birth of Lillian, which the trustees found attractive, since they planned to build a new school on the property. Somewhat incredibly, Joseph then decided to relocate his family to the home where his father had been murdered. The couple welcomed a second child, Charles J., into the household in December 1884. Joseph returned to work as a clerk in a grocery store, though city directories sometimes characterized his occupation as a "butcher." A cabinet card from the 1890s, one of the few photographic remnants from the Meierhofers, depicts a well-dressed Lillian and Charles ironically posing for the local photographer Louis E. Kirsten, whose family had played such a significant role in the trial.[16]

Joseph experienced some further tragedy in his life, despite the fact that his two children succeeded in their own ways. His wife, Jennie, died prematurely at the age of forty-four in April 1903, apparently owing to an untreated bout of appendicitis that produced peritonitis. Family lore suggests that Joseph had been driving his wife to Orange Memorial Hospital after she complained of stomach pains. Jennie began to feel better during the journey at which time they decided to return home, unfortunately allowing the poison to circulate throughout her system without treatment. Her funeral took place at the upscale Saint Cloud Presbyterian Church in West Orange, where a terse memorial announcement indicated only that "friends are invited." She was interred at Rosedale Cemetery in a family plot that did not include John Meierhofer. Shortly after Jennie's death, Joseph abandoned the farmhouse and moved with Lillian and Charles back to an address in downtown Orange. Lillian thrived academically. She became the valedictorian of the small and newly created West Orange High School and went on to a pedagogical career. By 1910, she was teaching in the local school system. Charles also proved quite successful. He graduated from the University of Pennsylvania and became a dentist, eventually setting up a practice in Elizabeth that spanned forty-five years. Joseph did not live long enough to appreciate his son's accomplishments. He contracted liver cancer and died in August 1911 at the age of fifty-one. His brief death notice made no mention of the Meierhofer trial or any religious ceremony, noting only that funeral services would take place at "his late residence" on North Jefferson Street in Orange and that his burial at Rosedale Cemetery would occur "at [the] convenience of family." It appears as though Joseph had abandoned the Roman Catholic faith that sustained his mother through imprisonment and instead raised his family in the Presbyterian tradition.[17]

Joseph's death precipitated change. In 1913, Charles J. Meierhofer and his uncle Theodore, who owned half of the farm owing to John dying intestate, sold the remainder of the property to Patrick H. Smith for ten thousand dollars. Lillian did not share in Joseph's piece of the Meierhofer inheritance, which had been deeded solely to Charles. Smith was an Irish-born general contractor who likely made the purchase at least partly on speculation, since he continued to live on Halsey Street in Newark for some time thereafter. By 1930, however, the Smiths had relocated to Saint Cloud Avenue, the former Swamp Road that had now been rebranded by realtors with a more attractive name befitting a romantic suburb. They perhaps built a new home on a section of the old Meierhofer property that had not been sold to the school board. Smith himself had transitioned from construction to working as a real estate broker as he grew older. He sold off some of the Meierhofer land in the 1930s to Rob and Bob Keller. In 1937, the Keller brothers established a popular roadhouse dining establishment on the site with a nostalgic 1920s-style decor that they named "Rod's." The restaurant, which now sports an English Tudor look after a 1960s remodeling, continues to exist as the Essex House. Lillian relocated to Bergen County after her father's death, where she secured a teaching position in the Ridgefield Park school system. At some point in the late 1920s, she married Edward M. Brueger, an insurance broker, at which time she gave up her career and settled into a northern New Jersey suburban lifestyle. She never had any children, though her husband had sired one by his previous marriage. Edward died in 1940 and Lillian passed away in 1955. Charles, for his part, married Agnes Van Middlesworth in the early 1920s. The couple initially moved to Westfield but spent much of the remainder of their lives in Elizabeth, until Charles died in 1961 and Agnes relocated to the Jersey Shore. They parented two daughters who both married and dispersed to other locations in New Jersey and Pennsylvania. The story of the Meierhofer murder has not been transmitted across the generations. Lillian and Charles clearly knew the story, since their childhood neighbors served as witnesses and observers at the trial, and their schoolmates no doubt heard about the tragic tale from their parents. Lillian, however, had no direct descendants. Charles's grandchildren knew nothing about this piece of family history, expressing surprise and interest when they first heard the story. Their ancestral knowledge dated back only to Joseph, and few artifacts and photographs documented the early history of the family excepting one rolling pin that Margaret apparently carried to the United States from Germany. Even more incredibly, they did not know that Joseph had a brother named Theodore, and when Charles's daughter married in 1939, neither his uncle Theodore nor any cousins appeared on the wedding guest list.[18]

Theodore Meierhofer also proved emotionally distraught after the verdict, but he at least received short-term support from Margaret's extended family. Following the murder and for some time subsequent to the execution, the fourteen-year-old lived with his uncle John Klem until he could finish basic schooling. Theodore seemed to have a particular affinity for horses and worked with equines as a stableman, coachman, and hostler for much of the late nineteenth and early twentieth centuries. Oddly, however, the U.S. census for 1900 lists his trade as "undertaker," though that seems something of an anomaly. In 1895, he married Catherine T. Hicks, a domestic servant in Orange and the daughter of Irish immigrants. The union produced four children who survived to adulthood: James, Thomas, George, and Mae. By the mid-1920s, Theodore had adapted to the automobile age and secured a position as a chauffeur for a private family in the wealthy suburban enclave of East Orange. He turned from that trade to house painting, however, and opened a business with his son James during the early years of the Great Depression. Theodore never owned a house but managed to rent in reasonably fashionable downtown neighborhoods owing to his success in the personal services and decorating trades. He retired from business in 1934 and lived comfortably until succumbing to heart disease five years later at the age of seventy-three. Two of his children followed closely in his footsteps. George, a naval veteran who served in World War I, also worked as an undertaker during the Depression but spent most of his civilian life as a driver in an auto livery service. He died prematurely of appendicitis in 1937, leaving behind his wife, Genevieve, and four children ranging in ages from a newborn through ten. James, popularly known as "Buzzie," never progressed beyond the eighth grade. He made a good living as a self-employed painter, continuing the business that he began with his father, and proudly served in the U.S. Navy during World War II. He married a divorced woman named Mary Mae Henry when he was in his late forties and never had children of his own. Buzzie especially became known in Caldwell for displaying a huge American flag from his second-floor Bloomfield Avenue apartment window every day in defiance of the property owners, who charged him an extra fee for violating their regulations. Thomas lived in Newark and worked in the hospitality industry, serving as superintendent at the fashionable Hotel Suburban on Harrison Street in East Orange. He and his wife, Susan, parented two children, Thomas and Joseph. Mae, who did finish high school, held a variety of stenographic and secretarial positions for school systems and commercial firms throughout her career. She eventually married a German-born draftsman named Hans Schwert in 1944, when she was thirty-seven years old, and the couple never had children. She passed away in 2001.[19]

Once again, the Meierhofer murder story died out at some early point for this branch of the family. Theodore's death certificate offers one clue to the short-lived nature of knowledge about the affair. When his children were questioned about the maiden name of his mother, the response came back "Don't know." Theodore, of course, had lived with Klem relatives as he came of age in Essex County but never apparently communicated the information to his progeny. His 1939 *Newark Evening News* obituary, perhaps not surprisingly, contained no mention of his parents or their fates, although such an omission appears incredible today. No surviving grandchildren of either Thomas or George had any knowledge of the murder when contacted, and their sense of family history dates back only to Theodore. Mae and James had no children, so had they been aware of the nature of their grandparents' demise, the consciousness ended with their deaths. Even the one family tree appearing on Ancestry.com that mentions Theodore, apparently mounted by a distant relative and containing several factual inaccuracies, fails to address the issue. It only references the fact that Mary "Kelm" (instead of Klem) Meierhofer "died" in 1881 in Newark and that her husband, John Meierhofer, "passed away" in 1879 without any explanatory context. One factor does differentiate this branch of the family from that of Joseph. Theodore, unlike his brother, apparently took Margaret's final pleas to heart and remained a practicing Catholic. His funeral took place at Our Lady Help of Christians in East Orange, and the rest of the immediate family seemed most closely affiliated with Saint John's Catholic Church in Orange, where many of his relatives have been buried in the adjacent parish graveyard. Generally, the two brothers apparently went their own separate ways following the execution, and their descendants have not remained in contact or shared information concerning their respective pasts.[20]

So the Meierhofer affair has receded into forgotten history. Professional historians have paid it little mind. Essex House restaurant patrons have no idea that their dining spot once served as the site for violence and intrigue. West Orange residents find it surprising that their densely populated commuter town featured small farms and contentious discord in the late nineteenth century. Meierhofer descendants express interest and astonishment at the forgotten familial episode. This all begs the question of whether the story needs to be retold and deserves renewed attention. Certainly, the incident appears inherently interesting on its own terms. But several broader themes that emerge from the tale contain both time-bound and contemporary cultural implications. Gilded Age Americans lived at a precarious historical moment. Military conflict, immigration, industrialization, urbanization, and technological change irrevocably altered traditions and lifestyles. Extraordinary accumulations of wealth became concentrated in a few hands. Income disparities increased to unprecedented levels. Large-scale national corporations became a pervasive and disruptive economic force, crippling many local communities and successfully crushing efforts to organize workers. Traditional crafts and trades buckled under the pressure of technological change and deskilling in the labor market. Family farms continued to decline as viable economic entities. Severe depressions in the 1870s and 1890s caused widespread unemployment, hunger, and suffering. The nation abandoned its experiment to reconstruct the South as the political system sank into a mire of corruption and deceit that produced power and profits for a fortunate few. When faced with disruptive change, many Americans instinctively fell back on nostalgia, myth, and comfortable fables. They convinced themselves that the nation shared ideological, ethical, and moral values that transcended the current historical disruptions. By embracing a radical conservatism and interpreting events through a reactive lens, they might stave off the forces of change that they failed to understand and that seemed to threaten foundational social structures. This overriding desire to restore a great America that never had existed in reality helps us make sense of the Meierhofer executions. Four mythological constructs appear particularly relevant.

The first involved democracy. The *Newark Daily Journal* accurately summarized this issue in a self-congratulatory editorial following the verdict when it spelled out the tremendous public cost associated with the case. The *Journal* proudly noted that the expenditures had been worth it so that "the State might ascertain who murdered, not a citizen of high station or wealth, but one of the lowliest men that was to be found within its borders—a poor, worn-out, demented, and ignorant farmer." The newspaper, citing the summation of Prosecutor Gustav Abeel, loftily proclaimed that "in the eyes of the State, the lives of all its citizens are alike sacred, and the shedding of the blood of even the meanest must call into exercise all the power of the commonwealth." Equality, of course, remained a chimerical concept in Gilded Age America. On the national and state levels, women still could not vote or even serve on juries, among a host of other restrictions. The protracted presidential election of 1876, hardly an advertisement for democratic government, only ended when Republicans agreed to halt Reconstruction and placate Southern Whites in exchange for installing the ineffective Rutherford B. Hayes as president. Southern violence and legal chicanery undermined constitutional amendments that supposedly assured African American suffrage. Mark Twain's novel *The Gilded Age: A Tale of Today* (1873) summarized and satirized the influence peddling, corruption, lobbying, and the speculative frenzy that characterized political life during the period had on Americans. And John Meierhofer's own life reflected the fact that even White male privilege did not guarantee democratic equality. After the Civil War, the government duly discharged him, provided him with a $207 bounty for his troubles, sent him home, and thanked him for his service. He never received any public assistance to help him cope with the traumatic wartime experiences that clearly affected his mental health. He became an object of derision and laughter within the community. He proved to be completely expendable, and passersby who heard shots coming from the farmhouse on the day of the murder and assumed that he had committed suicide did not even think it worth stopping to investigate further. The police appeared completely uninterested in his case. John's life became viewed as a paean to equality only after death conveniently removed him from the scene. Guilty verdicts and executions directed at two other marginalized people hardly served as a worthy democratic legacy for his sad and strange life.[21]

A second trial theme concerned justice. Newspaper accounts trumpeted "the State, as the administrator of even-handed justice" and the legal profession, which "has been glorified by this memorable trial." Pompous proclamations praised the prosecutorial and defense teams. Judge Depue received the highest admiration for impartial conduct and learned decision-making. Jurors emerged as sober and Solomon-like interpreters of evidence, carefully weighing testimony before rendering judgments. Americans needed to convince themselves, in an age that featured routine legal manipulation by the wealthy and powerful, that they lived in a fair and just society governed by carefully codified laws that applied equally to all. As the great Dutch historian Johan Huizinga reminded readers over eighty years ago in *Homo Ludens*, however, law often shares more affinity with play than justice, albeit a gamesmanship that has been subsumed in modern times under a veneer of seriousness. The legal game operates within a highly structured and rule-bound environment that privileges advocates who can arouse the most passion and enthusiasm among their audience of jurors and the general public. The Meierhofer and Lammens trials exemplified these points. Attorneys hurled unsubstantiated accusations, satirical remarks, and excoriating commentary at their opponents.

Witnesses engaged in gossip, personal invective, and slanderous asser-
tions. Prosecutor Abeel viewed both defendants with cold contempt,
ridiculing their testimonies. The trial featured wild gesticulations from
Lammens, emotional outbursts from both defendants, and Margaret dress-
ing in mourning clothes to indicate her sorrow over her departed husband.
Reporters gleefully graded the defendants on their dress and deportment.
All of these theatrics kept the audience amused, guaranteeing large crowds
in the courtroom and a wide readership in the press. The attorneys, having been trained and socialized into the norms and procedures of the bar
by their mentors, knew how to perform. Winning or losing became less
relevant than cementing their professional standing among their peers and
colleagues. They all succeeded on this score. For Depue, guiding the jury
deliberations while never sacrificing his reputation for impartiality became
his most important play. Jurors often appeared confused by the proceedings, as evidenced by their appeal for clemency, apparently unaware that
their conviction of Margaret would result in her execution. The Meierhofer and Lammens trials certainly revealed much about the legal system,
but it had little to do with ensuring equal justice for all. Tragically for Margaret and Frank, neither one had learned to play by the rules of the game.[22]

Third, the trial spoke directly to issues involving home and family. The
Meierhofer household hardly constituted the "haven in a heartless world"
that Victorians idealized in their literature and rhetoric. John and Margaret did not serve as the classic breadwinner father and nurturing mother
who could stem the tide of threats posed by modern civilization. Their
little family farm served as a home but also as a business, presided over by
a powerful woman who assumed traditionally masculine roles. The man
of the household existed in a state of complete subservience, unable to
make simple decisions or control his environment except through occasional outbursts of physical violence. When Frank Lammens materialized
at Margaret's front door, he personified the threat to Northern free labor
ideology posed by increased inequality and economic depression during the 1870s. He appeared as a mysterious and poverty-stricken member
of the "dangerous classes" without any family or support structure. His
relentlessly rootless lifestyle meant that he lived in a permanent state of
dependency as a hired laborer who would never settle down and achieve
his own competence. Fears about such men, many of whom had served in
the Civil War, proliferated among social reformers and average citizens.
Even worse, the Meierhofer household became identified as a site of female

sexual licentiousness. Margaret became vilified for her physical appearance, her alleged affairs, and her conduct with men throughout the neighborhood. The male boarders who populated her household did not merely serve as much-needed sources of income in this retelling. Instead, they violated domestic tranquility and appeared as suspicious intruders into households that should remain family-based. Further, the home became a site of domestic violence. Though Margaret had suffered at John's hands, she bore the brunt of the criticism. Her efforts to place him in an institution after several scary episodes served as evidence of motivation for the murder. When she refused to sleep with her husband, Margaret became accused of failing to fulfill her wifely responsibilities. Any attempt to control her husband's erratic behavior cast suspicion on Margaret as the true abuser in the relationship. During the late nineteenth century, gender roles appeared to be changing, and women increasingly demanded new rights and responsibilities. Reactionary Americans could not tolerate a household that operated in the manner of that managed by Margaret Meierhofer. It needed to be eradicated.

Finally, the issue of community also rose to the surface. Americans like to believe that their neighborhoods, towns, and small cities once existed as organic and cohesive communities. Such places provided stable institutions, supportive environments, friendly encouragement, and generous assistance to residents. The Meierhofer story reveals the dark side. Communities could also function as harsh and judgmental spaces. As exclusionist enclaves, they remained hostile to outsiders. They policed internal conformity, severely punished "deviants" who violated standard behavioral norms, and brooked no tolerance for different belief systems. West Orange consisted of four contiguous but institutionally independent and socially distinct communities in the 1870s: Llewellyn Park, Mountain Ridge, Saint Cloud, and the Valley. Margaret Meierhofer and her neighbors on the mountain lived in something of a netherworld disconnected from these physical spaces. No gathering places existed near the Northfield Road, excepting perhaps Jaillette's tavern and the public elementary school. Margaret and her family lived largely outside of any institutional structures. She would have needed to travel to Newark to find churches, social organizations, and businesses that catered to German immigrants. Instead, she existed in a world of dispersed households where neighbors often viewed one another with suspicion and distrust. During the trial, nearby residents regularly testified about how carefully they observed events at the Meierhofer farm. They always appeared to be keeping an eye on the premises, noting the arrival and departure of men whom they suspected to be sexual partners for Margaret. They carefully monitored her bedroom window, claiming to witness men climbing through and leaving at odd hours. On the day of the murder, numerous neighbors methodically noted the behavior of John and Frank throughout the morning with remarkable exactitude. Margaret received considerable scrutiny but little support. Viewed with suspicion and distrust by many mountain residents, she became the target of vituperative vilification throughout the trial. She served as a community threat on many levels, an aggressive and competent immigrant woman who successfully raised two children while dealing with her mentally unstable husband and their marginal economic status.

Margaret and Frank both constituted fundamental threats to home and family as defined by the reactive conservatives of their day. Their lives raised questions concerning the efficacy of the free labor system enshrined in capitalist ideology as well as the sanctity of family farms as reliable guarantors of a democratic republic. The trial spoke to the limitations of a judicial system that served the interests of an elite class of well-bred lawyers and judges much more successfully than that of clients and defendants. All three main characters in this tragedy exposed the limits of pious political proclamations concerning democracy and equality. Community and the "common good" remained elusive concepts in post–Civil War America. Institutional poverty characterized most towns and cities. The Meierhofer saga also illustrated the ways in which media outlets had begun to blend information and entertainment in new ways, a trend that soon would become exacerbated by the rise of the penny press and the consolidation of national news syndicates. Courtroom dramas proved especially amenable to sensationalism. During the twentieth century, a seemingly endless series of "trials of the century," from Leopold and Loeb through O. J. Simpson, thrilled and titillated national audiences in a variety of media. None of these developments proceeded without challenge. Within a generation, Progressive reformers would craft new institutional structures that attempted to ameliorate some of the worst excesses endemic to late-nineteenth-century socioeconomic systems. The state became more active in providing at least a rudimentary safety net for less fortunate citizens. Federal regulators eventually attempted to exert some oversight concerning media outlets. These controversial and contested trends, however, all remained far in the future.

Ultimately, the stories of Margaret Meierhofer and Frank Lammens proved too complex for contemporary legal and social systems to address in any sustained or systematic manner. Victorian Americans, however, always proved resourceful in finding other ways to bury their own inconvenient truths and enshrine their worn-out, laissez-faire mythologies. Execution offered an especially easy, socially acceptable, and seductive short-term solution for eradicating disruptive outliers. And so it happened to Margaret and Frank. And that ended that.

Notes

Chapter 1 The Gallows

1 Margaret's married name has been spelled myriad ways throughout the various sources and appears standardized throughout this manuscript as "Meierhofer." We have selected this spelling based on two especially credible sources. When the Benedictine monks at Saint Mary's in Newark baptized her oldest son, Joseph, in 1860, we can assume that they were familiar with the German usage, and they entered "Meierhofer" into the official church register. Further, when her youngest son, Theodore, died in 1939, the gravestone in Saint John's Cemetery also read "Meierhofer." Newspaper accounts, official state and federal records, census reports, and similar documents, however, include such variations as "Meierhoeffer," "Meierhoffer," "Meyerhofer," "Maerhoffer," "Maierhoeffer," "Meirhoffer," "Mihoffer," and even "Marcarhoffer." Variant spellings often appeared in the same document. For example, Margaret's official death certificate from the state of New Jersey referred to her as "Margaretha Meyerhofer" but noted that her death owed to "the conviction of murder of John Mierhoffer." Another good example occurred when Theodore died. The *Newark Evening News* printed his obituary under the name "Meierhoffer." His official death certificate referred to him as "Meierhoefer." As noted above, his tombstone is inscribed with "Meierhofer." So to avoid confusion throughout the book, we have decided on "Meierhofer."

2 "The Gallows. Two Murderers Pay the Penalty," *Newark Daily Advertiser*, 6 January 1881; "Expiation," *Newark Daily Journal*, 6 January 1881. Biographical information concerning the peripheral individuals mentioned in this chapter, as well as throughout the book, has been pieced together primarily from the 1870 and 1880 censuses and the city directories for the relevant communities. When additional biographical information has existed, we have cited additional sources. On Father Gerard Pilz, see James J. Horgan, *Pioneer College: The Centennial History of Saint Leo College, Saint Leo Abbey, and Holy Name Priory* (Saint Leo, Fla.: Saint Leo College

Press, 1996). For Rev. William S. Walter, see "A Distinguished Benedictine Monk," *Newark Daily Journal*, 19 June 1882, scrapbook, Benedictine Archives, Newark, N.J.

3 *Newark Daily Journal* and *Newark Daily Advertiser*, 6 January 1881. Ebenezer Davis was the son of a Baptist minister who had immigrated to the United States from England in 1848 with his parents and five siblings. He had served as an officer in the Civil War with the 15th New Jersey Volunteers, Company A & B, thereby earning the honorific title of colonel. See "New York Passenger and Crew Lists (Including Castle Garden and Ellis Island), 1820–1957," M237, 1820–1897, roll 073, https://www.ancestry.com/search/collections/7488/; and "U.S. Headstone Applications for Military Veterans, 1825–1941," https://www.ancestry.com/search/collections/2375/. Van Rensselaer's obituary can be found in *Newark Evening News*, 21 May 1885.

4 *Newark Daily Advertiser*, 6 January 1881. On Peter Van Pelt Hewlett, see William H. Shaw, *History of Essex and Hudson Counties, New Jersey* (Philadelphia: Everts & Peck, 1884), 1:342; and his obituary in *Newark Evening News*, 14 March 1906.

5 *Newark Daily Journal*, 6 January 1881.

6 *Newark Daily Journal*.

7 *Newark Daily Journal*.

8 Needless to say, an enormous literature exists around the invention and development of criminology. A useful starting point is the collection of essays in Peter Beckert and Richard F. Wetzell, eds., *Criminals and Their Scientists* (Oxford: Cambridge University Press, 2006), especially the articles by Mary S. Gibson, "Cesare Lombroso and Italian Criminology: Theory and Politics," and Nicole Hahn Rafter, "Criminal Anthropology: Its Reception in the United States and the Nature of Its Appeal." See also Richard Louis Dugdale, *The "Jukes": A Study in Crime, Pauperism, Disease, and Heredity. Also Further Studies of Criminals* (New York: G. P. Putnam's Sons, 1877); and Moriz Benedikt, *Anatomical Studies upon Brains of Criminals: A Contribution to Anthropology, Medicine, Jurisprudence, and Psychology*, trans. E. P. Fowler (New York: William Wood, 1881). Bertillon explained his system in Alphonse Bertillon, "The Bertillon System of Identification," *Forum* 11 (1891): 330–341.

9 On Alexander Dougherty, see his obituary in *Newark Daily Advertiser*, 1 December 1882. The autopsy results are described in *Newark Daily Advertiser* and *Newark Daily Journal* for 6 January 1881. Death certificates for "Margaretha Meyerhofer" and Frank Lammens can be found in the New Jersey State Archives, M154 and L49, 1881.

10 *Newark Daily Advertiser*, 7 January 1881; "After the Execution," *Newark Daily Journal*, 7 January 1881. Woodruff's advertisements can be found in *Holbrook's Newark City Directory for the Year Ending April 1, 1881* (Newark, N.J.: A. Stephen Holbrook, 1880).

11 Stuart Banner, *The Death Penalty: An American History* (Cambridge, Mass.: Harvard University Press, 2002), 76–84, discusses the dissection of criminals. Other sources concerning the death penalty on which the following discussion is based include David V. Baker, *Women and Capital Punishment in the United States: An Analytical History* (Jefferson, N.C.: McFarland, 2016); and Daniel Allen Hearn, *Legal Executions in New Jersey, 1691–1963* (Jefferson, N.C.: McFarland, 2005). On legislation in New Jersey, see "An Act for the Punishment of Crime," in William Paterson, ed., *Laws of the State of New Jersey* (New Brunswick, N.J.: Abraham

Blauvelt, 1800); "An Act for the Punishment of Crime," in New Jersey Legislature-General Assembly, *Acts of the Fifty-Third General Assembly of the State of New Jersey* (Trenton, N.J.: A. W. Phillips, 1828); and Edward Mussey Hartwell, "European and American Anatomy Acts Compared," *Boston Medical and Surgical Journal* 104 (20 January 1881): 56–58.

Newspapers consistently identified her brother John as living in East Newark in 1880, but this appears incorrect. No evidence exists that John ever moved away from his Livingston farm, where he remained until his death. Rather, the brother who lived in East Newark appears to be Balthazar Klem. City directories have him listed as being a machinist who lived in Newark and Orange during the late 1860s and 1870s and then at 16 Washington Street in East Newark in 1880. According to the 1910 census, Balthazar had emigrated from Germany in 1852, approximately the same time as the rest of the Klem family. The parish register at Saint Mary's in Newark also lists Balthazar Klem as the baptismal sponsor for Theodore Meierhofer in 1866, further cementing this connection.

12 *Newark Daily Journal*, 7 January 1881; "Trial by Rope," *New York Sun*, 8 January 1881.

13 *Newark Daily Journal*, 8 January 1881.

14 On Saint Mary's in Newark, see Joseph M. Flynn, *The Catholic Church in New Jersey* (Morristown, N.J.: Publishers Printing Company, 1904), 135–141; and Saint Mary's, Newark, annual reports for 1881 and 1882, Archives of the Archdiocese of Newark at Seton Hall University.

15 *Newark Daily Journal*, 8 January 1881; the estimate on the size of the church is from an interview with Father Augustine Curley, archivist of the Newark Benedictines, 28 February 2019; the translation of the Psalm is from the Douay-Rheims Bible: "Book of Psalms: Psalm 129," Douay-Rheims Bible Online, last accessed 27 October 2021, http://www.drbo.org/chapter/21129.htm.

16 *Rules and Regulations of the Cemetery of the Holy Sepulchre, Newark, N.J.* (Newark, N.J.: J. J. O'Connor, 1881). The Holy Sepulchre Cemetery file at the Archives of the Archdiocese of Newark at Seton Hall University contains considerable additional information concerning the cemetery. *Newark Daily Journal* 7 and 8 January 1881.

17 *Newark Daily Journal*, 6 and 7 January 1881.

18 *Newark Daily Journal*, 7 January 1881.

19 Banner, *Death Penalty*, presents an excellent historical overview of the legislative and cultural history of the death penalty.

20 Banner, 29–42.

21 Her actual name was Deignan, but she was referred to in all the contemporary literature as Durgan. The most interesting pamphlet to result from this trial and spectacle remains Rev. Mr. Brendan, *Life, Crimes, and Confession of Bridget Durgan, the Fiendish Murderess of Mrs. Coriel* (Philadelphia: C. W. Alexander, 1867), also available at https://publicdomainreview.org/collections/life-crimes-and-confession-of-bridget-durgan-1867/.

22 "Execution of Bridget Durgan," *New York Times*, 31 August 1867.

23 *New York Times*.

24 *New York Times*.

25 Van Hise, forty-seven years old at the time of the execution, needed both his public salary and private commissions to support his wife and six children ranging in age from one to twenty-four. He eventually left his janitorial job and became a

successful carpenter who operated a small business in Newark. An advertisement in the 1892–1893 Newark City Directory indicates that he eventually established a family business, James Van Hise and Son, that specialized in "Mill Wrighting, Shaft Hanging and Manufacturers of Water Tanks, Etc. Also Materials for Hat Factories. All Kinds of Jobbing Promptly Attended To," Newark City Directory, Ancestry, 1892–1893, p. 696, https://www.ancestry.com/imageviewer/collections/2469/images/11057231?usePUB=true&_phsrc=cR04&_phstart=successSource&usePUBJs=true&pId=577955803.

26 *Newark Daily Journal* and *Newark Daily Advertiser*, 6 January 1881.

27 *Newark Daily Advertiser*, 6 January 1881; *Newark Daily Journal*, 6 January 1881; Editorial, "'Trial by Rope,'" *Newark Daily Journal*, 8 January 1881; *New York Sun*, 7 January 1881. Interestingly enough, Meldrum—the chief of police—previously had worked as a hatter, indicating the fluidity of such public positions in nineteenth-century urban cultures.

28 *Newark Daily Journal*, 6 and 7 January 1881.

29 *New York Sun*, 8 January 1881.

30 Editorial, *Newark Daily Journal*, 8 January 1881.

Chapter 2   Communities

1 *The Oranges and Their Leading Business Men* (Newark, N.J.: Mercantile Publishing Company, 1890), 22, 26–27.

2 This discussion of Llewellyn Park is based largely on the following sources: Richard Guy Wilson, "Idealism and the Origin of the First American Suburb: Llewellyn Park, New Jersey," *American Art Journal* 11, no. 4 (1979): 79–90; Jane B. Davies, "Llewellyn Park in West Orange, New Jersey," *Magazine Antiques*, January 1975, 142–158; John Archer, "Country and City in the American Romantic Suburb," *Journal of the Society of Architectural Historians* 42, no. 2 (May 1983): 139–156; Susan Henderson, "Llewellyn Park, Suburban Idyll," *Journal of Garden History* 7, no. 23 (1987): 221–243; Witold Rybczynski, "How to Build a Suburb," *Wilson Quarterly* 19, no. 3 (Summer 1995): 114–127; and Robert Guter, "Historic Sites Survey: Llewellyn Park Survey and Nomination to the National Register of Historic Places," West Orange Historic Preservation Commission Archives, Planning Board, 1986, West Orange, N.J.

3 Richard Grubb and Associates, *Township of West Orange, Landmark Designation Report: Nichols-McKim Cottage, 45 Park Way (Block 112B/Lot 19)*, West Orange Historic Preservation Commission Archives, Planning Board, October 2011, West Orange, N.J.

4 Llewellyn Park, *Llewellyn Park: Country Homes for City People*, West Orange, N.J., n.d., brochure.

5 Llewellyn Park.

6 Llewellyn Park.

7 Davies, "Llewellyn Park in West Orange," 142. For a brief biography of Nichols, see Historic Northampton Museum and Education Center, "Northampton Meadows," last accessed 26 October 2021, http://www.historic-northampton.org/collections/edwardnichols.html; and on the Nichols-McKim Cottage, see Grubb and Associates, *Nichols McKim Cottage*.

8 On James Miller McKim, see Jeffrey Ruggles, *The Unboxing of Henry Brown* (Richmond: Library of Virginia, 2003), esp. 28–42; Ira Brown, "James Miller McKim and

Pennsylvania Abolitionism," *Pennsylvania History* 30 (January 1963): 56–72; and *The National Cyclopaedia of American Biography* (New York: James T. White, 1921), 2:529.

9 The statistics were compiled by analyzing the manuscript returns from the 1880 federal census, which are accessible through Ancestry.com. U.S. Census, West Orange, N.J., 1880, https://www.ancestry.com/imageviewer/collections/6742/images/4242210-00133?ssrc=&backlabel=Return. On the transformation of Llewellyn Park, see especially Davies, "Llewellyn Park in West Orange"; and Keith Spalding Robbins, "A History of the First Planned American Suburban Community: Llewellyn Park, West Orange" (BA thesis, George Washington University, 1985).

10 David Lawrence Pierson, *History of the Oranges to 1921: Reviewing the Rise, Development, and Progress of an Influential Community* (New York: Lewis, 1922), 3:587–588. The 1879 New York City Directory listed Marcy as having a medical practice at 330 Fifth Avenue and a home at 396 Fifth Avenue. The 1883 Orange City Directory noted that he was a physician in New York City but had a home at Mountain Ridge in West Orange. On Marcy, see Henry Whittemore, *The Founders and Builders of the Oranges* (Newark, N.J.: L. J. Hardham, 1896), 345–346. A brief but interesting obituary can be found in *The North American Journal of Homeopathy* (New York: Journal Publishing Club, 1901), 49:55–56.

11 On Randolph Marcy, see Whittemore, *Founders and Builders*, 346–347; as well as James Grant Wilson, ed., *Appleton's Cyclopaedia of American Biography* (New York: D. Appleton, 1888), 4:202–203. The standard work on George McClellan is Stephen W. Sears, *George B. McClellan: The Young Napoleon* (New York: Ticknor and Fields, 1988), from which much of the sketch in the following several paragraphs is taken. See also George McClellan, *McClellan's Own Story*, ed. William Cowper Prime (New York: Charles L. Webster, 1887).

12 McClellan, *McClellan's Own Story*, 16; McClellan to his mother, ca. February 1881, microfilm reel 39, George B. McClellan Papers, Library of Congress.

13 Whittemore, *Founders and Builders*; and Pierson, *History of the Oranges*, provide information on the early farmers and leading citizens of West Orange. Also see William H. Shaw, *History of Essex and Hudson Counties, New Jersey* (Philadelphia: Everts & Peck, 1884), 1:717–732. Several documents illustrate the connection between these early farmers and Saint Mark's Episcopal Church, including "Public Notice by Subscribers of the Protestant Episcopal Church in the Township of Orange," 1828; "Certificate of the Incorporation of Saint Mark's Church in Orange," 1828; and "Petition to See a Protestant Episcopal Church Established in Orange on or Contiguous to the Main Street and East of the Brook," 1828, all located in the Saint Mark's Files, Newark Episcopal Diocesan Archives, Newark, N.J. For a brief historical and architectural account of Saint Mark's, see the "St. Mark's National Register of Historic Places Nomination Form," 1977, National Park Service, Department of the Interior. On the Saint Cloud Presbyterian Church, see Ulana Zakalak, "Local Landmark Designation Report for St. Cloud Presbyterian Church," 2006, West Orange Historic Preservation Commission Archives, Planning Board, West Orange, N.J.; and Whittemore, *Founders and Builders*, 153–155.

14 For the Mountain Ridge residents, including McClellan and Adams, see U.S. Census, West Orange, 1880, 66–68. For a brief description of Mountain Ridge, see Robert Guter to Jeffrey Cahn, 3 February 1992, correspondence files, West Orange Historical Commission Archives, Planning Board, West Orange, N.J.; and Pierson, *History of the Oranges*, 3:587–588.

15 For William Henry Adams, see Charles Henry Parkhurst, *A Brief History of the Madison Square Presbyterian Church and Its Activities* (New York: Printed by request, 1906), 18; and Matthew Hale Smith, *Sunshine and Shadow in New York* (Hartford, Conn.: J. B. Burr, 1868), 502–510. Also see "Eugene Delano," obituary, *New York Times*, 3 April 1920; "Francis Beatty Thurber," obituary, *Brooklyn Eagle*, 5 July 1907; "Francis Beatty Thurber," obituary, *New York Times*, 5 July 1907; Francis Beatty Thurber, *From Coffee Cup to Plantation* (New York: American Grocer, 1881); and Emmanuel Rubin, "Jeannette Meyers Thurber and the National Conservatory of Music," *American Music* 8, no. 3 (Autumn 1990): 294–325.

16 For Benjamin F. Small, see his obituary, *Newark Daily Advertiser*, 2 June 1882; and Pierson, *History of the Oranges*, 3:588. His career movements have been pieced together by locating him in the U.S. Census listings for New Bedford, Massachusetts, 1850, and West Orange, N.J., 1870 and 1880. His membership in the Masons is documented in "Small, Benjamin F.," *Massachusetts, Mason Membership Cards, 1733–1990*, Ancestry, 21 November 1855, https://www.ancestry.com/search/collections/5061/. Information concerning Zebina Small was provided by the Dennis Township Historical Society, Dennis, Massachusetts. See Samuel L. Deyo, ed., *History of Barnstable County, Massachusetts* (New York: H. W. Blake, 1990), 885–887.

17 *Acts of the Ninety-Third Legislature of the State of New Jersey* (New Brunswick, N.J.: A. R. Speer, 1869); "Small," obituary, *Newark Daily Advertiser*. This analysis of the Saint Cloud neighborhood was drawn from the U.S. Census, West Orange, N.J., 1880, 63–67. See also Alison Haley and Patrick Harshbarger, *An Intensive-Level Architectural Survey of Selected Properties within the St. Cloud Neighborhood and the Main Street Corridor in the Township of West Orange, Essex County, New Jersey*, West Orange Historic Preservation Commission Archives, Planning Board, September 2014, West Orange, N.J.

18 A lively account of Fuller's life can be found in Smith, *Sunshine and Shadow*, 544–547. See also Daniel Willard Fiske, *The Book of the First American Chess Congress: Containing the Proceedings of That Celebrated Assemblage, with the Papers Held in Its Sessions, the Games Played in the Grand Tournament, and the Stratagems Entered in the Problem Tourney; Together with Sketches of the History of Chess in the Old and New Worlds* (New York: Rudd and Carleton, 1859), 412; "William J. A. Fuller," obituary, *New York Times*, 12 March 1887; and "W. J. A. Fuller," obituary, *New York Tribune*, 12 March 1887.

19 William Edgar Sackett, *Modern Battles of Trenton: A History of New Jersey's Politics and Legislation from the Year 1868 to the Year 1894* (Trenton, N.J.: John L. Murphy, 1895), 223; U.S. Census, West Orange, N.J., 1870 and 1880. A search for Fuller turns up several passports in the late nineteenth century that are documented in *U.S. Passport Applications, 1795–1925*, Ancestry.com, 2007, https://www.ancestry.com/search/collections/1174/. His controversial will, which called for his cremation and forbade any mourning attire, can be found in *New York Wills and Probate Records, 1659–1999*, "Wills," vol. 401–402, Ancestry, 1887–1889, https://www.ancestry.com/search/collections/8800/.

20 A vast literature exists concerning the Panic of 1873. One useful recent overview can be found in Richard White, *The Republic for Which It Stands: The United States during Reconstruction and the Gilded Age, 1865–1896* (New York: Oxford University Press, 2017).

21 "Small," obituary, *Newark Daily Advertiser.*

22 This demographic data has been culled by analyzing the U.S. Census, West Orange, N.J., 1870 and 1880. All West Orange residents who held occupations for those two years were characterized as being in one of several sectors: farming, hatting, shoemaking, laborers and other industrial jobs, artisans and craftspersons (including carpenters, printers, machinists, masons, cigar makers, blacksmiths), service fields (domestic servants, coachmen, gardeners, cooks, nursemaids, waiters and waitresses), commercial and financial services (including merchants, grocers, real estate, banking, stocks, insurance agents), and the professions (doctors, lawyers, teachers, artists, editors, and undertakers). In instances below where I analyzed the ethnic composition of the population, I only surveyed those residents fifteen years of age and older so that I could obtain a portrait of the adult population. Fifteen typically constituted the age at which many children obtained their initial jobs, and few West Orange residents at this time sent their children to either high schools or academic institutions. The town itself only provided primary and grammar schools, which meant that anyone wishing to send their children to high school needed to pay tuition to Orange. Further, if I had surveyed children under fifteen years of age, the population would have skewed toward native-born residents. Many children under fifteen were first-generation Americans who had been born after their Irish or German parents established families in the United States.

23 Richard Edwards, *Industries of New Jersey, Essex County* (New York: Historical, 1882), 760; Shaw, *Essex and Hudson*, 1:746–750; Pierson, *History of the Oranges*, 3:637–642. The best contemporary scholarly source on hatting, which contains considerable information concerning Orange, is David Bensman, *The Practice of Solidarity: American Hat Finishers in the Nineteenth Century* (Urbana: University of Illinois Press, 1985), esp. 1–17, 27–28, 131–149.

24 Pierson, *History of the Oranges*, 638; Bensman, *Practice of Solidarity*, 42–61; Amos Alonzo Stagg and Wesley Winans Stout, *Touchdown!* (New York: Longmans, Green, 1927), 46.

25 U.S. Census, West Orange, N.J., 1880, provides the data used to draw this portrait of the valley neighborhoods and streets.

26 U.S. Census, West Orange, N.J., 1880. On the Stetsons generally and Napoleon in particular, see Whittemore, *Founders and Builders*, 262–264.

27 Stagg and Stout, *Touchdown!*, 46–50; Robin Lester, *Stagg's University: The Rise, Decline, and Fall of Big-Time Football at Chicago* (Urbana: University of Illinois Press, 1995), 7–8. On the shoe industry, see Alan Dawley, *Class and Community* (Cambridge, Mass.: Harvard University Press, 1978).

28 The Stagg family's employment and residential patterns have been reconstructed through examining the U.S. Census, West Orange and Irvington, N.J., 1860, 1870, 1880, 1900, 1910, and 1920. Lester, *Stagg's University*, reconstructs the career of Amos Alonzo Stagg.

29 Samuel Crane Williams, *Historical Sketch of the Growth and Development of the Town of West Orange, New Jersey, 1862–1937* (West Orange, N.J.: Samuel Crane Williams, 1937), 6–11, provides an excellent overview of West Orange's mid-nineteenth century topography. This analysis of West Orange farmers is based on the U.S. Census, West Orange, N.J., 1870.

30 *Orlando Williams* (West Orange, N.J.: Privately printed, 1911).

31 U.S. Census, West Orange, N.J., 1880.

32 Williams, *Historical Sketch*, 30–40.
33 *Baldwin's Orange Directory, Containing the Names and Business Addresses of All Residents of Orange, East Orange, West Orange, and South Orange, for the Year Ending May 1, 1883* (Orange, N.J.: Chronicle Book and Job Printing Office, 1882), contains the data on which this analysis was based. Shaw, *Essex and Hudson*, also contains a useful list of Orange's civic, business, and social institutions, 1:750–754.

Chapter 3   Murder

1 *Newark Daily Advertiser*, 1 October 1879.
2 "A Revival of Business," *Newark Daily Advertiser*, 2 September 1879. On the sources and consequences of the Panic of 1873, as well as the way in which it played itself out in the urban north, a good source remains Richard White, *The Republic for Which It Stands: The United States during Reconstruction and the Gilded Age, 1865–1896* (New York: Oxford University Press, 2017), chap. 7.
3 "Opening of the Schools," *Newark Daily Advertiser*, 26 August 1879. It is difficult to find much secondary information concerning John C. Pierson, though it seems likely that he might be John Claiborne Pierson, who was twenty-three years old in 1880, had been born in Pennsylvania, and was living with his mother (a school-teacher) in nearby Bloomfield at least since 1870. The Orange City Directories for 1874 and 1883 list the schools in West Orange and indicate the expansion of elementary educational institutions from one to four during the decade.
4 "The Next Term of Courts," *Newark Daily Advertiser*, 26 August 1879.
5 Horace Stetson's comments are contained in George Waring, ed., *Report of the Social Statistics of Cities* (Washington, D.C.: Government Printing Office, 1886), 1:716–722.
6 *Newark Daily Advertiser*, 2 September 1879; "Weather Report for October," *Newark Daily Advertiser*, 1 November 1879.
7 *Newark Daily Advertiser*, 6 August 1879 and 1 September 1879; Waring, *Social Statistics of Cities*, 1:718–719. *Orange Journal*, 27 March 1880, summarizes the annual report of the police department.
8 *Newark Daily Advertiser*, 2 and 11 October 1879.
9 Margaret related her own story and background on the witness stand, and her testimony was covered and indeed virtually transcribed in the *Newark Daily Journal* and *Newark Daily Advertiser* for 23 January 1880. Her basic life story was corroborated through a variety of other sources, including additional trial testimony reported in the newspapers, the 1860 and 1880 U.S. censuses, and her death certificate in the New Jersey State Archives. A few useful introductions to German immigration to the United States during this period include Kathleen Neils Conzen, "Germans," in *Harvard Encyclopedia of American Ethnic Groups*, ed. Stephan Thernstrom (Cambridge, Mass.: Harvard University Press, 1980), 400–425; LaVern J. Rippley, *The German-Americans* (Boston: Twayne, 1976), 74–79; and Gunter Moltmann, "The Pattern of German Emigration to the United States in the Nineteenth Century," in *America and the Germans: An Assessment of a Three-Hundred Year History*, ed. Frank Trommler and Joseph McVeigh (Philadelphia: University of Pennsylvania Press, 1985), 14–24.

10 Conzen, "Germans," 405–425; Tyler Anbinder, *City of Dreams: The 400-Year Epic History of Immigrant New York* (New York: Houghton Mifflin Harcourt, 2016), chap. 9.

11 The 1860 census for Orange and Livingston serves as the source of this information concerning the Klem family in Livingston and the Meierhofers in Orange. In the 1910 census, Michael Klem (living in West Orange, Ward 4, District 0227) is listed as a seventy-four-year-old widower who emigrated from Germany in 1850. This would mean that he arrived a couple of years before Margaret. On the other hand, this may have been an approximation, or he may have misremembered the exact year, so it is difficult to draw a firm conclusion about the migration of the entire family. Information concerning the Harrisons is taken from the U.S. censuses for 1860, 1870, and 1880.

12 John's precise age, like virtually every other demographic factor concerning his life, appears difficult to pinpoint. The 1860 federal census for Orange lists him as being thirty-seven years old, which would have placed his birthdate in 1823. His Civil War records list him as having been mustered in at the age of forty-two in 1864, which would have him being born around 1822. The Rosedale Cemetery records, on the other hand, list him as being "50 years old" at the time of his death in 1879, which would have meant that he was born in 1829. This last date may have been an approximation, since the circumstances of his demise likely meant that no one provided exact details to the cemetery. I have been unable to locate the Klem-Meierhofer marriage records, and baptismal records for the couple's two children remain silent concerning the age of the parents.

13 Essex County deed books, G11, 1860, pp. 402–405 and C12, 1864, pp. 189–190, County Hall of Records, Newark, N.J.

14 *Orange Journal*, 11 October 1879; U.S. Census, Livingston, N.J. 1870; Essex County deed book, C12, pp. 189–190.

15 Margaret describes these financial arrangements in her 23 January 1880 testimony, as recounted in the *Newark Daily Journal* and *Newark Daily Advertiser*.

16 *Orange Journal*, 11 October 1879; *Newark Daily Advertiser*, 10 and 11 October 1879. The article "A Tramp Kills a Farmer," *New York Times*, 11 October 1879, observed that "Mrs. Meierhoeffer has a bad reputation, and was not liked by her neighbors."

17 Margaret provided this testimony, which appeared in the *Newark Daily Journal* and *Newark Daily Advertiser* newspapers on 23 January 1880. For Joseph's testimony, see *Newark Daily Advertiser*, 21 January 1880.

18 Catharine Klem's death is recorded in "Return of Deaths in the City of Newark, County of Essex, State of New Jersey, from the 1st Day of June 1871 to the 1st Day of June 1872," vol. AS, 17 April 1872, p. 309, New Jersey State Archives. Catherine Greiner's confinement to the Camden Street Insane Asylum in Newark, as well as her escape and visit to Margaret, is discussed in the *Newark Daily Journal*, 4 January 1881, scrapbook, Benedictine Archives, Newark, N.J. U.S. Census, West Orange, N.J., 1880, lists the Michael Klem household. Joseph Meierhofer recounted his life history in his testimony, captured in *Newark Daily Advertiser*, 21 January 1880.

19 White, *Republic*, esp. chap. 4, "Home," offers an excellent overview of the period from which this paragraph and the following one draw inspiration.

20 "John Maierhoeffer," Muster in Roll, Company H, vol. 2, 1861–1865, New Jersey State Archives, Trenton, N.J.; "Dead, Dead, Dead," *National Police Gazette*, 22

January 1881; "Trying to Save Two Lives," *Newark Daily Journal*, 11 February 1880; *Newark Daily Advertiser*, 11 October 1879, 24 January 1880.

21 "The Double Execution," *New Jersey Freie Zeitung*, 6 January 1881; *Newark Daily Advertiser*, 11 October 1879; *Orange Journal*, 6 January 1881; *Newark Daily Advertiser*, 20, 21, and 23 January 1880.

22 Edwin G. Burrows and Mike Wallace, *Gotham: A History of New York City to 1898* (New York: Oxford University Press, 1999), 895; William Gillette, *Jersey Blue: Civil War Politics in New Jersey, 1854–1865* (New Brunswick, N.J.: Rutgers University Press, 1999), 241, 243.

23 U.S. Civil War Draft Registration Records, 1863–1865, New Jersey 4th Congressional District, Ancestry, June 1863, https://www.ancestry.com/search/collections/1666/. Meierhofer received a $33.33 bounty upon enlistment with an additional $33.33 due to him at a future date. He also received a $44.85 clothing allowance. When he mustered out of the army, the government provided a final $207 payment for his services, which was sent to Margaret. The $207 appears exceptional, given the fact that he was not wounded and since he served as a private. All other enlisted men in the company received disbursements between $25 and $50, so this appears quite unusual, and there was no explanation. Record group R, box 83, Adjutant General's Office, Civil War, 1861–1865, regimental records, folders 10, 25, 26, 28, and 41, include this information as well as "The Thirty-Ninth Regiment New Jersey Volunteers" history. A large literature exists on the Petersburg campaign. For a relatively recent treatment, see A. Wilson Greene, *The Final Battles of the Petersburg Campaign: Breaking the Backbone of the Rebellion* (Knoxville: University of Tennessee Press, 2008).

24 See, for example, Brian Matthew Jordan, *Marching Home: Union Veterans and Their Unending Civil War* (New York: Norton, 2015); Michael Adams, *Living Hell: The Dark Side of the Civil War* (Baltimore, Md.: Johns Hopkins University Press, 2016); Judith Pizarro, Roxanne Cohen Silver, and JoAnn Prause, "Physical and Mental Health Costs of Traumatic Experiences among Civil War Veterans," *Archives of General Psychiatry* 63 (February 2006): 193–200; and Judith Andersen, "'Haunted Minds': The Impact of Combat Exposure on the Mental and Physical Health of Civil War Veterans," in *Years of Change and Suffering: Modern Perspectives on Civil War Medicine*, ed. James M. Schmidt and Guy R. Hasegawa (Roseville, Minn.: Edinborough, 2009).

25 Saint Mary's in Newark Baptismal Register, 10 June 1866, Benedictine Archives, Newark, N.J. *Newark Daily Advertiser*, 4 and 5 February 1880; *Newark Daily Journal*, 5 February 1880; U.S. Census, "Henry Richey," 1870, p. 11.

26 *Newark Daily Advertiser*, 20, 21, 22, 23, and 24 January 1880, and 5 February 1880; "Now, the Verdict," and "The Meierhofer Trial," *Newark Daily Journal*, 13 February 1880.

27 "Lammens' Last Chance," *Newark Daily Journal*, 22 December 1880.

28 The biographical sketch of Lammens in this paragraph and the succeeding pages has been cobbled together from his personal statements and the scant corroborative evidence that exists. As mentioned in the text, virtually no written documentation concerning his life has been located, raising the possibility that he completely invented and fabricated his own history. Still, this effort to describe his life constitutes a best guess and possesses some consistency. On Dutch immigration, see especially Robert P. Swierenga, *Faith and Family: Dutch Immigration and*

Settlement in the United States, 1820–1940 (New York: Holmes and Meier, 2000); and Hans Krabbandam, *Freedom on the Horizon: Dutch Immigration in America, 1840–1940* (Grand Rapids, Mich.: Eerdmans, 2009). *Newark Daily Advertiser*, 5 and 6 February 1880; "The West Orange Tragedy," *Newark Daily Journal*, 13 October 1879; *Orange Daily Journal*, 8 January 1881, all discuss Lammens's origins in Holland. He claimed to have been born in Zeeland, Holland.

29 *Newark Daily Advertiser*, 5 and 6 February 1880; "Lammens' Defense," *Newark Daily Journal*, 5 February 1880; "The Murder Trial," *Newark Daily Journal*, 6 February 1880; "Lammens and a Juror Unwell," *Newark Daily Journal*, 7 February 1880; "Frank Lammens' Wife," *Newark Daily Journal*, 28 December 1880.

30 On asylums, which boast an enormous literature, a good brief introduction is David Wright, "Getting Out of the Asylum: Understanding the Confinement of the Insane in the Nineteenth Century," *Social History of Medicine* 10 (1997): 137–155. A classic study of nineteenth-century American insane asylums is David Rothman, *The Discovery of the Asylum: Social Order and Disorder in the New Republic* (Boston: Little, Brown, 1971). See also Benjamin Reiss, *Theaters of Madness: Insane Asylums and Nineteenth-Century American Culture* (Chicago: University of Chicago Press, 2008); and Carl Yanni, *The Architecture of Madness: Insane Asylums in the United States* (Minneapolis: University of Minnesota Press, 2007). On Auburn, see *Second Annual Report of the Inspectors and Superintendent of the New York Asylum for Insane Convicts at Auburn* (Albany, N.Y.: Comstock and Cassidy, 1863), esp. 20–21; *Third Annual Report of the Inspectors and Superintendent of the New York Asylum for Insane Convicts at Auburn* (Albany, N.Y.: Comstock and Cassidy, 1864), esp. 10–11; *Fourth Annual Report of the Inspectors and Superintendent of the New York Asylum for Insane Convicts at Auburn* (Albany, N.Y.: Comstock and Cassidy, 1864); and *Eighth Annual Report of the Inspectors and Superintendent of the New York Asylum for Insane Convicts at Auburn* (Albany, N.Y.: Comstock and Cassidy, 1868).

31 Todd DePastino, *Citizen Hobo: How a Century of Homelessness Shaped America* (Chicago: University of Chicago Press, 2003), offers a good overview of the tramping phenomenon and dates the creation of the term to describe men who traveled the country with no means of visible support to 1873. Prior to that time, tramping simply referred to a long walk or march. *Harper's Weekly*, 2 September 1876, pp. 718–719; Francis Wayland, "The Tramp Question," in *Proceedings of the Conference of Charities Held in Connection with the General Meeting of the American Social Science Association at Saratoga, September, 1877* (Boston: A. Williams, 1877), 111–126.

32 State of New Jersey, *Revision of the Statutes of New Jersey. Published under the Authority of the Legislature* (Trenton, N.J.: John L. Murphy, 1877), 1208–1210; Kenneth Kusmer, *Down and Out, on the Road: The Homeless in American History* (New York: Oxford University Press, 2002), esp. 53–54; Tim Cresswell, *The Tramp in America* (London: Reaktion, 2001).

33 *Newark Daily Journal*, 4 and 5 February 1880, and 14 October 1880.

34 *Newark Daily Advertiser*, 4, 5, and 6 February 1880; "The Trial Resumed," *Newark Daily Journal*, 4 February 1880; "Lammens' Defense," *Newark Daily Journal*, 5 February 1880; "The Murder Trial," *Newark Daily Journal*, 6 February 1880.

35 "More about Frank Lammens," *Newark Daily Journal*, 9 October 1879; "Murder in West Orange," *Newark Daily Journal*, 10 October 1879; "The Meierhofer

Tragedy," *Newark Daily Journal*, 21 January 1880; *New York Times*, 11 October 1879; *Newark Daily Advertiser*, 14 and 15 October 1879, and 20 January 1880. On Jacqui, see his obituary in *Newark Evening News*, 30 August 1894, as well as U.S. Census, Orange, N.J., District 107, 1880, p. 15; Orange City Directories, 1874 and 1883; "First German Presbyterian Church, Register of Baptisms, Births, Marriages, and Deaths," last accessed 26 October 2021, Ancestry, https://search.ancestry .com/cgi-bin/sse.dll?indiv=1&dbid=61048&h=263523&tid=&pid=&queryId= baea86a2d341a19651e4c30483801500&usePUB=true&_phsrc=cR07&_phstart= successSource.

36 *Newark Daily Advertiser*, 14 October 1879, and 23 January 1880.

37 *Newark Daily Advertiser*, 20 January 1880, 10 and 11 October 1879, and 6 February 1880.

38 *Newark Daily Advertiser*, 13 and 14 October 1879; *Orange Journal*, 11 October 1879.

Chapter 4   Trial

1 William H. Shaw, *History of Essex and Hudson Counties, New Jersey* (Philadelphia: Everts & Peck, 1884), 1:323–324.

2 Shaw, *Essex and Hudson*, 1:286–287, 890-e; *Newark Evening News*, 21 May 1885, for Van Rensselaer's obituary.

3 "An Act Respecting Coroners," in *Revision of the Statutes of New Jersey Published under the Authority of the Legislature by Virtue of an Act Approved April 4, 1871* (Trenton, N.J.: John L. Murphy, 1877), 169–174, https://books.google.com/books ?id=SAtQAAAAYAAJ&printsec=frontcover&source=gbs_ViewAPI#v=onepage &q&f=false; New Jersey State Constitution, 1844, art. VII, sec. II, para. 7, https:// www.state.nj.us/state/archives/docconst44.html. The twelve jurors were Charles E. Dodd, Jonathan P. Ennis, Samuel Toombs, Edwin W. Hine, Abram Mandeville, Robert E. Parsons, Richard N. French, J. Eugene Smith, and John B. Rose. All except Rose, who resided in Newark, were in Orange. Their profiles were gleaned from the U.S. Census, 1880, as well as from the Orange City Directory, 1883; *Newark Daily Journal*, 11 and 13 October 1879.

4 *Newark Daily Advertiser*, 11, 14, and 15 October 1879; "The West Orange Tragedy," *Newark Daily Journal*, 13 October 1879; "The West Orange Tragedy— The Inquest," *Newark Daily Journal*, 14 October 1879; "The West Orange Inquest," *Newark Daily Journal*, 15 October 1879.

5 *Newark Daily Advertiser*; *Newark Daily Journal*.

6 *Newark Daily Advertiser*; *Newark Daily Journal*.

7 Charles Hopkins Hartshorne, "New Jersey's Antiquated Courts, 1844–1905," in *Jersey Justice: Three Hundred Years of the New Jersey Judiciary*, ed. Carla Vivian Bello and Arthur Vanderbilt II (Newark, N.J.: Institute for Continuing Legal Education, 1978), esp. 155–156; Charles E. Ernman Jr., "The Movement for Judicial Reorgani-zation in New Jersey, 1875–1935," in Bello and Vanderbilt, *Jersey Justice*, 167–184; Charles Hopkins Hartshorne, *Courts and Procedure in England and New Jersey* (Newark, N.J.: Soney & Sage, 1905). A good overview of Progressive legal reform can be found in Michael Willrich, *City of Courts: Socializing Justice in Progressive Era Chicago* (New York: Cambridge University Press, 2003). For an interesting biography of Hartshorne, see "Obituaries," *New Jersey Law Journal* 41, no. 9 (Sep-tember 1918): 287–288.

8 Julian P. Boyd, *Fundamental Laws and Constitutions of New Jersey* (Princeton, N.J.: D. Van Nostrand, 1964).

9 Edward Quinton Keasby, *Courts and Lawyers of New Jersey, 1661–1912* (New York: Lewis Historical, 1912), 2:768–773; *Cyclopedia of New Jersey Biography* (Newark, N.J.: Memorial History, 1916), 227–229; Shaw, *Essex and Hudson*, 1:247; "David A. Depue, Eminent Jurist, Has Gone to His Last Reward," *Newark Evening News*, 4 April 1902. Some of Depue's physical characteristics can be discerned on his passport in *U.S. Passport Applications, 1795–1925*, roll 353, Ancestry, 10 June 1890–16 June 1890, https://www.ancestry.com/search/collections/1174/, and others from photographs that appear in the above sources. Other information concerning Depue's family, acquaintances, and schoolmaster can be gleaned from the U.S. Census, Belvidere, Warren County, N.J., 1850, 1860, and 1870; U.S. Census, Easton, Northampton County, Pa., 1840, 1850; and U.S. Census, Newark, Essex County, N.J., 1870 and 1880.

10 Keasby, *Courts and Lawyers*, 768–773; U.S. Census, Essex County, Newark, N.J., 1880.

11 "Many Mourners at Late Jurist's Bier," *Newark Evening News*, 7 April 1902; Shaw, *Essex and Hudson*, 1:247.

12 Minute book, Essex County Court of Oyer and Terminer, 25 October 1876–23 December 1880, New Jersey State Archives, Trenton, N.J.; *Newark Daily Journal*, 16 December 1879.

13 Shaw, *Essex and Hudson*, 1:171–172; *Newark Evening News*, 5 and 7 January 1884; U.S. Census, Essex County, Newark, N.J., 1870 and 1880.

14 Shaw, *Essex and Hudson*, 1:284–285; *New York Times*, 15 February 1909; *Newark Evening News*, 15 February 1909; U.S. Census, Essex County, Newark, N.J., 1880.

15 *Newark Daily Journal*, 16 December 1879; Mary Depue Ogden, *Memorial Cyclopedia of New Jersey* (Newark, N.J.: Memorial History Company, 1915), 2:220; *Newark Evening News*, 12 February 1912; *Newark Daily Advertiser*, 24 August 1883; *New York Times*, 24 August 1883; U.S. Census, Essex County, Newark, N.J., 1860, 1870, and 1880.

16 Minute book, Essex County Court of Oyer and Terminer, 13 and 16 January 1880, New Jersey State Archives, Trenton, N.J.; *Newark Daily Advertiser*, 13 and 16 January 1880; *Newark Daily Journal*, 13 January 1880.

17 On John Haviland, see Matthew Baigell, "John Haviland in Philadelphia, 1818–1826," *Journal of the Society of Architectural Historians* 25, no. 3 (September 1966): 197–208; and Max Page, "From 'Miserable Dens' to the 'Marble Monster': Historical Memory and the Design of Courthouses in Nineteenth Century Philadelphia," *Pennsylvania Magazine of History and Biography* 19, no. 4 (October 1995): 299–343. On the Egyptian Revival movement, the best source is Joy M. Giguere, *Characteristically American: Memorial Architecture, National Identity and the Egyptian Revival* (Knoxville: University of Tennessee Press, 2014).

18 New Jersey State Legislature, *Revision of the Statutes of the State of New Jersey Published under the Authority of the Legislature by Virtue of an Act Approved April 4, 1871* (Trenton, N.J.: John L. Murphy, 1877), 526; "New Jersey Women Called for a Jury," *New York Times*, 12 October 1920; *Newark Daily Advertiser*, 19 January 1880. The twelve jurors were Stephen Simonson (foreman), Charles P. Valentine, William Cherry, Jeremiah Baldwin, Cyrus Williams, John Richard, Jacob Hammacher, Ezra Axtell, Aaron O. Maines, William Ridler, Samuel Doughty, and Jacob Vermillyea.

Their profiles were compiled from U.S. Census, Essex County, Newark, N.J., 1880, as well as the Newark City Directory, 1880, and the Orange City Directory, 1883.

19 "The Meierhofer Tragedy," *Newark Daily Journal*, 20 January 1880; "Mrs. Meierhofer's Defense," *Newark Daily Journal*, 23 January 1880; "Mrs. Meierhofer's Defense," *Newark Daily Journal*, 24 January 1880; *Newark Daily Advertiser*, 19, 23, and 24 January 1880. The succeeding paragraphs also draw on these newspaper accounts, which covered her testimony. Some biographical information concerning the visitors to the Meierhofer house has been compiled from the U.S. Census, 1880, and Newark and Orange City Directories, 1880.

20 Lammens's testimony was chronicled in the *Newark Daily Journal* and *Newark Daily Advertiser* on 4, 5, and 6 February 1880.

21 See "The West Orange Tragedy," *Newark Daily Journal*, 20 January 1880; "The Meierhofer Tragedy," *Newark Daily Journal*, 21 January 1880; "Lammens' Defense," *Newark Daily Journal*, 5 February 1880; "The Murder Trial," *Newark Daily Journal*, 6 February 1880; "The Testimony Closed," *Newark Daily Journal*, 9 February 1880; "Nearing the End," *Newark Daily Journal*, 12 February 1880; and "Now, the Verdict!," *Newark Daily Journal*, 13 February 1880.

22 *Newark Daily Journal* and *Newark Daily Advertiser*, 23 January 1880 and 5 February 1880.

23 *Newark Daily Advertiser*, 13 October 1879, 5 and 9 February 1880; *Newark Daily Journal*, 9 February 1880.

24 *Newark Daily Journal* and *Newark Daily Advertiser*, 23 January 1880, and 5, 10, 11, 12, and 13 February 1880.

25 *Newark Daily Journal* and *Newark Daily Advertiser*, 22 January 1880 and 9 February 1880.

26 *Newark Daily Journal* and *Newark Daily Advertiser*, 21 and 26 January 1880, and 5 and 12 February 1880.

27 Minute book, Essex County Court of Oyer and Terminer, 19 January 1880 and 9 February 1880; *Newark Daily Journal* and *Newark Daily Advertiser*, 20 October 1879, and 7, 9, and 10 February 1880; Allan Pinkerton, *Strikers, Communists, Tramps, and Detectives* (New York: G. W. Carleton, 1878), 49, 66.

28 *Orange Journal*, 14 February 1880; *Newark Daily Advertiser*, 6 February 1880; *Newark Daily Journal*, 6 February 1880.

29 *Newark Daily Journal*, 20 and 22 January 1880, and 4 and 9 February 1880; *Newark Daily Advertiser*, 26 and 28 January 1880, and 4 and 6 February 1880.

30 *Newark Daily Journal*, 13 February 1880, reprints Depue's complete final charge to the jury and is the source of all quotes in this and the succeeding paragraph.

31 *Newark Daily Journal*, 14 February 1880.

Chapter 5   Prison

I am using the term *prison* here, but *jail* would actually be more appropriate and correct, since Margaret Meierhofer and Frank Lammens were confined to the Essex County Jail in Newark until their executions. Jails typically are operated by county governments for the temporary confinement of persons who have been accused of minor crimes. Prisons, administered by state and federal authorities, tend to be reserved for convicted felons. Possibly for convenience sake, Margaret and Frank remained in the jail despite their felony convictions. The alternative would have been to transfer them to the New Jersey

State Prison in Trenton or perhaps the Caldwell Penitentiary, which housed convicted felons in Essex County. Largely for literary reasons and owing to the fact that *prisons* popularly serves as a synonym for *jails*, I have used the terms interchangeably throughout the chapter. But readers should remain aware of the distinction.

1 William H. Shaw, *History of Essex and Hudson Counties, New Jersey* (Philadelphia: Everts & Peck, 1884), 1:214. The Old Essex County Jail website, constructed by Columbia University graduate students, details the history of the prison, "Home," last accessed 26 October 2021, https://www.oldessexcountyjail.org/.

2 B. T. Pierson, *Directory of the City of Newark for 1838–1839* (Newark, N.J.: G. P. Scott, 1838); U.S. Census, Essex County, Newark, N.J., 1860, Ward 4; U.S. Census, Essex County, Newark, N.J., 1870, Ward 7, p. 47; U.S. Census, Essex County, Newark, N.J., 1880, Ward 48, p. 62; *Newark Daily Advertiser*, 30 May 1893; Joseph Atkinson, quoted in Frank J. Urquhart, *A History of the City of Newark, New Jersey: Embracing Practically Two and A Half Centuries* (New York: Lewis Historical, 1913), 2:701.

3 *Newark Daily Advertiser*, 30 May 1893; U.S. Census, Essex County, Newark, N.J., 1870, Ward 7, p. 47; New Jersey Bureau of Statistics of Labor and Industries, *Annual Report* (Trenton, N.J.: Bureau of Labor Statistics, 1882), 410.

4 *Newark Daily Journal*, 18 November 1879; U.S. Census, Essex County, Newark, N.J., 1870, p. 42; Urquhart, *City of Newark*, 2:868.

5 *Newark Daily Journal*, 21 November 1879.

6 Minute book, Essex County Court of Oyer and Terminer, 15 January 1880, New Jersey State Archives, Trenton, N.J.; *New York Times*, 6 December 1879 and 17 January 1880.

7 Minute book, Essex County Court of Oyer and Terminer, 15 January 1880, New Jersey State Archives, Trenton, N.J.

8 Minute book, Essex County Court of Oyer and Terminer, 15 January 1880, New Jersey State Archives, Trenton, N.J.; Shaw, *Essex and Hudson*, 1:271–272; U.S. Census, Essex County, Newark, N.J., 1880, 1900.

9 Bureau of Statistics, *Annual Report*, 412–426.

10 U.S. Census, Essex County, Newark and Caldwell, N.J., 1880.

11 "Lammens and Mrs. Meierhofer," *Newark Daily Journal*, 16 February 1880.

12 "A Verdict of Guilty," *Newark Daily Journal*, 14 February 1880; "A Ray of Hope for Lammens," *Newark Daily Journal*, 13 March 1880.

13 "The Meierhofer Murder," *Newark Daily Journal*, 20 March 1880.

14 *Newark Daily Journal*, 20 March 1880.

15 "Striving to Save Lammens," *Newark Daily Journal*, 27 March 1880; "Lammens Once More," *Newark Daily Journal*, 9 April 1880.

16 *Newark Daily Journal*, 9 April 1880; "Arguing Lammens' Application," *Newark Daily Journal*, 16 April 1880.

17 "The Meierhofer Case," *Newark Daily Journal*, 19 July 1880.

18 "Lammens and Mrs. Meierhofer," *Newark Daily Journal*, 16 February 1880. On Wynkoop, see *Necrological Report Presented to the Alumni Association of Princeton Theological Seminary at Its Annual Meeting, May 7, 1907* (Princeton, N.J.: Princeton University Press, 1907); William Wynkoop McNair, "The Evangelization of Our Italians," *Assembly Herald* 11, no. 8 (August 1905): 404–409; Charles L. Thompson, "The Rev. William Wynkoop McNair: An Appreciation," *Assembly Herald* 11, no. 8

(August 1905): 403–404; and "Portage Presbyterian Church History," last accessed 26 October 2021, https://portagepresbyterian.com/ppchistory.html.

19 *Newark Daily Journal*, 15 and 17 March 1880; "At the Jail," *Newark Daily Journal*, 22 April 1880; *Newark Daily Advertiser*, 15 and 16 March 1880; U.S. Census, Essex County, Newark, N.J., 1880; Russell Gasero, *Historical Directory of the Reformed Church in America* (Grand Rapids, MI: William B. Eerdmans, 2001); *Acts and Proceedings of the Seventy-Sixth General Synod of the Reformed Church in America* (New York: Board of Publication of the Reformed Church in America, 1882), 444; "Rev. Frederick Kern," Find-A-Grave.com, last accessed 26 October 2021, https://www.findagrave.com/memorial/99869078/frederick-kern.

20 "Lammens' Second Trial," *Newark Daily Journal*, 11 October 1880; "Lammens' New Trial," *Newark Daily Journal*, 12 October 1880; "The West Orange Murder," *Newark Daily Journal*, 13 October 1880. On Ketcham, see Newark City Directory, 1880; and U.S. Census, Essex County, Newark, N.J., 1880. On Hagaman, see *New York Times*, 24 August 1883; and *Newark Daily Advertiser*, 24 August 1883.

21 *Newark Daily Advertiser*, 12 October 1880; *Newark Daily Journal*, 11, 12, and 13 October 1880; "Lammens' Second Trial," *Newark Daily Journal*, 15 October 1880.

22 *Newark Daily Journal*, 12 and 15 October 1880.

23 "Nearing the End," *Newark Daily Journal*, 12 February 1880; "Pleading for Lammens," *Newark Daily Journal*, 18 October 1880; "Appealing to the Jury," *Newark Daily Journal*, 19 October 1880.

24 "The Jury Charged," *Newark Daily Journal*, 20 October 1880.

25 *Newark Daily Journal*, 18 October 1880; "Lammens Again Convicted," *Newark Daily Journal*, 21 October 1880; "The Courts," *Newark Daily Journal*, 22 October 1880; *Newark Daily Advertiser*, 22 October 1880.

26 *Newark Daily Advertiser*, 22 April 1880; "To Die on the Gallows," *Newark Daily Journal*, 6 November 1880.

27 "Their Doom Sealed," *Newark Daily Journal*, 14 December 1880; "Told That They Must Die," *Newark Daily Journal*, 15 December 1880; "In Lammens's Behalf," *Newark Daily Journal*, 16 December 1880; "Lammens' Last Chance," *Newark Daily Journal*, 22 December 1880; "Lammens' Last Hope Vanishes," *Newark Daily Journal*, 29 December 1880.

28 "Petition in Behalf of Mrs. Meierhofer," *Newark Daily Journal*, 6 December 1880; *Newark Evening News*, 11 October 1899.

29 James J. Horgan, *Pioneer College: The Centennial History of Saint Leo College, Saint Leo Abbey, and Holy Name Priory* (Saint Leo, Fla.: Saint Leo College Press, 1996), provides a biography of Gerard Pilz; "To Die on the Gallows," *Newark Daily Journal*, 6 November 1880; "Told That They Must Die," *Newark Daily Journal*, 15 December 1880; "To Be Hanged on Thursday," *Newark Daily Journal*, 3 January 1881; "The Last Few Hours," *Newark Daily Journal*, 4 January 1881; "The Eve of the Execution," *Newark Daily Journal*, 5 January 1881.

30 *Newark Daily Journal* and *Newark Daily Advertiser*, 3, 4, and 5 January 1881; "Expiation!," *Newark Daily Journal*, 6 January 1881; *New York Sun*, 7 January 1881. The De Vallerot story has been pieced together from the following sources: "Passenger List of Vessels Arriving at New York, 1820–1897," microfilm # 62, 1 June 1846 and 10 July 1846, National Archives and Records Administration, College Park, Md.; U.S. Census, New York, 1870; *New York City Directories*, 1867, 1870, 1871; U.S. Census, Essex County, Newark, N.J., 1880; Newark City Directories, 1875, 1877,

1879, 1882; Louis De Vallerot, Holy Sepulchre Cemetery Day Book, 1879–1880, Archives of the Archdiocese of Newark at Seton Hall University; *Last Will and Testament of Marie De Vallerot*, Ancestry, 24 February 1922, https://www.ancestry .com/imageviewer/collections/8800/images/005238331_00208?usePUB=true &_phsrc=cR029&_phstart=successSource&usePUBJs=true&pId=7788219; and U.S. Census, 1910, Okanogan, Wash.
31 "To Be Hanged on Thursday," *Newark Daily Journal*, 3 January 1881; "The Eve of the Execution," *Newark Daily Journal*, 5 January 1881; "Expiation!," *Newark Daily Journal*, 6 January 1881.
32 "To Die on the Gallows," *Newark Daily Journal*, 6 November 1880; "Told That They Must Die," *Newark Daily Journal*, 15 December 1880; "In Lammens's Behalf," *Newark Daily Journal*, 16 December 1880; "The Eve of the Execution," *Newark Daily Journal*, 5 January 1881; "Expiation!," *Newark Daily Journal*, 6 January 1881.
33 "Frank Lammens' Wife," *Newark Daily Journal*, 28 December 1880; "Husband and Wife," *Brooklyn Daily Eagle*, 29 December 1880.
34 *Newark Daily Journal*, 6 January 1881; "A Woman on the Gallows," *New York Sun*, 7 January 1881. Concerning Theodore Crane, see *Newark Evening News*, 29 May 1919; and U.S. Census, Essex County, Newark, N.J., 1880.

Chapter 6 Memory

1 *Newark Daily Advertiser*, 31 December 1881.
2 Candice Millard, *Destiny of the Republic: A Tale of Madness, Medicine, and the Murder of a President* (New York: Doubleday, 2011), is an excellent recent study of the assassination and the ways in which incompetent medical practice contributed to Garfield's death.
3 *Newark Daily Advertiser*, 31 December 1881; Millard, *Destiny*, 247–248.
4 *Newark Sunday Call*, 29 May 1881, scrapbook, Benedictine Archives, Newark, N.J.; "John Meirhoefer," Headstones Provided for Deceased Civil War Veterans, 1861–1904, National Archives and Records Administration microfilm, Ancestry, https://www.ancestry.com/search/collections/1195/.
5 This portrait of the town has been drawn primarily from the U.S. Census, Essex County, West Orange, N.J., 1900.
6 Andre Millard, *Edison and the Business of Invention* (Baltimore, Md.: Johns Hopkins University Press, 1990), esp. 7–21, 60–87, 111–135; Paul Israel, *Edison: A Life of Invention* (New York: John Wiley & Sons, 1998), 248–249, 260–276.
7 Joseph Fagan, *West Orange* (Charleston, S.C.: Acadia, 2009); Acroterion, "Cultural Resources of West Orange, N.J.," West Orange Historic Preservation Commission, July 1992, pp. 20–25; *Orange Journal*, 20 July 1880; U.S. Census, Essex County, West Orange, N.J., 1880; "Susan Jaillette," *New Jersey Death and Burials Index, 1798–1971*, Ancestry, https://search.ancestry.com/cgi-bin/sse.dll?indiv=1&dbid=2540&h =501287009&tid=&pid=&queryId=0386f610282dae5f0d25c634ed94377e& usePUB=true&_phsrc=cR030&_phstart=successSource.
8 Stephen W. Sears, *George B. McClellan: The Young Napoleon* (New York: Ticknor and Fields, 1988); *Newark Daily Advertiser*, 24 August 1883; *New York Times*, 24 August 1883; *Newark Evening News*, 7 January 1884; *Newark Evening News*, 21 May 1885.

9 *Newark Evening News*, 4, 5, and 7 April 1902, 15 February 1909, and 21 February 1912; *New York Times*, 15 February 1909; William H. Shaw, *History of Essex and Hudson Counties, New Jersey* (Philadelphia: Everts & Peck, 1884), 1:284–285.

10 Barbara Petrick, *Mary Philbrook: The Radical Feminist in New Jersey* (Trenton: New Jersey Historical Commission, 1981); *New Jersey Law Journal* 44, no. 1 (January 1921): 32.

11 "Jail Construction: Materials and Technology," Old Essex County Jail, last accessed 26 October 2021, https://www.oldessexcountyjail.org/construction-materials -technology/; Roger Neustadter, "The 'Deadly Current': The Death Penalty in the Industrial Age," *Journal of American Culture* (September 1989): 79–87; Stuart Banner, *The Death Penalty: An American History* (Cambridge, Mass.: Harvard University Press, 2002), 189; Millard, *Business of Invention*, 104–107; Israel, *Edison*, 326–330.

12 U.S. Census, Essex County, West Orange, N.J., 1900; Peter J. Wosh, "Guide to Northern New Jersey Catholic Parish and Institutional Records," 1981, Seton Hall University Archives; Temple Sharey Tefilo-Israel, "TSTI History," last accessed 26 October 2021, https://www.tsti.org/tsti-history; Yoland Skeete, *When Newark Had a Chinatown: My Personal Journey* (Pittsburgh, Pa.: Dorrance, 2016).

13 Joshua Strong, *Our Country: Its Possible Future and Its Present Crisis* (New York: American Home Missionary Society, 1885), esp. 30, 40–45. Strong published another edition after the census of 1890 appeared, which seemed to exacerbate the trends that he revealed.

14 Daniel Allen Hearn, *Legal Executions in New Jersey: A Comprehensive Registry, 1691–1963* (Jefferson, N.C.: McFarland, 2005), 146–149; David V. Baker, *Women and Capital Punishment in the United States: An Analytical History* (Jefferson, N.C.: McFarland, 2016), 99–102; Kerry Segrave, *Women and Capital Punishment in America, 1840–1899: Death Sentences and Executions in the United States and Canada* (Jefferson, N.C.: McFarland, 2008), 111–113.

15 Robert Wilhelm, "Who Shot Meierhoffer?," *Murder by Gaslight*, 12 January 2019, http://www.murderbygaslight.com/2019/01/who-shot-meierhoffer.html.

16 *Newark Daily Journal*, 14 February 1880; *Newark Daily Advertiser*, 17 and 18 February 1880; U.S. Census, Essex County, Orange, N.J., 1860; U.S. Census, Essex County, West Orange, N.J., 1900; Essex County deed book, U21, 1882, pp. 25–27, Essex County Hall of Records, Newark, N.J.; Louis E. Kirsten, "Lillian and Charles Meierhofer," cabinet card, courtesy of Patricia Brunker.

17 *Newark Evening News*, 18 April 1903, 11 and 12 August 1911, and 13 September 1961; U.S. Census, Essex County, West Orange, N.J., 1900; U.S. Census, Essex County, Orange, Ward 2, 1910; Orange City Directories, 1902, 1903, 1904, 1910; "Elizabeth Jane Meierhoffer," death certificate, 17 April 1903, New Jersey State Archives, Trenton, N.J.; "Phillip Joseph Meierhoffer," death certificate, 10 August 1911, New Jersey State Archives, Trenton, N.J.; Interment records, Rosedale Cemetery, sec. S, lot 122, Montclair, N.J.

18 Essex County deed book, Q52, 1913, pp. 246–247 and 445–447, Essex County Hall of Records, Newark, N.J.; Fagan, *West Orange*, 45; U.S. Census, Essex County, Newark, N.J., 1920; U.S. Census, Bergen County, Ridgefield Park, N.J., 1920; U.S. Census, Essex County, West Orange, N.J., 1930; U.S. Census, Union County, Westfield, N.J., 1930; *Newark Evening News*, 13 September 1961 and 6 October 1968; "Lillian Brueger," Find-A-Grave.com, https://www.ancestry.com/discoveryui-content/

view/185831436:60525?tid=&pid=&queryId=479da0d5435b1ef851ccf6c4ef1979eb
&_phsrc=cR032&_phstart=successSource; Jean Geater to Peter Wosh, email,
24 and 25 August 2020; Patricia Brunker to Peter Wosh, email, 25, 26, and 27
August 2020.

19 U.S. Census, Essex County, East Orange, N.J., 1930 and 1940; U.S. Census, Essex
    County, Orange, N.J., 1860, 1880, 1900, 1910, 1940; U.S. Census, Essex County,
    Newark, N.J., 1940; "James Edward Meierhofer," draft registration card, Ancestry,
    1940, https://www.ancestry.com/discoveryui-content/view/301064027:2238?tid=
    &pid=&queryId=2fa07621edcdb1ec65bbd8fd0e80d761&_phsrc=cR035&_phstart
    =successSource; "Theodore Meierhoefer," death certificate, 11 December 1939, and
    "George Meierhofer," death certificate, 31 October 1937, New Jersey State Archives,
    Trenton, N.J.; *Newark Evening News*, 12 December 1939; Orange City Directories,
    1902, 1904, 1910; "Theodore Meierhofer," "Catherine T. Hicks," graves located at
    Saint John's Cemetery in Orange by the author; "George Francis Meierhofer,"
    Find-A-Grave.com, https://www.findagrave.com/memorial/95611387/george
    -francis-meierhofer%3F; and George Meierhofer to Peter Wosh, email, 27 and
    28 August 2020.

20 "Theodore Meierhofer," death certificate, 11 December 1939, New Jersey State
    Archives, Trenton, N.J.; *Newark Evening News*, 12 December 1939; George Meier-
    hofer to Peter Wosh, email, 27 and 28 August 2020; Thomas Meierhofer to Peter
    Wosh, telephone call, 5 September 2020.

21 *Newark Daily Journal*, 13 February 1880; Civil War records, adjutant general's office,
    39th regiment allotment roll, Company H, folder 10, New Jersey State Archives,
    Trenton, N.J.

22 *Newark Daily Journal*, 13 February 1880; Johan Huizinga, *Homo Ludens: A Study of
    the Play-Element in Culture* (Boston, Mass.: Beacon, 1955).

Index

Page numbers in *italics* refer to figures.

About the Authors

PETER J. WOSH directed the archives/public history graduate education program in the history department at New York University from 1994 until his retirement in 2016. He previously served as an archivist at both the American Bible Society in New York (1984–1994) and Seton Hall University in South Orange, New Jersey (1978–1984). His books include *Waldo Gifford Leland and the Origins of the American Archival Profession* (2011), *Covenant House: Journey of a Faith-Based Charity* (2005), and *Spreading the Word: The Bible Business in Nineteenth-Century America* (1994). He is a fellow of the Society of American Archivists.

PATRICIA L. SCHALL (1945–2020) was professor emeritus at Saint Elizabeth University in Morristown, New Jersey. She served in a variety of leadership capacities there from 1992 until her retirement in 2016, including being head of the education department and the director of various graduate education programs. She previously taught English at Watchung Hills Regional High School from 1968 to 1980 and directed the Educational Media Center at Seton Hall University. Her publications include *Protecting the Right to Teach and Learn: Power, Politics, and Public Schools* (1981), and she served as a former president of the New Jersey Council of Teachers of English.